The GUITAR BOOK

BY

ADAM KADMON

the author of the world famous

GUITAR GRIMOIRE SERIES

A GUITAR GRIMOIRE

PUBLICATION

Produced by

⭐ METATRON INC.

for

CARL FISCHER®
65 Bleecker Street, New York, NY 10012

Copyright © 1999 by Carl Fischer, LLC
International Copyright Secured.

GT101

ISBN 0-8258-3900-9

MW00902796

For more information on **The Guitar Grimoire**® Series and other music instructional products
by Adam Kadmon check out the following websites:
http://www.guitargrimoire.com
http://www.adamkadmon.com

CONTENTS

CHORD EQUIVALENTS

3 AND 4 NOTE CHORDS

M	Major	(1, 3, 5)
$^-$	Minor	(1, ♭3, 5)
sus2	Suspended Second	(1, 2, 5)
sus(4)	Suspended Fourth	(1, 4, 5)
♭5	Flatted Fifth	(1, 3, ♭5)
°	Diminished	(1, ♭3, ♭5)
+	Augmented	(1, 3, #5)
♭6	Flatted Sixth	(1, 3, 5, ♭6)
$^-$♭6	Minor Flatted Sixth	(1, ♭3, 5, ♭6)
6	Major Sixth	(1, 3, 5, 6)
$^-$6	Minor Sixth	(1, ♭3, 5, 6)
°7	Diminished Seventh	(1, ♭3, ♭5, ♮7)
Q(3)	Quartal or Double Fourth	(1, 4, ♭7)
7	Dominant	(1, 3, 5, ♭7)
$^-$7	Minor Seventh	(1, ♭3, 5, ♭7)
7sus2	Dominant Suspended Second	(1, 2, 5, ♭7)
7sus	Dominant Suspended	(1, 4, 5, ♭7)
7♭5	Dominant Flatted Fifth	(1, 3, ♭5, ♭7)
ø	Half Diminished	(1, ♭3, ♭5, ♮7)
7$^+$	Dominant Augmented	(1, 3, #5, ♭7)
△	Delta or Major Seventh	(1, 3, 5 ,7)
$^-$△	Minor Delta or Minor Major	(1, ♭3, 5, 7)
△sus2	Delta Sus2 or Major Seventh Suspended Second	(1, 2, 5, 7)
△sus	Delta Sus or Major Seventh Suspended Fourth	(1, 4, 5, 7)
△♭5	Delta Flatted Fifth or Major Seventh Flatted Fifth	(1, 3, ♭5, 7)
△°	Delta Diminished or Major Seventh Diminished	(1, ♭3, ♭5, 7)
△$^+$	Delta Augmented or Major Seventh Augmented	(1, 3, #5, 7)
$^-$△$^+$	Minor Delta Augmented or Minor Major Seventh Augmented (1, ♭3, #5, 7)	

THE BUILDING BLOCKS OF MUSIC

In order to understand music, one must understand the basics of harmony and theory. Music is sound. But for now imagine that it is a set of 12 equal blocks (fig. 1). The distance from one block to the next is a half-step. From block 1 to block 2 is a half-step, from 8 to block 9 is a half-step, etc.

1	2	3	4	5	6	7	8	9	10	11	12

fig. 1

1		2		3	4		5		6		7

fig. 2

7 of these 12 tones or blocks have been given positions of "major" importance (fig. 2). Looking at the diagram we only see 7 numbers, but there are still 12 tones or blocks. The empty blocks are reserved for flats ♭ and sharps ♯. The distance from block 1 to the first empty block is still a half-step. The blocks that are numbered are the tones that make up the Major scale.

The various combinations of half-steps are called intervals. Basically, an interval is the distance between two tones. The names of the intervals are then divided into two sets: the majors and the perfects. The majors are 2, 3, 6, and 7; the perfects are 1, 4, 5, and 8. 1 would be a unison, such as two instruments playing the same note. An 8 would be the octave. Altering the intervals with flats or sharps changes them from major and perfect into minor, diminished, and augmented (fig. 3).

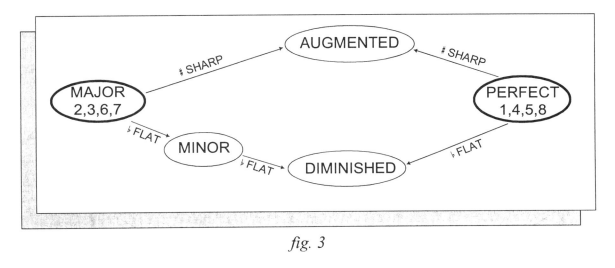

fig. 3

In essence:
- Flat a major — get a minor
- Flat a minor — get a diminished
- Flat a perfect — get a diminished
- Sharp a major — get an augmented
- Sharp a perfect — get an augmented

The entire set of major and perfect intervals are called diatonic intervals.

Let's look at an easy way for memorizing interval distances by counting the amount of blocks. There are 12 building blocks within the Major scale. Therefore, an interval has to consist of so many building blocks. We'll demonstrate first with a major 2nd. There are 3 blocks in a major 2nd (fig. 4), but the distance from the 2 to the 3 is also a major 2nd (fig. 5).

1		2		3	4		5		6		7

1		2

fig. 4

1		2		3	4		5		6		7

1		2

fig. 5

Fig. 6 is a complete chart of intervals showing you a breakdown in building block format. Also observe, the chart tells you how many half- and whole steps make up each interval.

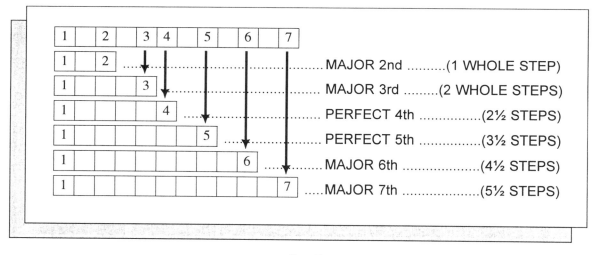

1													1 BLOCK = UNISON ....(0 STEPS)

1 | ♭2 | 2 BLOCKS = MINOR 2nd ....(½ STEPS)
1 | | 2 | 3 BLOCKS = MAJOR 2nd ....(1 WHOLE STEP)
1 | | | ♭3 | 4 BLOCKS = MINOR 3rd ....(1½ STEPS)
1 | | | | 3 | 5 BLOCKS = MAJOR 3rd ....(2 WHOLE STEPS)
1 | | | | | 4 | 6 BLOCKS = PERFECT 4th ....(2½ STEPS)
1 | | | | | | ♭5 | 7 BLOCKS = DIMINISHED 5th ....(3 WHOLE STEPS)
1 | | | | | | | 5 | 8 BLOCKS = PERFECT 5th ....(3½ STEPS)
1 | | | | | | | | ♭6 | 9 BLOCKS = MINOR 6th ....(4 WHOLE STEPS)
1 | | | | | | | | | 6 | 10 BLOCKS = MAJOR 6th ....(4½ STEPS)
1 | | | | | | | | | | ♭7 | 11 BLOCKS = MINOR 7th ....(5 WHOLE STEPS)
1 | | | | | | | | | | | 7 | 12 BLOCKS = MAJOR 7th ....(5½ STEPS)

fig. 6

Now let's look at all the individual components of the Major scale in building block breakdown (fig. 7).

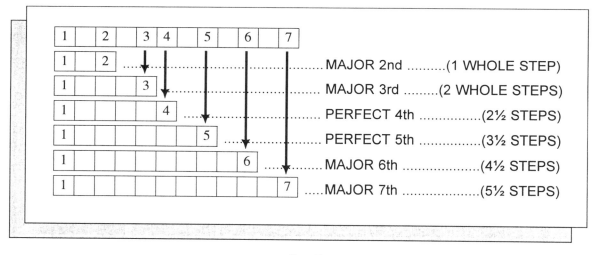

1		2		3	4		5		6		7	

1 | | 2 | .... MAJOR 2nd ....(1 WHOLE STEP)
1 | | | | 3 | .... MAJOR 3rd ....(2 WHOLE STEPS)
1 | | | | | 4 | .... PERFECT 4th ....(2½ STEPS)
1 | | | | | | 5 | .... PERFECT 5th ....(3½ STEPS)
1 | | | | | | | | 6 | .... MAJOR 6th ....(4½ STEPS)
1 | | | | | | | | | | 7 | .....MAJOR 7th ....(5½ STEPS)

fig. 7

We can clearly see here the individual intervals. We have a 2nd, 3rd, 4th, 5th, 6th, and 7th. With the block diagram we can also see exactly how many steps make up each interval.

Using the same building block breakdown method, we can also analyze the intervallic relationship between the intervals themselves.

Fig. 8 clearly shows us the distance of the intervals from the intervals. For instance, from the major 2nd to the major 3rd is a major 2nd or a whole step. From the 3rd to the 4th is a minor 2nd or a half-step, etc.

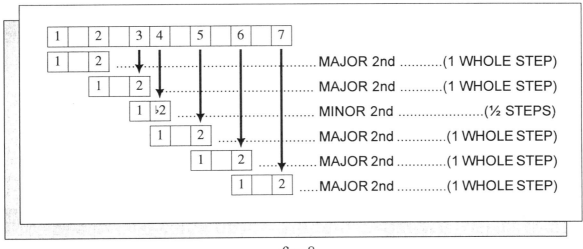

fig. 8

In studying the altered intervals, many of them will look differently on paper and in theory, but sonically, they are the same (fig. 9).

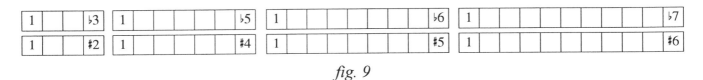

fig. 9

Notice the numbers to the right of each set above are different between the upper and the lower, yet each has the same number of blocks. The minor 3rd is the same as the augmented 2nd, the diminished 5th is the same as the augmented 4th, the minor 6th is the same as the augmented 5th, and the minor 7th is the same as the augmented 6th.

In the next example, the diminished 7th (a double-flat 7th) is the same as the major 6th in sound; although in theory, they also are two very different intervals (fig. 10).

| 1 | | | | | | | 6 |
| 1 | | | | | | | ♭♭7 |

fig. 10

The complete group of intervals which make up the scale, in this case the Major scale, can be theoretically repeated infinitely in both directions; although, in practice there are only so many octaves the human ear can hear (fig. 11).

← | 1 | 2 | 3 | 4 | 5 | 6 | 7 | 1 | 2 | 3 | 4 | 5 | 6 | 7 | → *fig. 11*

This is the mathematics of music theory. It is important that you memorize the numerics behind the building blocks, in order to form a solid foundation for your musical creations.

SCALES AND MODES

A scale is a sequence of tones comprised of varying intervals. Modes can be described as scales based upon the tones of the main scale. The Major scale has 7 modes, because it has 7 tones. The 1st mode of any modal system is the scale itself. For many scales, the individual modes have been given names because they are used as scales themselves.

The modes of the Major scale are the Ionian, Dorian, Phrygian, Lydian, Mixolydian, Aeolian, and Locrian. The Major scale is the Ionian mode (Major scale = Ionian). Of all the scales, the Major is the only one that has a different name for the 1st mode.

The II mode of any scale is based upon the 2nd tone of the main scale, in this case the Major scale. A mode uses the exact tones of the main scale; however, what was a 2 becomes a 1, what was a 3 becomes a 2, etc. (fig. 12).

1	2	3	4	5	6	7	1	2	3	4	5	6	7
	1	2	♭3	4	5	6	♭7						

fig. 12

The process then continues for the other modes. For the III mode, the 3 becomes the 1, the 4 becomes the 2, etc. (fig. 13).

1	2	3	4	5	6	7	1	2	3	4	5	6	7
		1	♭2	♭3	4	5	♭6	♭7					

fig. 13

For the IV mode, the 4 becomes the 1, the 5 becomes the 2, etc. (fig. 14).

1	2	3	4	5	6	7	1	2	3	4	5	6	7
			1	2	3	♯4	5	6	7				

fig. 14

For the V mode, the 5 becomes the 1, the 6 becomes the 2, etc. (fig. 15).

1	2	3	4	5	6	7	1	2	3	4	5	6	7
				1	2	3	4	5	6	♭7			

fig. 15

For the VI mode, the 6 becomes the 1, the 7 becomes the 2, etc. (fig. 16).

1	2	3	4	5	6	7	1	2	3	4	5	6	7
					1	2	♭3	4	5	♭6	♭7		

fig. 16

For the VII mode, the 7 becomes the 1, the 1 becomes the 2, the 2 becomes the 3, etc. (fig. 17).

1	2	3	4	5	6	7	1	2	3	4	5	6	7
						1	♭2	♭3	4	♭5	♭6	♭7	

fig. 17

In the examples above, every mode has 7 tones; however, it some kind of a 2, some kind of a 3, some kind of a 4, etc. In other words, though you are using the same tones, the numeric value changes when you shift the tone center — that is the tone which you now designate as 1.

At the bottom of the title pages, the relative relationship of each mode to the main scale is graphed out for you along with the numeric formula for each mode (fig. 18).

NUMERIC SCALE / MODE CHART

		1	2	3	4	5	6	7	1	2	3	4	5	6	7
I	IONIAN	1	2	3	4	5	6	7	1	2	3	4	5	6	7
II	DORIAN		1	2	♭3	4	5	6	♭7						
III	PHRYGIAN			1	♭2	♭3	4	5	♭6	♭7					
IV	LYDIAN				1	2	3	#4	5	6	7				
V	MIXOLYD.					1	2	3	4	5	6	♭7			
VI	AEOLIAN						1	2	♭3	4	5	♭6	♭7		
VII	LOCRIAN							1	♭2	♭3	4	♭5	♭6	♭7	
		1		2		3	4	5		6		7			

fig. 18

As you study the numeric formulas for each scale or mode, there is a simple 4-step system which will help you in understanding how the tones become flats or sharps. Fig. 19 demonstrates the application of this 4-step rule. When you compare your tones to the Major, the number of boxes to the left or right of the original tone decides whether standard flats and sharps or double flats and sharps are used. 1 box over is a standard, 2 boxes is a double (fig. 19).

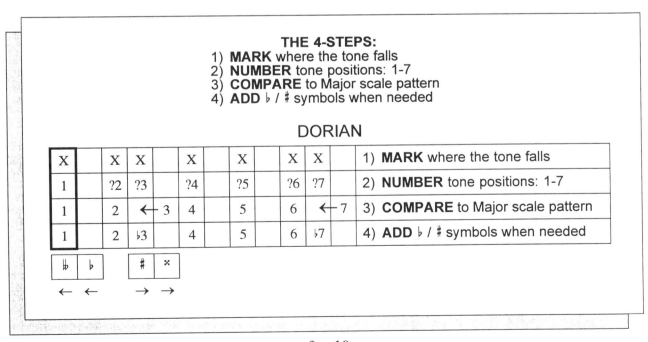

fig. 19

MODES AND RELATIVE SCALES

Scales and modes are the foundation of your compositon and improvisation. Modes are treated as scales. Just as we can change the pitch of the main scale, in order to play in one of the 12 keys, the same concept or principle can be used when using a mode. The mode generator chart of the title pages will show you the main scale equivalent for each mode (fig. 20).

The concept and principles behind **The Quick Mode Generator Chart** are the same regardless of what instrument you play.

The letters in column I indicate the pitch of the starting point. In other words it tells you what key you are in. The other columns tell you what key the relative scale is in. Column I also denotes the key for the keyboard patterns to the left.

Let's demonstrate this below with a G Mixolydian (fig. 21). The Mixolydian is the V mode of the Major scale.

Beneath column I we go down to the G, because that will be our starting pitch or key. Over to where it meets column V we come to a C, therefore, if we are playing a G Mixolydian we are actually playing a C Major with the root note shifted to the G.

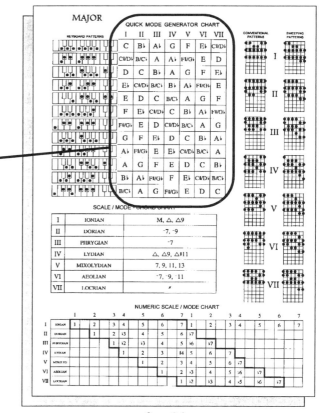

fig. 20

> **Step 1** Place left finger on desired key in column I.
>
> **Step 2** Place right finger on column of desired mode (in roman numerals at the top).
>
> **Step 3** Run fingers across and down until they meet.
>
> The point where they meet is the relative scale.

It's as simple as 1 - 2 - 3 !

QUICK MODE GENERATOR CHART

| KEY | | | | MODE | | |
I	II	III	IV	V	VI	VII
C	B♭	A♭	G	F	E♭	C#/D♭
C#/D♭	B/C♭	A	A♭	F#/G♭	E	D
D	C	B♭	A	G	F	E♭
E♭	C#/D♭	B/C♭	B♭	A♭	F#/G♭	E
E	D	C	B/C♭	A	G	F
F	E♭	C#/D♭	C	B♭	A♭	F#/G♭
F#/G♭	E	D	C#/D♭	B/C♭	A	G
G	F	E♭	D	C	B♭	A♭
A♭	F#/G♭	E	E♭	C#/D♭	B/C♭	A
A	G	F	E	D	C	B♭
B♭	A♭	F#/G♭	F	E♭	C#/D♭	B/C♭
B/C♭	A	G	F#/G♭	E	D	C

fig. 21

6

INTERVALS AND INSTRUMENT

Now that we've learned about intervals, the building blocks of music, let's see how they tie into our instrument. We are going to take two octaves of the intervals which make up the Major scale and see how they match up to the guitar in the key of F.

Looking at the diagram, (fig. 22) we can see that each block corresponds to a fret. Putting your 1st finger on the 1st string, the 1st fret will give a 1, in this case an F. On the 3rd fret you'll have your Major 2nd, on the 5th fret your Major 3rd, etc.

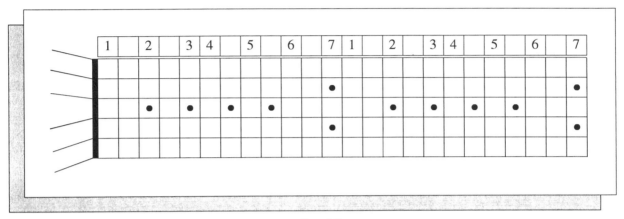

fig. 22

An example for the keyboard, in the key of C, shows that the blocks which make up the Major scale align with the "white" keys (fig. 23).

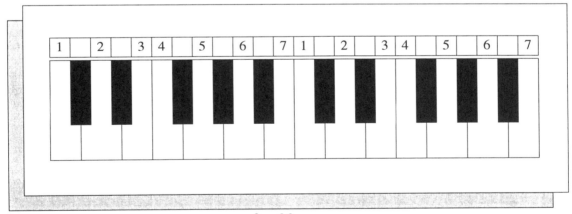

fig. 23

To change keys change the pitch of the starting note, in other words shift the mathematical formula to the appropriate pitch or key. In this case the formula is the Major scale.

We have included **Interval Maps** for the scales and chords in this book. On the interval maps the numbers in the white circles represent the numerics (1,2,3,4,5,6,7) for all 12 keys. The key is stated above each fretboard. Open notes are represented by the circles above the fretboard. Interval maps are useful reference tools in composition and study.

The interval maps change in relation to pitch, that is why there are 12 interval maps for every scale. The pitch map or **Pitch Indicator Chart**, see page 157, never changes (unless you get into open tunings).

INTERVAL MAPS

A unique feature of the Guitar Grimoire Series are the Interval Maps. As stated on the previous page, an Interval Map shows the relationships between the tones of the scale or chord on the fretboard. Each key has its own diagram for quick reference. Figures 24 and 25 show examples of interval maps for the Major scale and chord in the key of F respectively. The circled notes represent the notes used in the scale or chord, and any combination can be chosen for compositions. So, interval maps take the guesswork out of choosing notes in a solo. Just pick any circled note on the fretboard and you know it will automatically fit for the key of the chord or scale you are playing in.

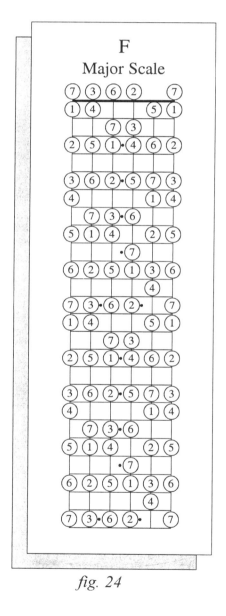

fig. 24

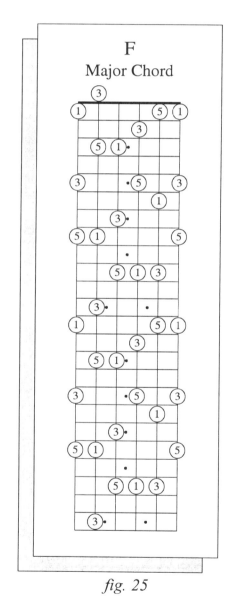

fig. 25

MAJOR

QUICK MODE GENERATOR CHART

KEYBOARD PATTERNS

I	II	III	IV	V	VI	VII
C	B♭	A♭	G	F	E♭	C#/D♭
C#/D♭	B/C♭	A	A♭	F#/G♭	E	D
D	C	B♭	A	G	F	E♭
E♭	C#/D♭	B/C♭	B♭	A♭	F#/G♭	E
E	D	C	B/C♭	A	G	F
F	E♭	C#/D♭	C	B♭	A♭	F#/G♭
F#/G♭	E	D	C#/D♭	B/C♭	A	G
G	F	E♭	D	C	B♭	A♭
A♭	F#/G♭	E	E♭	C#/D♭	B/C♭	A
A	G	F	E	D	C	B♭
B♭	A♭	F#/G♭	F	E♭	C#/D♭	B/C♭
B/C♭	A	G	F#/G♭	E	D	C

CONVENTIONAL PATTERNS   SWEEPING PATTERNS

I

II

III

IV

V

VI

VII

SCALE / MODE - CHORD CHART

I	IONIAN	M, △, △9
II	DORIAN	⁻7, ⁻9
III	PHRYGIAN	⁻7
IV	LYDIAN	△, △9, △#11
V	MIXOLYDIAN	7, 9, 11, 13
VI	AEOLIAN	⁻7, ⁻9, ⁻11
VII	LOCRIAN	∅

NUMERIC SCALE / MODE CHART

		1	2	3	4	5	6	7	1	2	3	4	5	6	7
I	IONIAN	1	2	3	4	5	6	7	1	2	3	4	5	6	7
II	DORIAN		1	2	♭3	4	5	6	♭7						
III	PHRYGIAN			1	♭2	♭3	4	5	♭6	♭7					
IV	LYDIAN				1	2	3	#4	5	6	7				
V	MIXOLYD					1	2	3	4	5	6	♭7			
VI	AEOLIAN						1	2	♭3	4	5	♭6	♭7		
VII	LOCRIAN							1	♭2	♭3	4	♭5	♭6	♭7	

F MAJOR = G DORIAN ~ A PHRYGIAN ~ B♭ LYDIAN ~ C MIXOLYDIAN ~ D AEOLIAN ~ E LOCRIAN

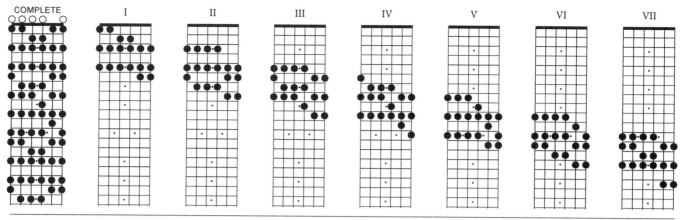

F♯ / G♭ MAJOR = A♭ DORIAN ~ B♭ PHRYGIAN ~ B / C♭ LYDIAN ~ C♯ / D♭ MIXOLYDIAN ~ E♭ AEOLIAN ~ F LOCRIAN

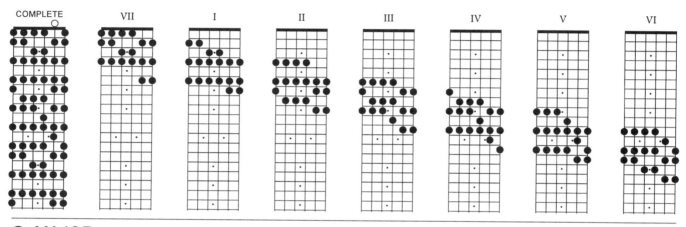

G MAJOR = A DORIAN ~ B / C♭ PHRYGIAN ~ C LYDIAN ~ D MIXOLYDIAN ~ E AOELIAN ~ F♯ / G♭ LOCRIAN

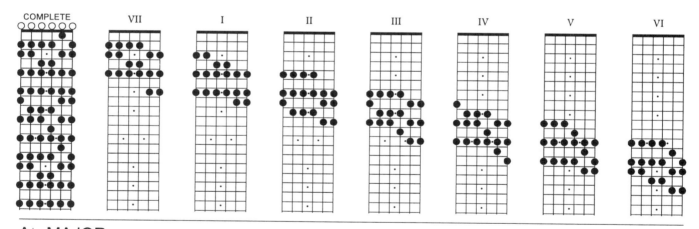

A♭ MAJOR = B♭ DORIAN ~ C PHRYGIAN ~ C♯ / D♭ LYDIAN ~ E♭ MIXOLYDIAN ~ F AEOLIAN ~ G LOCRIAN

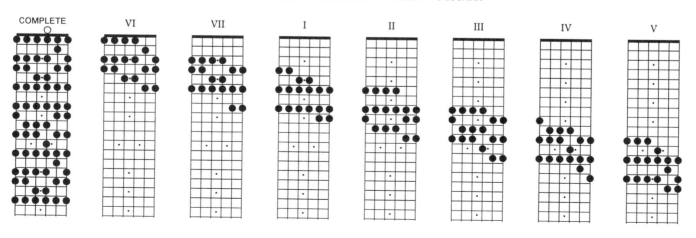

A MAJOR = B / C♭ DORIAN ~ C♯ / D♭ PHRYGIAN ~ D LYDIAN ~ E MIXOLYDIAN ~ F♯ / G♭ AEOLIAN ~ A♭ LOCRIAN

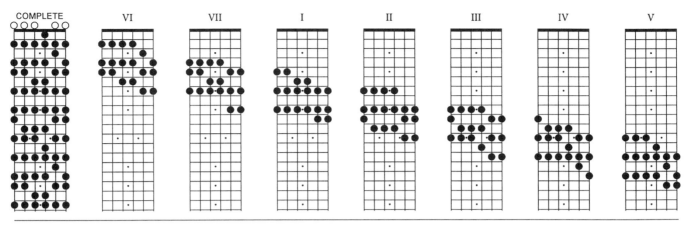

B♭ MAJOR = C DORIAN ~ D PHRYGIAN ~ E♭ LYDIAN ~ F MIXOLYDIAN ~ G AEOLIAN ~ A LOCRIAN

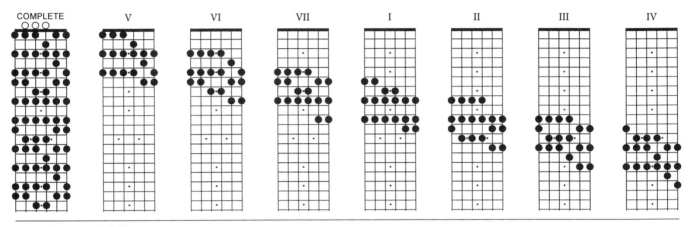

B / C♭ MAJOR = C♯ / D♭ DORIAN ~ E♭ PHRYGIAN ~ E LYDIAN ~ F♯ / G♭ MIXOLYDIAN ~ A♭ AEOLIAN ~ B♭ LOCRIAN

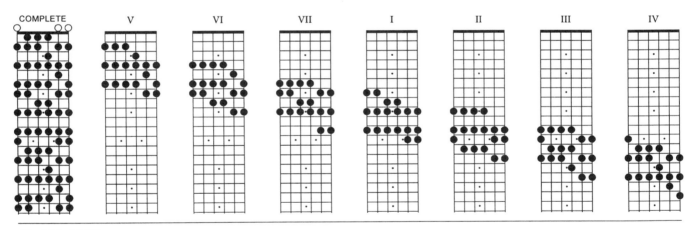

C MAJOR = D DORIAN ~ E PHRYGIAN ~ F LYDIAN ~ G MIXOLYDIAN ~ A AEOLIAN ~ B / C♭ LOCRIAN

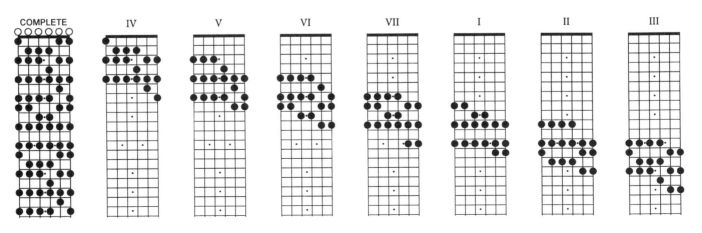

C# / D♭ MAJOR = E♭ DORIAN ~ F PHRYGIAN ~ F#/G♭ LYDIAN ~ A♭ MIXOLYDIAN ~ B♭ AEOLIAN ~ C LOCRIAN

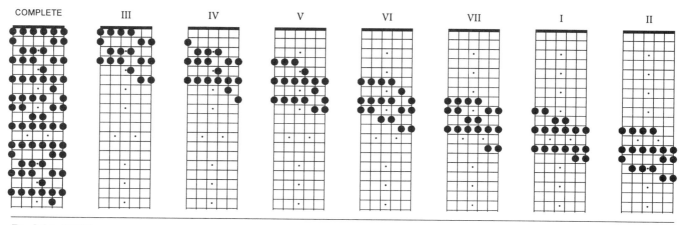

D MAJOR = E DORIAN ~ F#/G♭ PHRYGIAN ~ G LYDIAN ~ A MIXOLYDIAN ~ B/C♭ AEOLIAN ~ C#/D♭ LOCRIAN

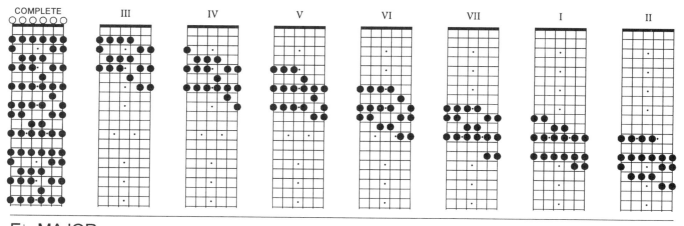

E♭ MAJOR = F DORIAN ~ G PHRYGIAN ~ A♭ LYDIAN ~ B♭ MIXOLYDIAN ~ C AEOLIAN ~ D LOCRIAN

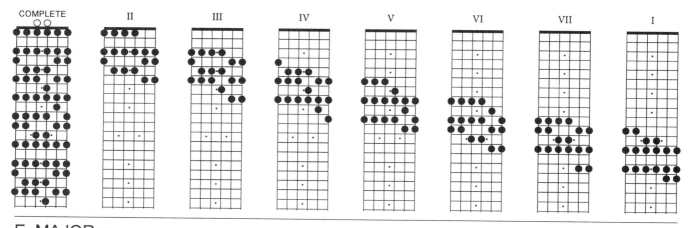

E MAJOR = F#/G♭ DORIAN ~ A♭ PHRYGIAN ~ A LYDIAN ~ B/C♭ MIXOLYDIAN ~ C#/D♭ AEOLIAN ~ E♭ LOCRIAN

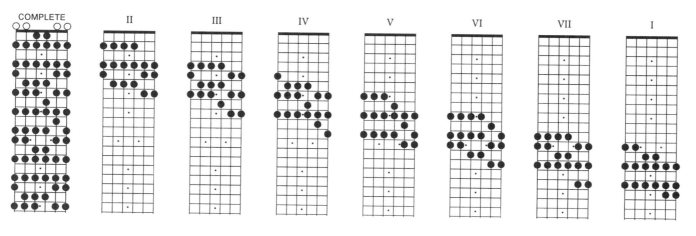

12

MAJOR

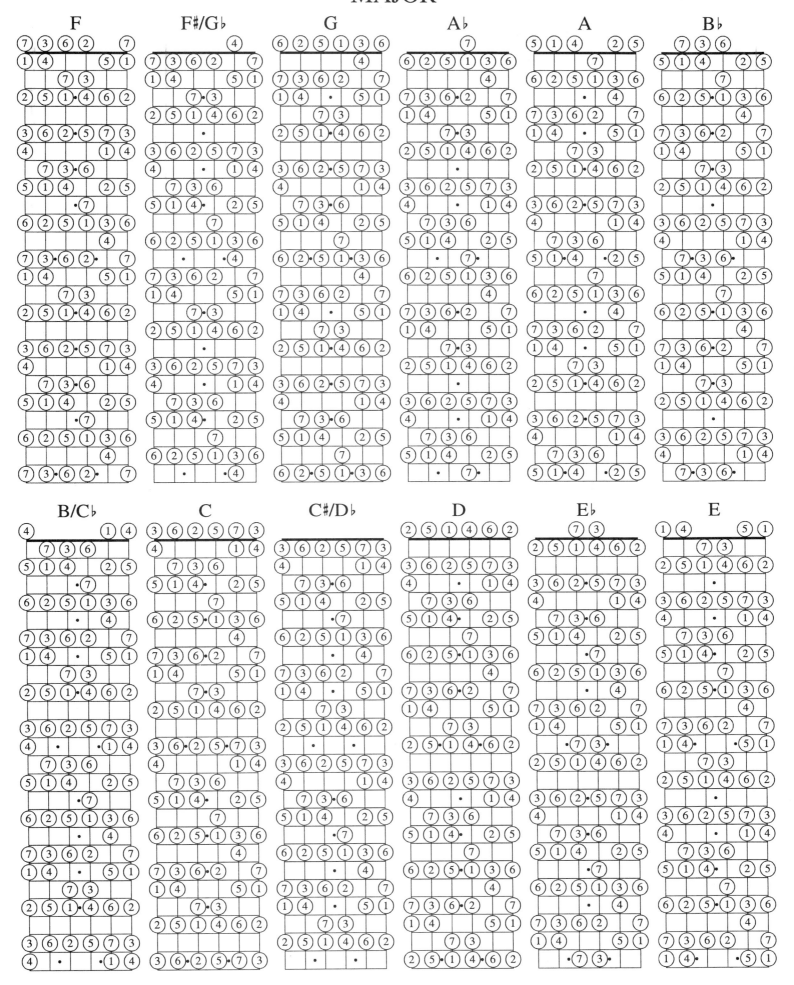

DORIAN   II MAJOR

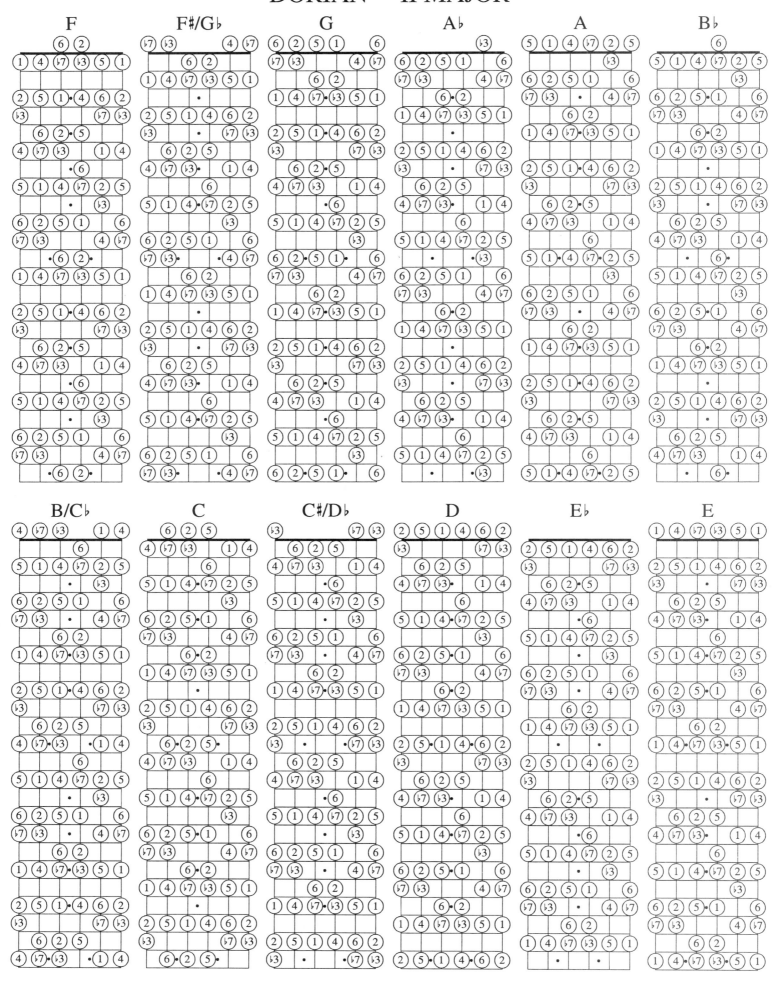

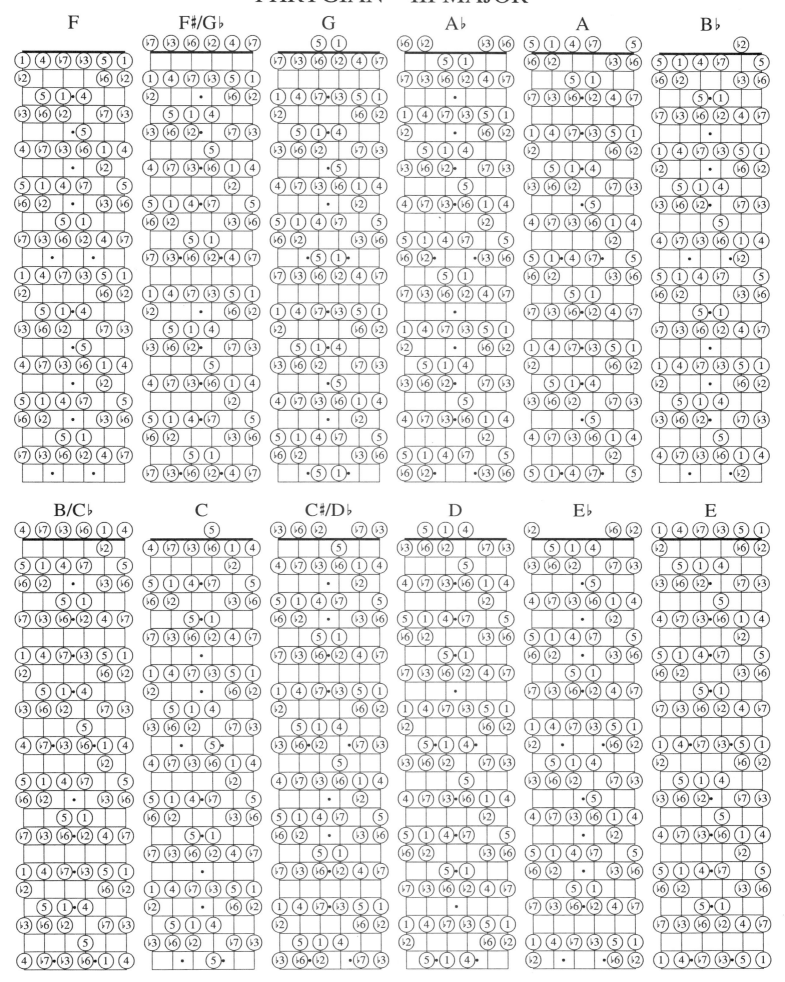

15

LYDIAN IV MAJOR

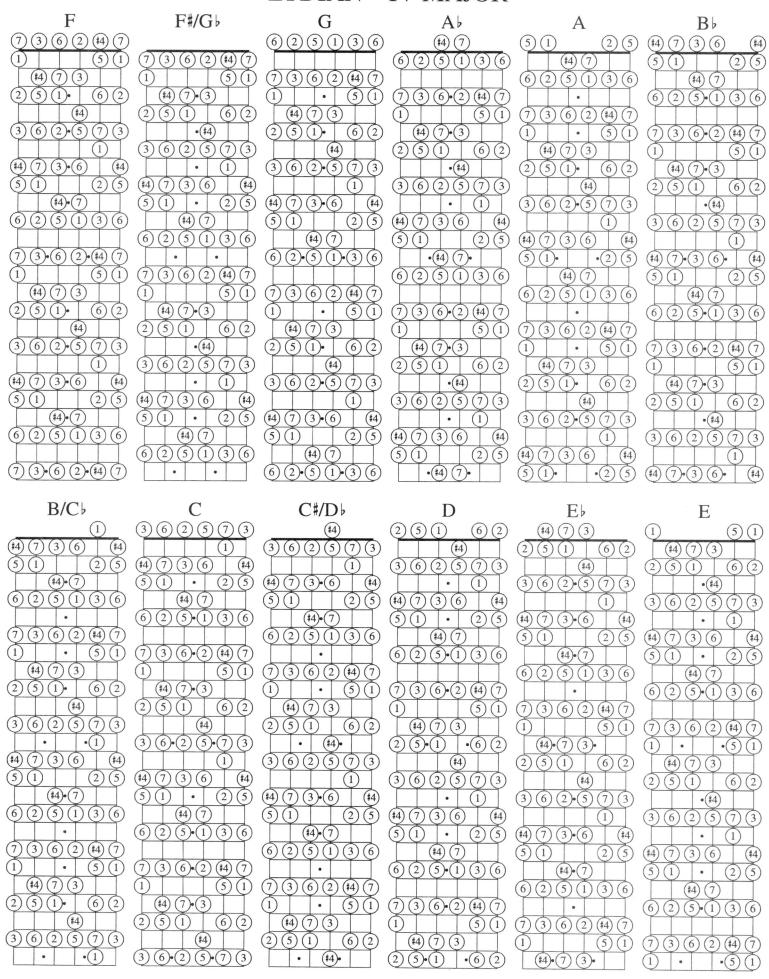

MIXOLYDIAN V MAJOR

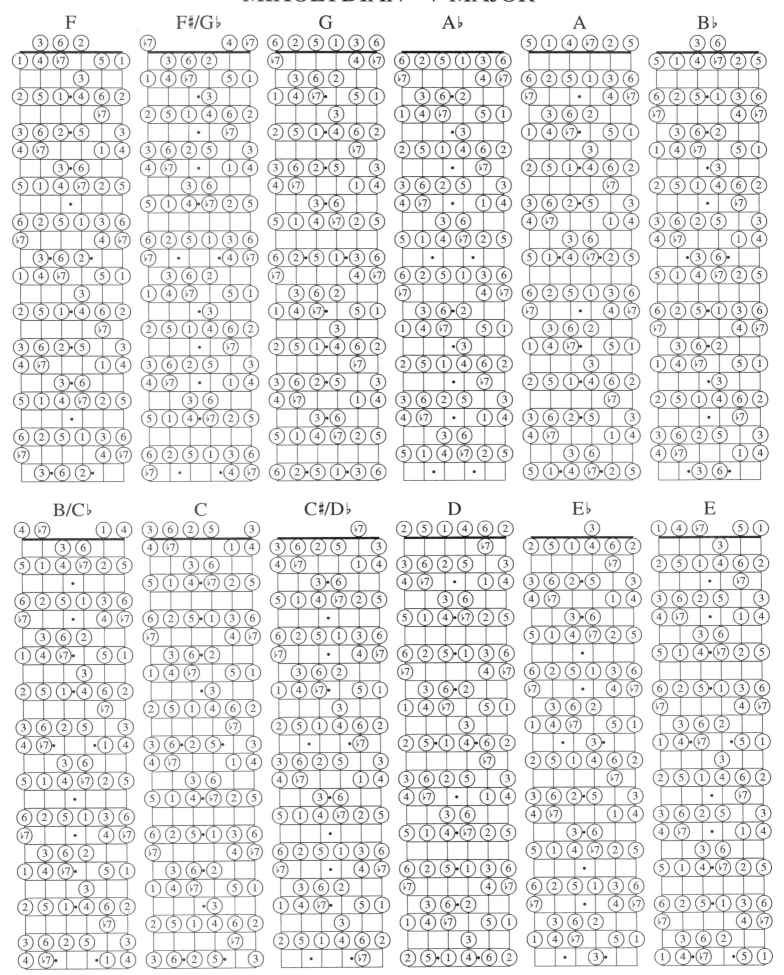

17

AEOLIAN   VI MAJOR

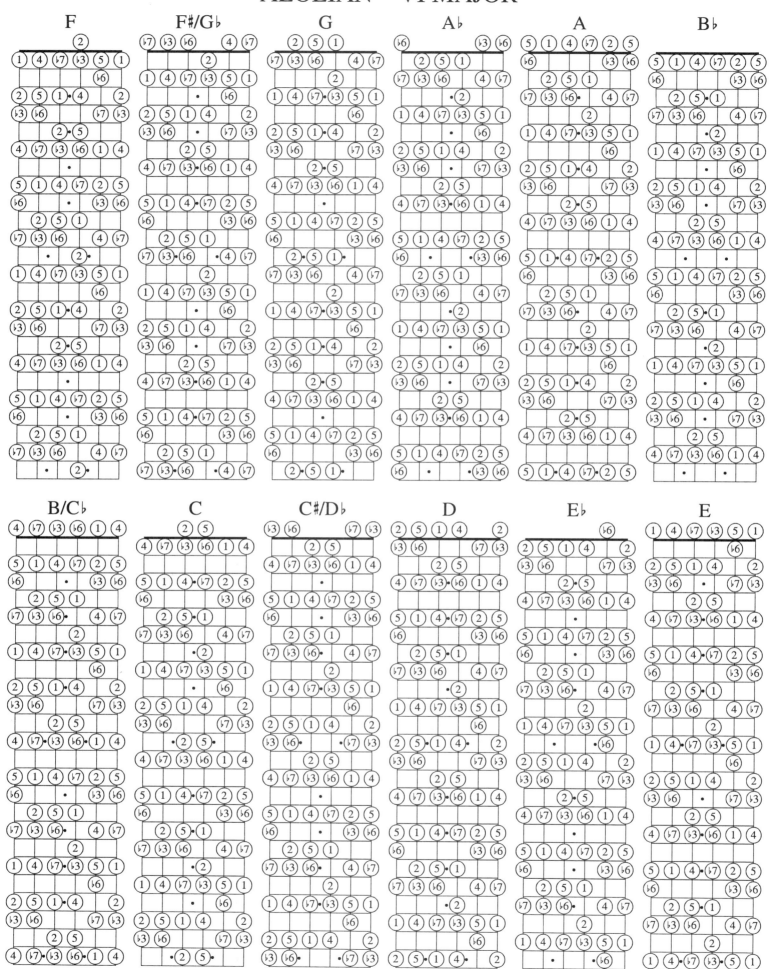

LOCRIAN VII MAJOR

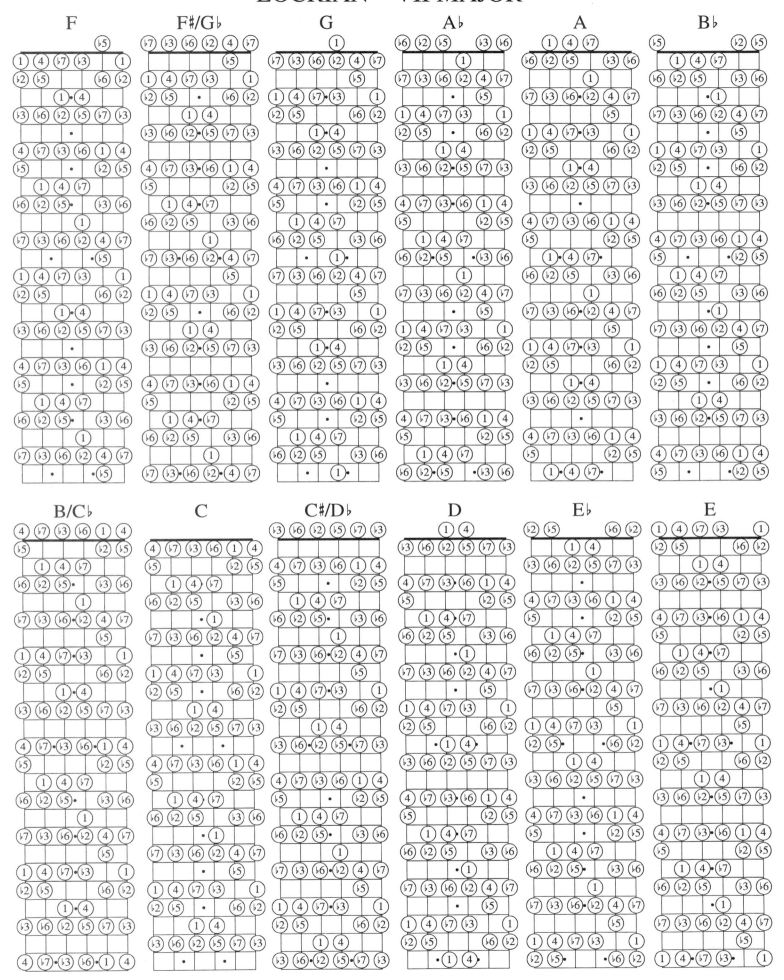

19

MELODIC MINOR

KEYBOARD PATTERNS

QUICK MODE GENERATOR CHART

	I	II	III	IV	V	VI	VII
	C	B♭	A	G	F	E♭	C#/D♭
	C#/D♭	B/C♭	B♭	A♭	F#/G♭	E	D
	D	C	B/C♭	A	G	F	E♭
	E♭	C#/D♭	C	B♭	A♭	F#/G♭	E
	E	D	C#/D♭	B/C♭	A	G	F
	F	E♭	D	C	B♭	A♭	F#/G♭
	F#/G♭	E	E♭	C#/D♭	B/C♭	A	G
	G	F	E	D	C	B♭	A♭
	A♭	F#/G♭	F	E♭	C#/D♭	B/C♭	A
	A	G	F#/G♭	E	D	C	B♭
	B♭	A♭	G	F	E♭	C#/D♭	B/C♭
	B/C♭	A	A♭	F#/G♭	E	D	C

CONVENTIONAL PATTERNS / SWEEPING PATTERNS

(I, II, III, IV, V, VI, VII)

SCALE / MODE - CHORD CHART

I	MELODIC MINOR	⁻△, ⁻6
II	DORIAN ♭2	⁻7
III	LYDIAN AUGMENTED	△⁺, △♭5
IV	LYDIAN DOMINANT	7♭5
V	HINDU	7♭13, 7⁺
VI	LOCRIAN ♮2	∅9
VII	SUPER LOCRIAN	ALT

NUMERIC SCALE / MODE CHART

		1		2	3	4		5		6		7	1		2		3	4		5		6		7
I	MELODIC	1		2	♭3	4		5		6		7	1		2	♭3		4		5		6		7
II	DORIAN ♭2			1	♭2	♭3		4		5		6	♭7												
III	LYD AUG				1	2		3		#4		#5	6		7										
IV	LYD DOM					1		2		3		#4	5		6	♭7									
V	HINDU							1		2		3	4		5	♭6		♭7							
VI	LOCRIAN ♮2									1		2	♭3		4	♭5		♭6		♭7				
VII	SUPER LOC											1	♭2		♭3	♭4		♭5		♭6		♭7		

20

F MELODIC = G DORIAN ♭2 ~ A♭ LYDIAN AUGMENTED ~ B♭ LYDIAN DOMINANT ~ C HINDU ~ D LOCRIAN ♭2 ~ E SUPER LOCRIAN

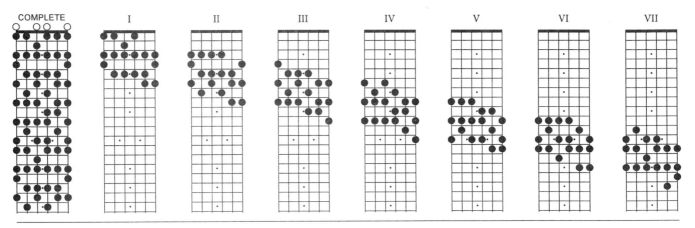

F#/G♭ MELODIC = A♭ DORIAN ♭2 ~ A LYDIAN AUGMENTED ~ B / C♭ LYDIAN DOMINANT ~ C♯ / D♭ HINDU ~ E♭ LOCRIAN ♭2 ~ F SUPER LOCRIAN

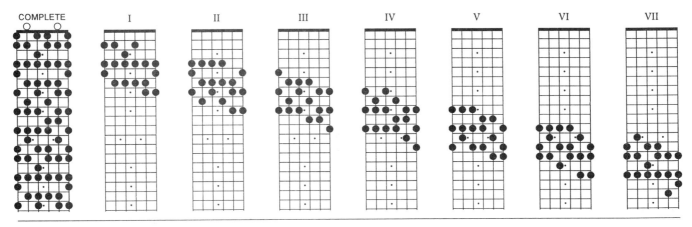

G MELODIC = A DORIAN ♭2 ~ B♭ LYDIAN AUGMENTED ~ C LYDIAN DOMINANT ~ D HINDU ~ E LOCRIAN ♭2 ~ F♯ / G♭ SUPER LOCRIAN

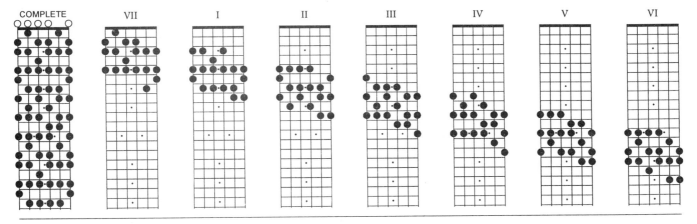

A♭ MELODIC = B♭ DORIAN ♭2 ~ B / C♭ LYDIAN AUGMENTED ~ C♯ / D♭ LYDIAN DOMINANT ~ E♭ HINDU ~ F LOCRIAN ♭2 ~ G SUPER LOCRIAN

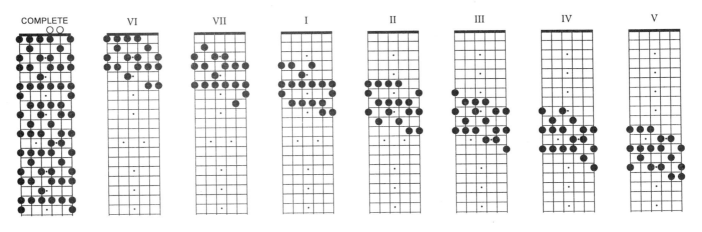

A MELODIC = B / C♭ DORIAN ♭2 ~ C LYDIAN AUGMENTED ~ D LYDIAN DOMINANT ~ E HINDU ~ F# / G♭ LOCRIAN ♭2 ~ A♭ SUPER LOCRIAN

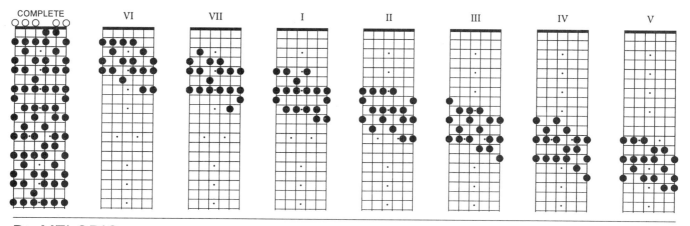

B♭ MELODIC = C DORIAN ♭2 ~ C# / D♭ LYDIAN AUGMENTED ~ E♭ LYDIAN DOMINANT ~ F HINDU ~ G LOCRIAN ♭2 ~ A SUPER LOCRIAN

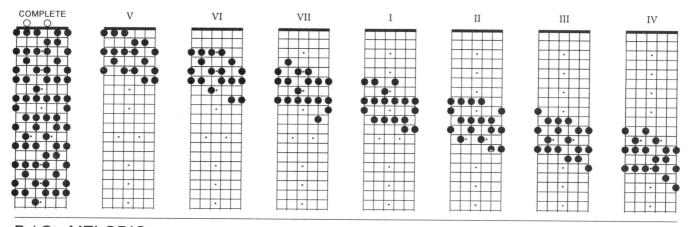

B / C♭ MELODIC = C# / D♭ DORIAN ♭2 ~ D LYDIAN AUGMENTED ~ E LYDIAN DOMINANT ~ F# / G♭ HINDU ~ A♭ LOCRIAN ♭2 ~ B♭ SUPER LOCRIAN

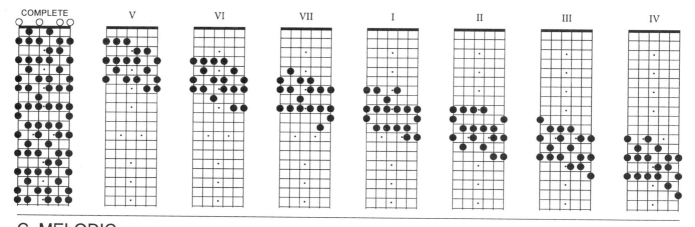

C MELODIC = D DORIAN ♭2 ~ E♭ LYDIAN AUGMENTED ~ F LYDIAN DOMINANT ~ G HINDU ~ A LOCRIAN ♭2 ~ B / C♭ SUPER LOCRIAN

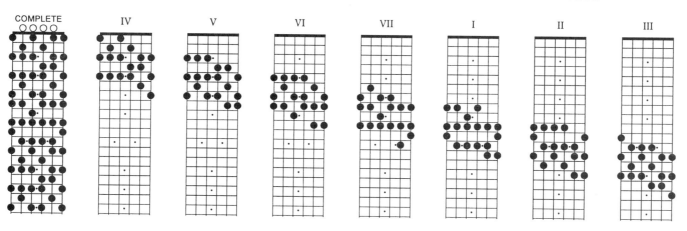

C♯ / D♭ MELODIC = E♭ DORIAN ♭2 ~ E LYDIAN AUGMENTED ~ F♯ / G♭ LYDIAN DOMINANT ~ A♭ HINDU ~ B♭ LOCRIAN ♭2 ~ C SUPER LOCRIAN

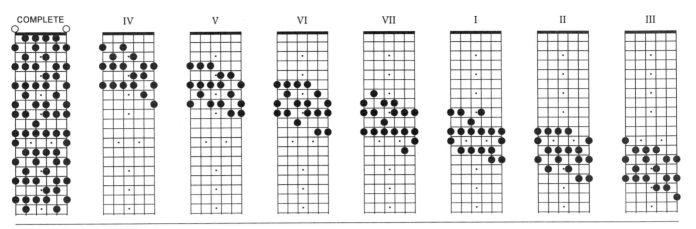

D MELODIC = E DORIAN ♭2 ~ F LYDIAN AUGMENTED ~ G LYDIAN DOMINANT ~ A HINDU ~ B / C♭ LOCRIAN ♭2 ~ C♯ / D♭ SUPER LOCRIAN

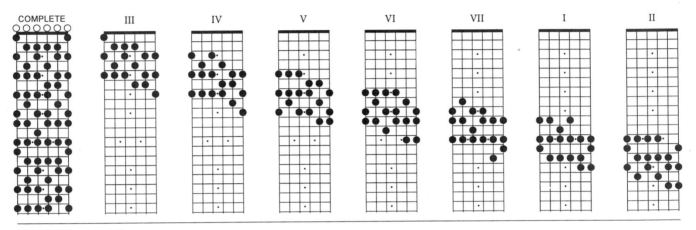

E♭ MELODIC = F DORIAN ♭2 ~ F♯ / G♭ LYDIAN AUGMENTED ~ A♭ LYDIAN DOMINANT ~ B♭ HINDU ~ C LOCRIAN ♭2 ~ D SUPER LOCRIAN

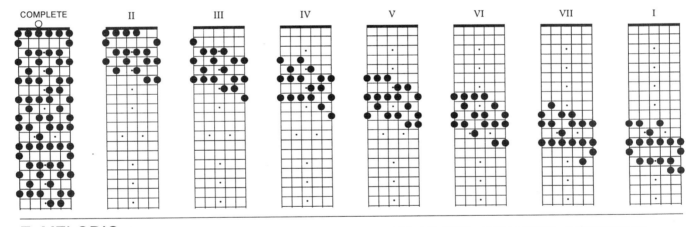

E MELODIC = F♯ / G♭ DORIAN ♭2 ~ G LYDIAN AUGMENTED ~ A LYDIAN DOMINANT ~ B / C♭ HINDU ~ C♯ / D♭ LOCRIAN ♭2 ~ E♭ SUPER LOCRIAN

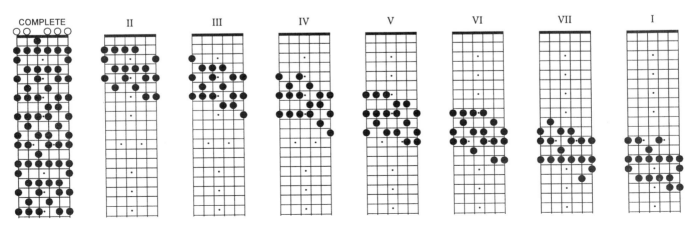

23

MELODIC MINOR

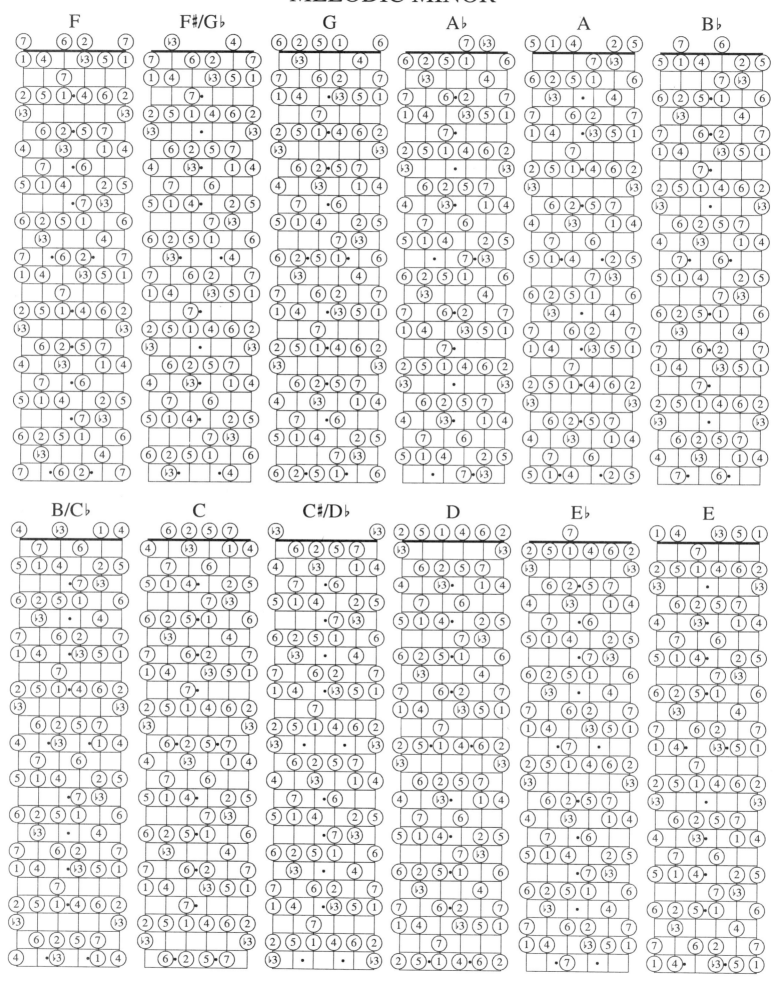

24

HARMONIC MINOR

KEYBOARD PATTERNS

QUICK MODE GENERATOR CHART

I	II	III	IV	V	VI	VII
C	B♭	A	G	F	E	C#/D♭
C#/D♭	B/C♭	B♭	A♭	F#/G♭	F	D
D	C	B/C♭	A	G	F#/G♭	E♭
E♭	C#/D♭	C	B♭	A♭	G	E
E	D	C#/D♭	B/C♭	A	A♭	F
F	E♭	D	C	B♭	A	F#/G♭
F#/G♭	E	E♭	C#/D♭	B/C♭	B♭	G
G	F	E	D	C	B/C♭	A♭
A♭	F#/G♭	F	E♭	C#/D♭	C	A
A	G	F#/G♭	E	D	C#/D♭	B♭
B♭	A♭	G	F	E♭	D	B/C♭
B/C♭	A	A♭	F#/G♭	E	E♭	C

CONVENTIONAL PATTERNS   SWEEPING PATTERNS

I, II, III, IV, V, VI, VII

SCALE / MODE - CHORD CHART

I	HARMONIC MINOR	-△, -♭6
II	LOCRIAN ♮6	∅ , °7
III	IONIAN #5	△+
IV	DORIAN #4	∅ , ° , -7, -6, ∅9, °9, -9
V	PHRYGIAN ♮3	+, 7, 7+, 7♭9
VI	LYDIAN #2	M, m, 6, △, -△
VII	ALT ♮7	♭5, ° , °7

NUMERIC SCALE / MODE CHART

		1		2		3	4		5		6		7	1		2		3	4		5		6		7
I	HARMONIC MINOR	1		2	♭3		4		5	♭6			7	1		2	♭3		4		5	♭6			7
II	LOCRIAN ♮6			1	♭2		♭3		4	♭5			6	♭7											
III	IONIAN #5				1		2		3	4			#5	6		7									
IV	DORIAN #4						1		2	♭3			#4	5		6	♭7								
V	PHRYGIAN ♮3								1	♭2			3	4		5	♭6		♭7						
VI	LYDIAN #2									1			#2	3		#4	5		6		7				
VII	ALT ♮7												1	♭2		♭3	♭4		♭5		♭6		♭7		

F HARMONIC MINOR = G LOCRIAN ♮6 ~ A♭ IONIAN AUG ~ B♭ DORIAN ♯4 ~ C PHRYGIAN MAJ ~ C♯ / D♭ LYDIAN ♯2 ~ E ALT ♮♭7

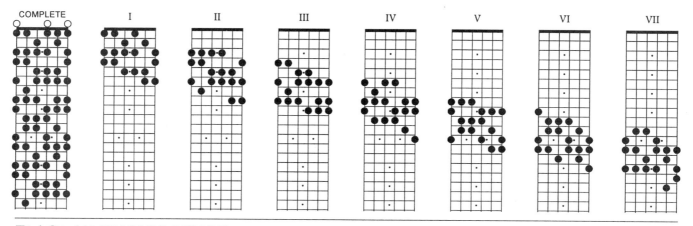

F♯ / G♭ HARMONIC MINOR = A♭ LOCRIAN ♮6 ~ A IONIAN AUG ~ B / C♭ DORIAN ♯4 ~ C♯ / D♭ PHRYGIAN MAJ ~ D LYDIAN ♯2 ~ F ALT ♮♭7

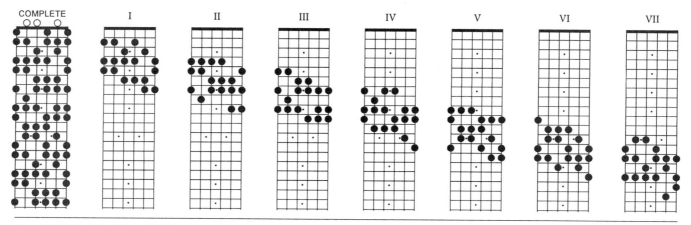

G HARMONIC MINOR = A LOCRIAN ♮6 ~ B♭ IONIAN AUG ~ C DORIAN ♯4 ~ D PHRYGIAN MAJ ~ E♭ LYDIAN ♯2 ~ F♯ / G♭ ALT ♮♭7

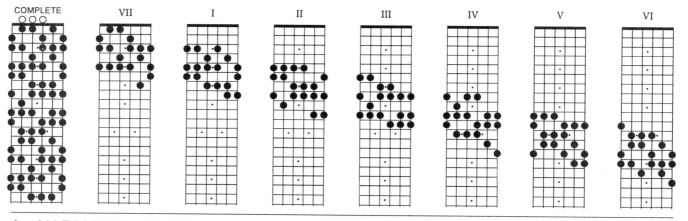

A♭ HARMONIC MINOR = B♭ LOCRIAN ♮6 ~ B / C♭ IONIAN AUG ~ C♯ / D♭ DORIAN ♯4 ~ E♭ PHRYGIAN MAJ ~ E LYDIAN ♯2 ~ G ALT ♮♭7

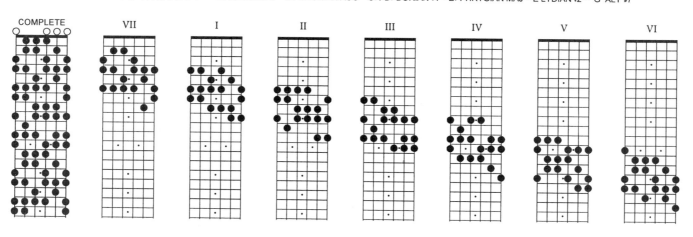

26

A HARMONIC MINOR = B / C♭ LOCRIAN ♮6 ~ C IONIAN AUG ~ D DORIAN ♯4 ~ E PHRYGIAN MAJ ~ F LYDIAN ♯2 ~ A♭ ALT ♮♭7

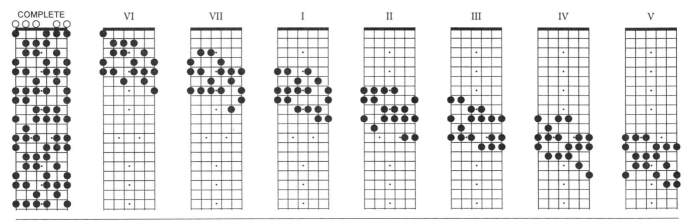

B♭ HARMONIC MINOR = C LOCRIAN ♮6 ~ C♯ / D♭ IONIAN AUG ~ E♭ DORIAN ♯4 ~ F PHRYGIAN MAJ ~ F♯ / G♭ LYDIAN ♯2 ~ A ALT ♮♭7

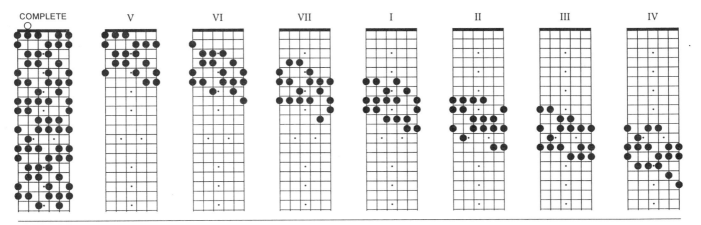

B / C♭ HARMONIC MINOR = C♯ / D♭ LOCRIAN ♮6 ~ D IONIAN AUG ~ E DORIAN ♯4 ~ F♯ / G♭ PHRYGIAN MAJ ~ G LYDIAN ♯2 ~ B♭ ALT ♮♭7

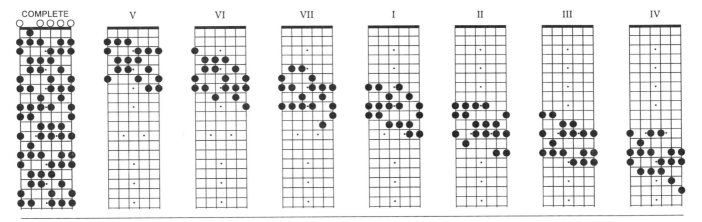

C HARMONIC MINOR = D LOCRIAN ♮6 ~ E♭ IONIAN AUG ~ F DORIAN ♯4 ~ G PHRYGIAN MAJ ~ A♭ LYDIAN ♯2 ~ B / C♭ ALT ♮♭7

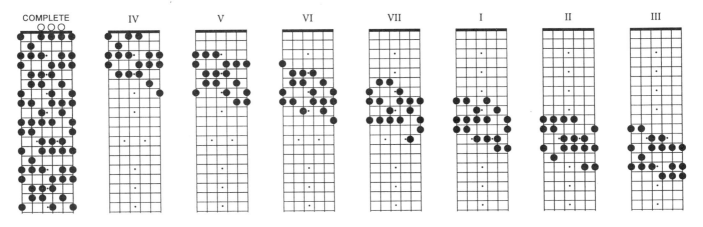

C# / Db HARMONIC MINOR = Eb LOCRIAN ♮6 ~ E IONIAN AUG ~ F♯ / Gb DORIAN ♯4 ~ Ab PHRYGIAN MAJ ~ A LYDIAN ♯2 ~ C ALT ♯♯7

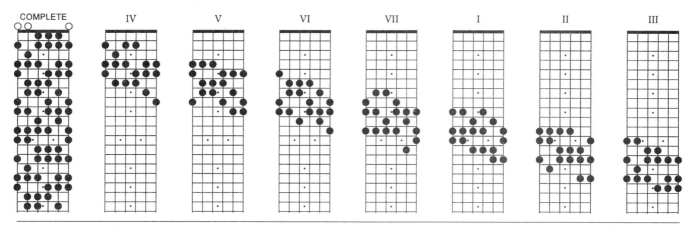

D HARMONIC MINOR = E LOCRIAN ♮6 ~ F IONIAN AUG ~ G DORIAN ♯4 ~ A PHRYGIAN MAJ ~ Bb LYDIAN ♯2 ~ C♯ / Db ALT ♯♯7

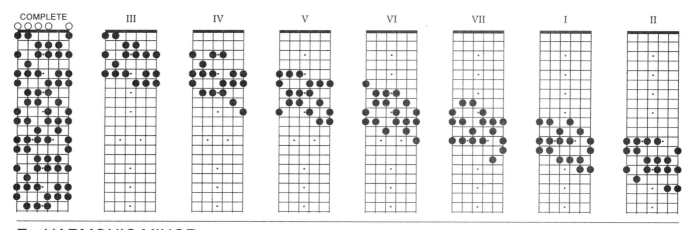

Eb HARMONIC MINOR = F LOCRIAN ♮6 ~ F♯ / Gb IONIAN AUG ~ Ab DORIAN ♯4 ~ Bb PHRYGIAN MAJ ~ B / Cb LYDIAN ♯2 ~ D ALT ♯♯7

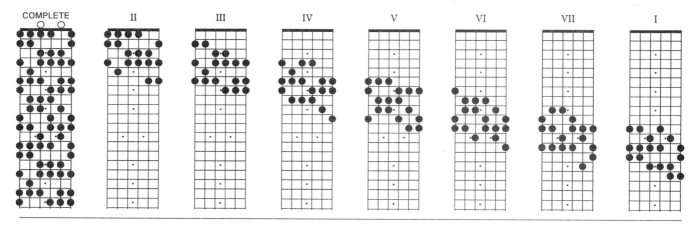

E HARMONIC MINOR = F♯ / Gb LOCRIAN ♮6 ~ G IONIAN AUG ~ A DORIAN ♯4 ~ B / Cb PHRYGIAN MAJ ~ C LYDIAN ♯2 ~ Eb ALT ♯♯7

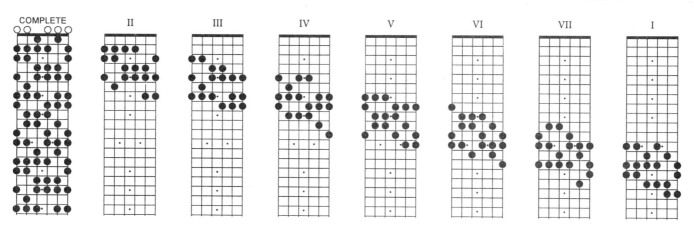

28

HARMONIC MINOR

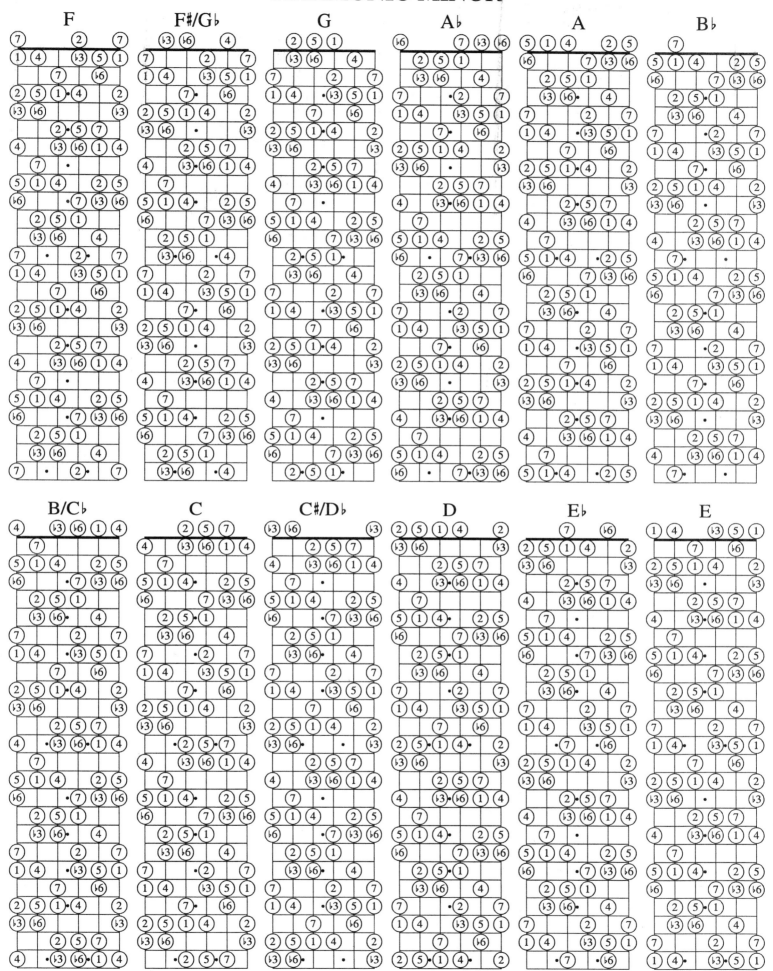

29

HARMONIC MAJOR

KEYBOARD PATTERNS

QUICK MODE GENERATOR CHART

I	II	III	IV	V	VI	VII
C	B♭	A♭	G	F	E	C#/D♭
C#/D♭	B/C♭	A	A♭	F#/G♭	F	D
D	C	B♭	A	G	F#/G♭	E♭
E♭	C#/D♭	B/C♭	B♭	A♭	G	E
E	D	C	B/C♭	A	A♭	F
F	E♭	C#/D♭	C	B♭	A	F#/G♭
F#/G♭	E	D	C#/D♭	B/C♭	B♭	G
G	F	E♭	D	C	B/C♭	A♭
A♭	F#/G♭	E	E♭	C#/D♭	C	A
A	G	F	E	D	C#/D♭	B♭
B♭	A♭	F#/G♭	F	E♭	D	B/C♭
B/C♭	A	G	F#/G♭	E	E♭	C

CONVENTIONAL PATTERNS / SWEEPING PATTERNS (I, II, III, IV, V, VI, VII)

SCALE / MODE - CHORD CHART

I	HARMONIC MAJOR	△, △⁺, △sus2, △sus, ♭6
II	DORIAN ♭5	ø, °7, °9
III	PHRYGIAN ♭4	7, 7⁺, ⁻7, ♭9, #9, ♭13
IV	LYDIAN ♭3	⁻△, △°, ⁻6, °7
V	DOMINANT ♭2	7, 6, 7sus, ♭9, 11, 13
VI	LYDIAN AUGMENTED #2	△⁺, ⁻△⁺, △♭5
VII	LOCRIAN ♮7	°, °7

NUMERIC SCALE / MODE CHART

		1	2	3	4	5	6	7	1	2	3	4	5	6	7
I	HARMONIC MAJOR	1	2	3	4	5 ♭6		7	1	2	3	4	5 ♭6		7
II	DORIAN ♭5		1	2 ♭3	4 ♭5		6 ♭7								
III	PHRYGIAN ♭4			1 ♭2	♭3 ♭4		5 ♭6	♭7							
IV	LYDIAN ♭3				1	2 ♭3	#4 5		6	7					
V	DOMINANT ♭2					1 ♭2	3 4		5	6 ♭7					
VI	LYDIAN AUG #2						1	#2 3	#4	#5 6		7			
VII	LOCRIAN ♮7							1 ♭2	♭3	4 ♭5	♭6 ♭7				

F HARMONIC MAJOR = G DORIAN ♭5 ~ A PHRYGIAN ♭4 ~ B♭ LYDIAN ♭3 ~ C DOMINANT ♭2 ~ C♯ / D♭ LYDIAN AUG ♯2 ~ E LOCRIAN ♮7

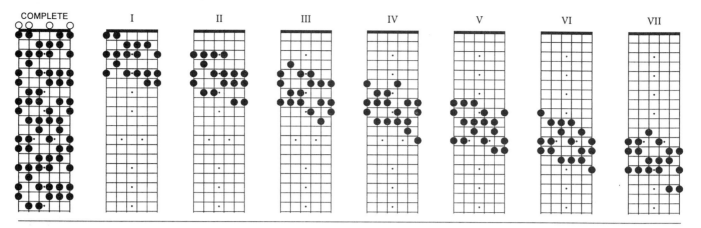

F♯ / G♭ HARMONIC MAJOR = A♭ DORIAN ♭5 ~ B♭ PHRYGIAN ♭4 ~ B/C♭ LYDIAN ♭3 ~ C♯/D♭ DOMINANT ♭2 ~ D LYDIAN AUG ♯2 ~ F LOCRIAN ♮7

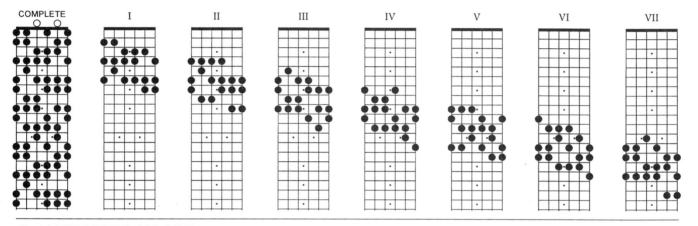

G HARMONIC MAJOR = A DORIAN ♭5 ~ B / C♭ PHRYGIAN ♭4 ~ C LYDIAN ♭3 ~ D DOMINANT ♭2 ~ E♭ LYDIAN AUG ♯2 ~ F♯ / G♭ LOCRIAN ♮7

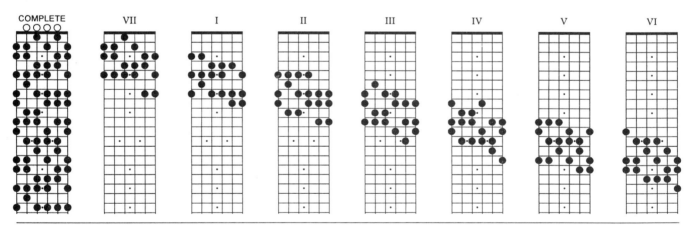

A♭ HARMONIC MAJOR = B♭ DORIAN ♭5 ~ C PHRYGIAN ♭4 ~ C♯ / D♭ LYDIAN ♭3 ~ E♭ DOMINANT ♭2 ~ E LYDIAN AUG ♯2 ~ G LOCRIAN ♮7

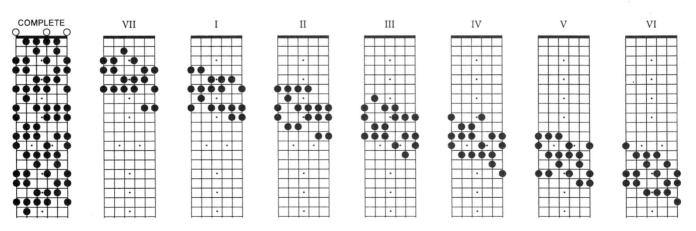

31

A HARMONIC MAJOR = B / C♭ DORIAN ♭5 ~ C♯ / D♭ PHRYGIAN ♭4 ~ D LYDIAN ♭3 ~ E DOMINANT ♭2 ~ F LYDIAN AUG ♯2 ~ A♭ LOCRIAN ♮7

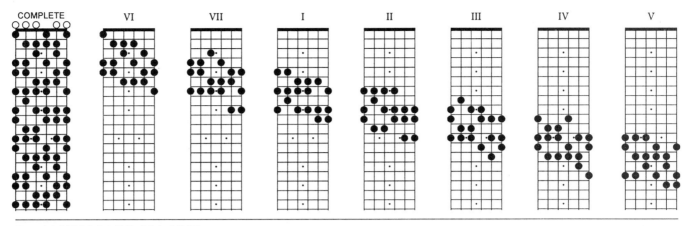

B♭ HARMONIC MAJOR = C DORIAN ♭5 ~ D PHRYGIAN ♭4 ~ E♭ LYDIAN ♭3 ~ F DOMINANT ♭2 ~ F♯ / G♭ LYDIAN AUG ♯2 ~ A LOCRIAN ♮7

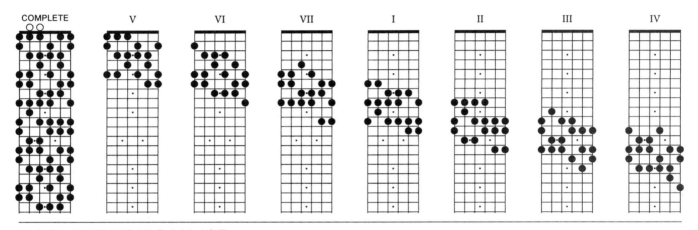

B / C♭ HARMONIC MAJOR = C♯/D♭ DORIAN ♭5 ~ E♭ PHRYGIAN ♭4 ~ E LYDIAN ♭3 ~ F♯/G♭ DOMINANT ♭2 ~ G LYDIAN AUG ♯2 ~ B♭ LOCRIAN ♮7

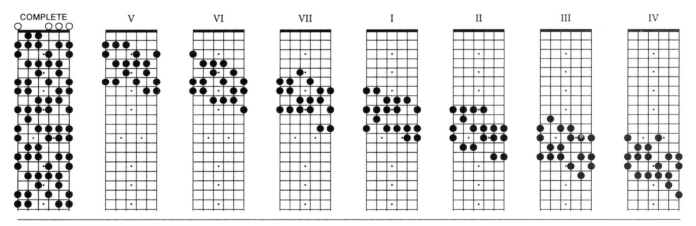

C HARMONIC MAJOR = D DORIAN ♭5 ~ E PHRYGIAN ♭4 ~ F LYDIAN ♭3 ~ G DOMINANT ♭2 ~ A♭ LYDIAN AUG ♯2 ~ B / C♭ LOCRIAN ♮7

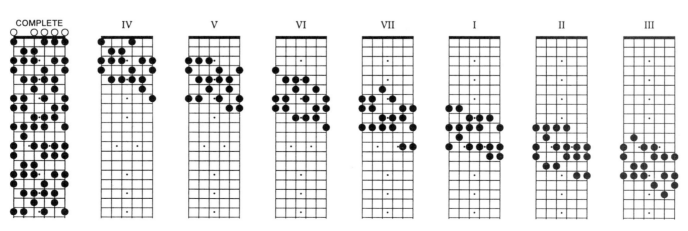

C♯ / D♭ HARMONIC MAJOR = E♭ DORIAN ♭5 ~ F PHRYGIAN ♭4 ~ F♯ / G♭ LYDIAN ♭3 ~ A♭ DOMINANT ♭2 ~ A LYDIAN AUG ♯2 ~ C LOCRIAN ♯7

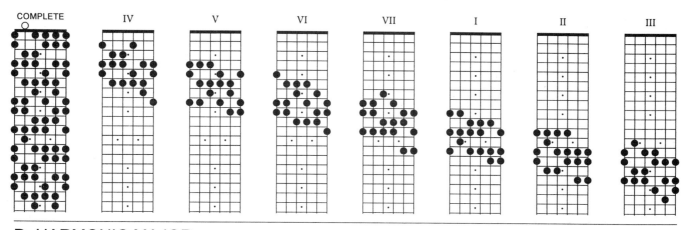

D HARMONIC MAJOR = E DORIAN ♭5 ~ F♯ / G♭ PHRYGIAN ♭4 ~ G LYDIAN ♭3 ~ A DOMINANT ♭2 ~ B♭ LYDIAN AUG ♯2 ~ C♯ / D♭ LOCRIAN ♯7

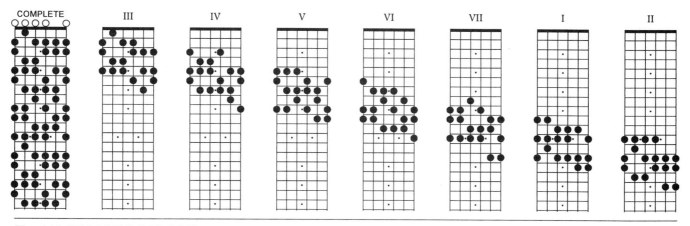

E♭ HARMONIC MAJOR = F DORIAN ♭5 ~ G PHRYGIAN ♭4 ~ A♭ LYDIAN ♭3 ~ B♭ DOMINANT ♭2 ~ B / C♭ LYDIAN AUG ♯2 ~ D LOCRIAN ♯7

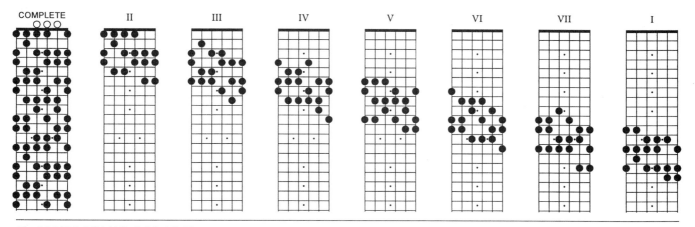

E HARMONIC MAJOR = F♯ / G♭ DORIAN ♭5 ~ A♭ PHRYGIAN ♭4 ~ A LYDIAN ♭3 ~ B / C♭ DOMINANT ♭2 ~ C LYDIAN AUG ♯2 ~ E♭ LOCRIAN ♯7

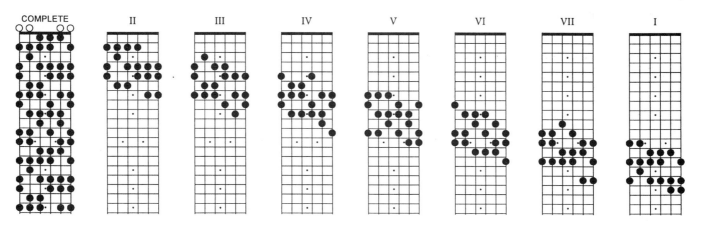

33

HARMONIC MAJOR

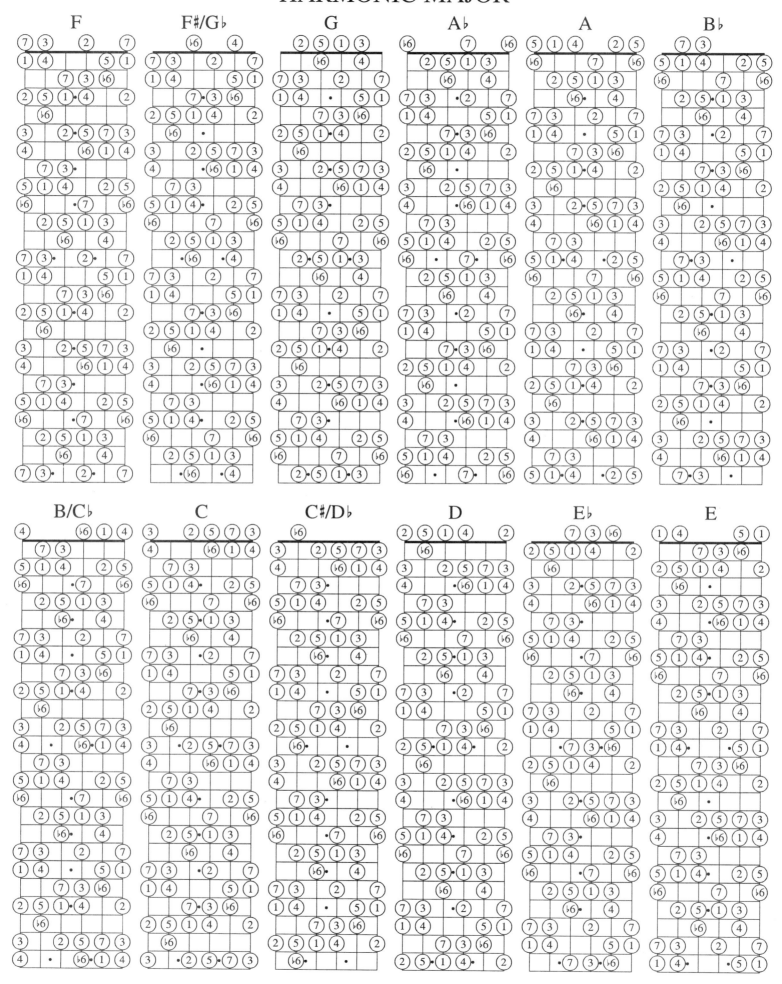

MINOR PENTATONIC

QUICK MODE GENERATOR CHART

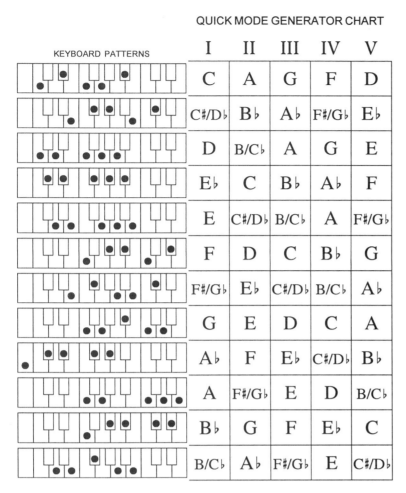

KEYBOARD PATTERNS

I	II	III	IV	V
C	A	G	F	D
C#/Db	Bb	Ab	F#/Gb	Eb
D	B/Cb	A	G	E
Eb	C	Bb	Ab	F
E	C#/Db	B/Cb	A	F#/Gb
F	D	C	Bb	G
F#/Gb	Eb	C#/Db	B/Cb	Ab
G	E	D	C	A
Ab	F	Eb	C#/Db	Bb
A	F#/Gb	E	D	B/Cb
Bb	G	F	Eb	C
B/Cb	Ab	F#/Gb	E	C#/Db

CONVENTIONAL PATTERNS — I, II, III, IV, V

SWEEPING A — I, II, III, IV, V

SWEEPING B — I, II, III, IV, V

SCALE / MODE - CHORD CHART

I	MINOR PENTATONIC	-7
II	MAJOR PENTATONIC	sus2, M, 6
III	MODE 3	sus2, sus
IV	MODE 4	Q(3)
V	MODE 5	sus2, sus

The Minor Pentatonic is the most common pentatonic scale. The Minor Pentatonic can be interspersed with the Dorian, Phrygian, and Aeolian (of the Major scale), because the tones of the Minor Pentatonic are contained in all the above modes, as well as other scales.

NUMERIC SCALE / MODE CHART

		1		2		3	4		5		6		7	1		2		3	4		5		6		7
I	MINOR PENT	1				b3	4		5				b7	1				b3	4		5				b7
II	MAJOR PENT			1			2		3			5		6											
III	MODE 3					1		2			4		5			b7									
IV	MODE 4						1		b3		4				#5		b7								
V	MODE 5								1		2			4		5		6							

35

F MINOR PENTATONIC = A♭ MAJOR PENTATONIC

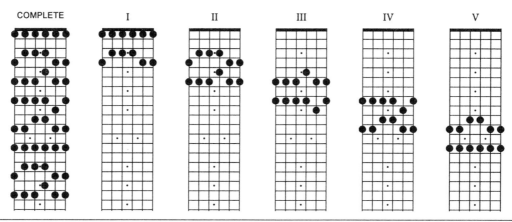

F# / G♭ MINOR PENTATONIC = A MAJOR PENTATONIC

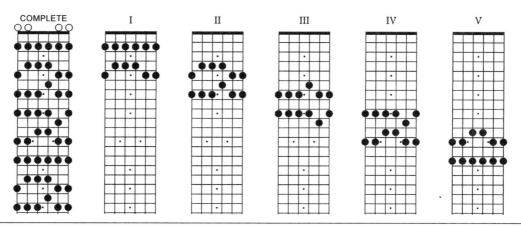

G MINOR PENTATONIC = B♭ MAJOR PENTATONIC

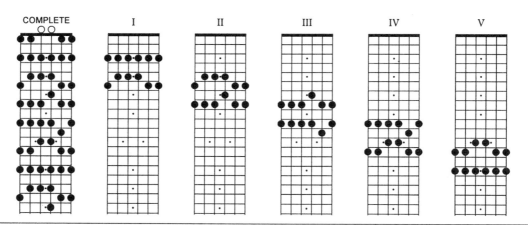

A♭ MINOR PENTATONIC = B / C♭ MAJOR PENTATONIC

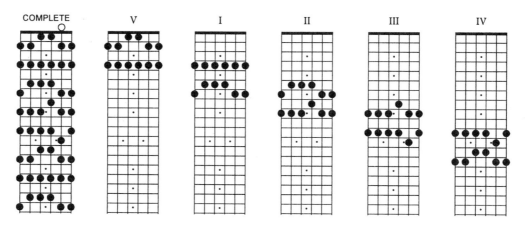

A MINOR PENTATONIC = C MAJOR PENTATONIC

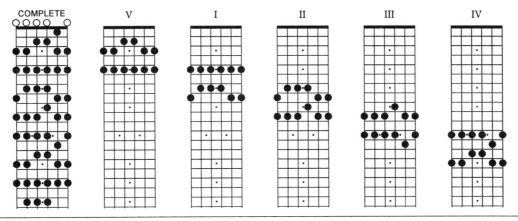

B♭ MINOR PENTATONIC = C♯ / D♭ MAJOR PENTATONIC

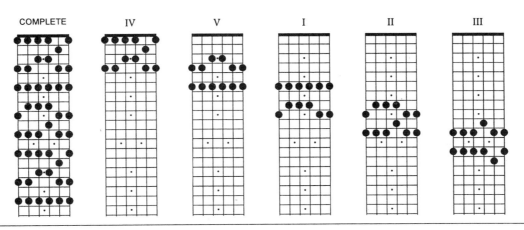

B / C♭ MINOR PENTATONIC = D MAJOR PENTATONIC

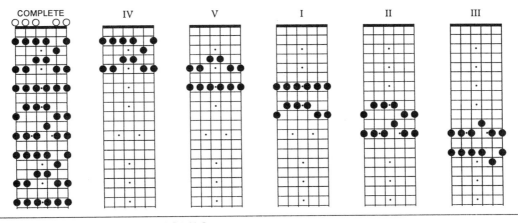

C MINOR PENTATONIC = E♭ MAJOR PENTATONIC

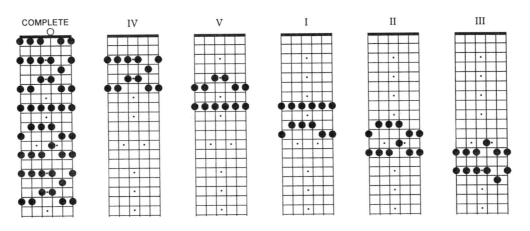

C# / Db MINOR PENTATONIC = E MAJOR PENTATONIC

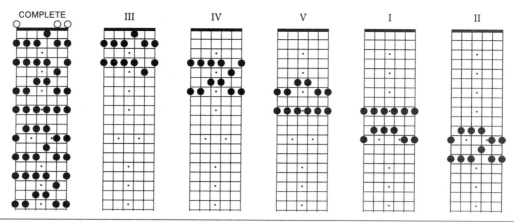

D MINOR PENTATONIC = F MAJOR PENTATONIC

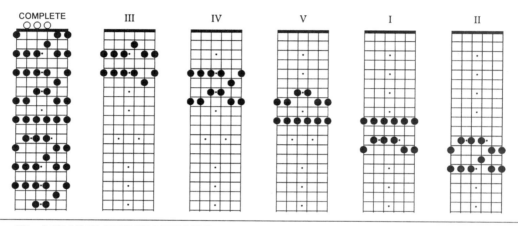

Eb MINOR PENTATONIC = F# / Gb MAJOR PENTATONIC

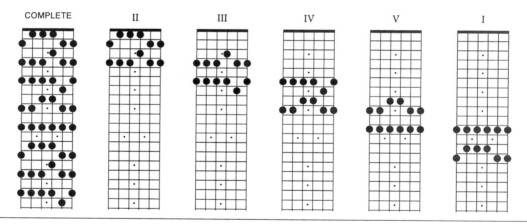

E MINOR PENTATONIC = G MAJOR PENTATONIC

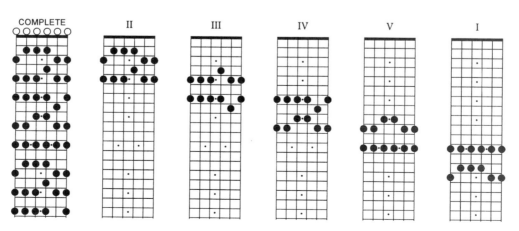

MINOR PENTATONIC

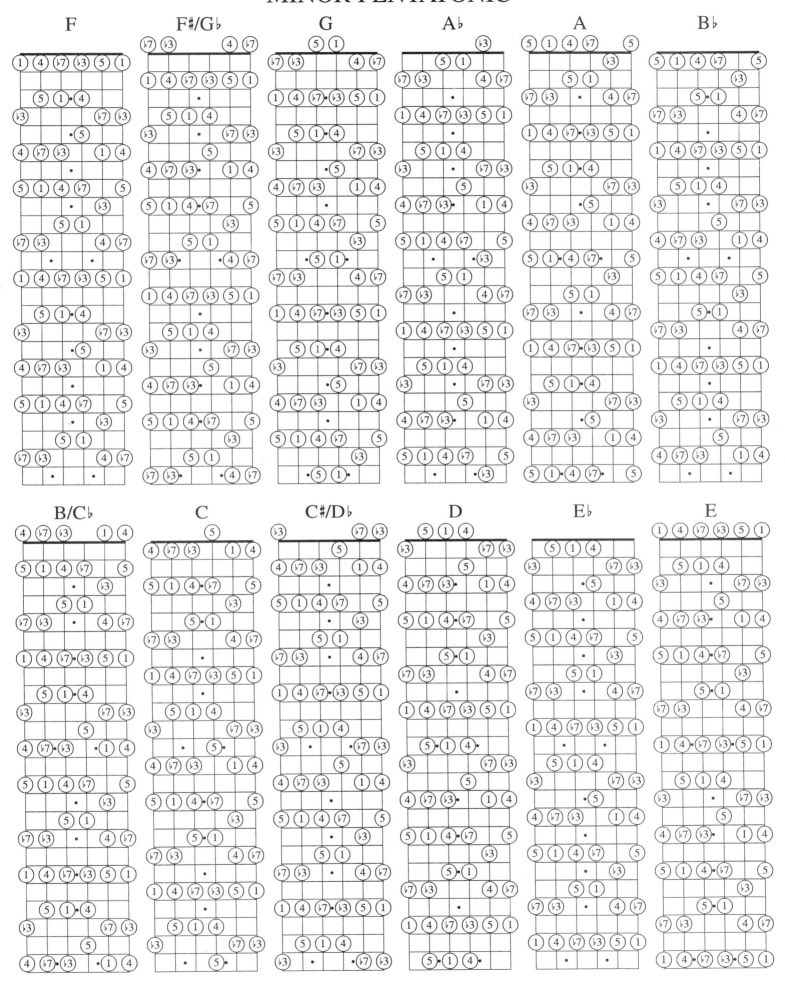

MAJOR PENTATONIC

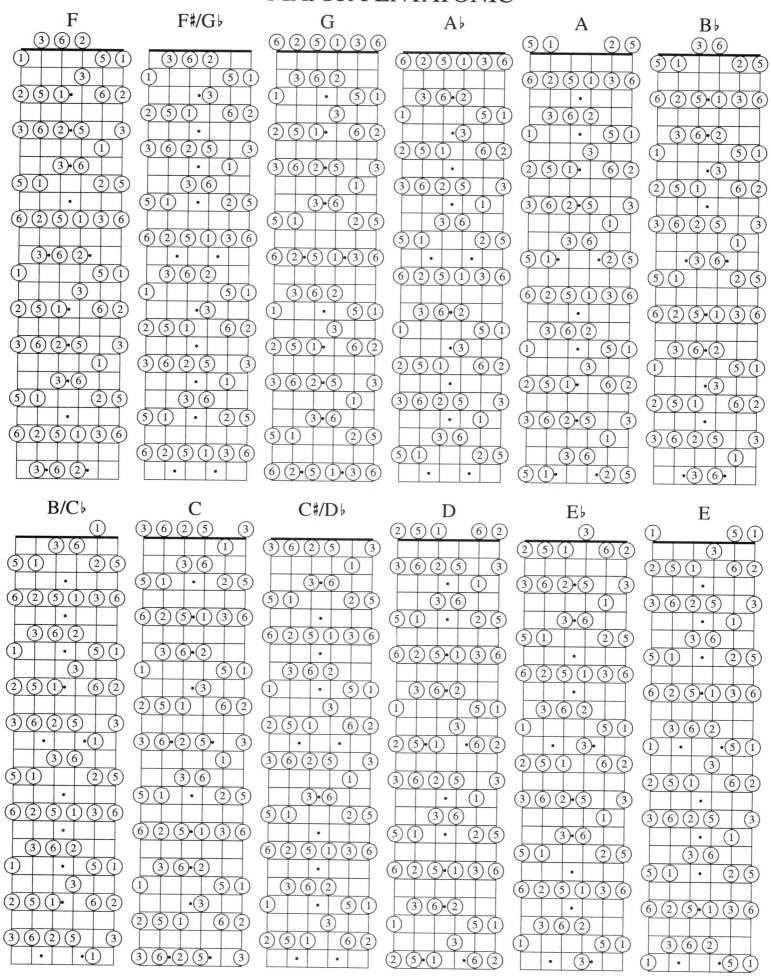

CHORDS

A chord is defined as 3 or more tones played simultaneously; an interval can be considered a 2 tone chord, as in a Power chord. A basic chord "formula" is to use every other tone of the scale. For example, a Major chord contains 1, 3, 5. A Major 7th chord is 1, 3, 5, 7 (fig. 26).

Major Scale	1		2		3	4		5		6		7
Major Chord	1				3			5				↓
Major 7th △7	1				3			5				7

fig. 26

What about those big fancy chords like 9ths, 11ths, and 13ths? Using 2 octaves of our Major scale, we can clearly see that a 9th is a 2nd, an 11th is a 4th, and the 13th is a 6th (fig. 27). This should help remove the mystery behind big chords.

Major Scale	1		2		3	4		5		6		7	1		2		3	4		5		6		7
Major 9th	1				3			5				7			9									
Major 11th	1				3			5				7			9				11					
Major 13th	1				3			5				7			9				11				13	

fig. 27

To play inversions merely bounce the lowest tone up an octave (fig. 28).

Major Scale	1		2		3	4		5		6		7	1		2		3	4		5		6		7
Major Chord	1				3			5																
1st Inversion					3			5				1												
2nd Inversion								5				1						3						

fig. 28

CHORD NAMING

Certain guidelines help musicians communicate. To understand numeric chord formulas, you must understand the chord naming system in this text. In fig. 29 the 7 symbols denote the status of specific tones within the chord. Flat and sharp symbols are used when altering any other tones. Do not use - and + as flats and sharps.

CHORD NAMING CHART

	SYMBOL	DENOTES STATUS OF	CHANGE	RESULT	NAME	EXAMPLE & FORMULA
3 tone	−	3	♭	♭3	MINOR	C⁻ = 1, ♭3, 5
	+	5	♯	♯5	AUGMENTED	C⁺ = 1, 3, ♯5
	°	3,5	♭	♭3,♭5	DIMINISHED	C° = 1, ♭3, ♭5
4 tone	△	7	same	7	DELTA	C△ = 1, 3, 5, 7
	7	7	♭	♭7	DOMINANT	C7 = 1, 3, 5, ♭7
	∅	3,5,7	♭	♭3,♭5,♭7	HALF-DIMINISHED	C∅ = 1, ♭3, ♭5, ♭7
	°7	7 of ∅	extra ♭	♭♭7	DIMINISHED 7th	C°7 = 1, ♭3, ♭5, ♭♭7

fig. 29

VOICING CHORDS

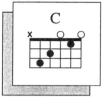

fig. 30

The chord symbol to the left (fig. 30) is probably the one you are most familiar with for a C chord. More correctly however, it is a "voicing" for a C chord. The more thorough approach for the guitarist would be to visualize the C chord in it's entirety, that is every note possible for C, on the entire fretboard (fig. 31). This allows the guitarist total freedom to voice the C chord anyway that is needed to complete the composition.

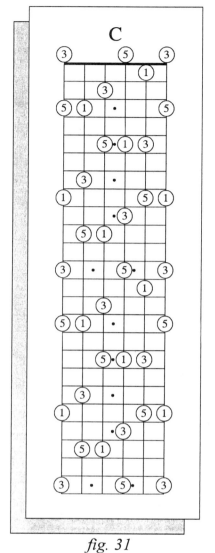

fig. 31

Any combination of notes from the diagram above (fig. 31) will be a voicing for a C chord and will work anywhere that a C chord is to be played.

In figure 32, highlighted circles represent the chord voicing. Notice how the chord voicings are derived from the complete fretboard.

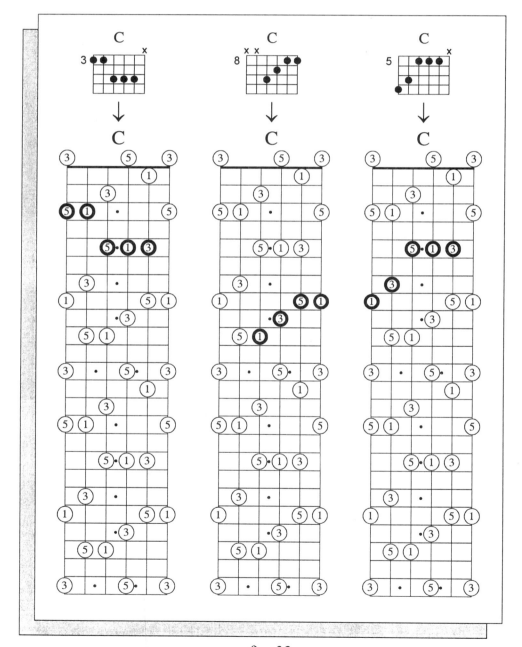

fig. 32

CHORD VOICINGS AND SCALES

Along with an Interval Map each chord has an Example Page. Next to every chord voicing are two compatible scale patterns. These patterns allow you to solo over the chord, in the designated scale without having to change positions (fig. 33). A more complete study of this concept is found in **The Guitar Grimoire® Chords & Voicings** book.

The chord voicings used on the example pages are movable chords, that is they are voicings whose pattern shape remain the same but are movable up and down the fretboard to change the pitch of the chord. Fig. 34 demonstrates how a voicing for the F chord taken from the Major Example Page can be moved anywhere up and down the fretboard.

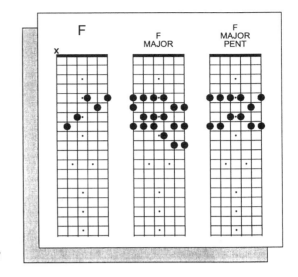

fig. 33

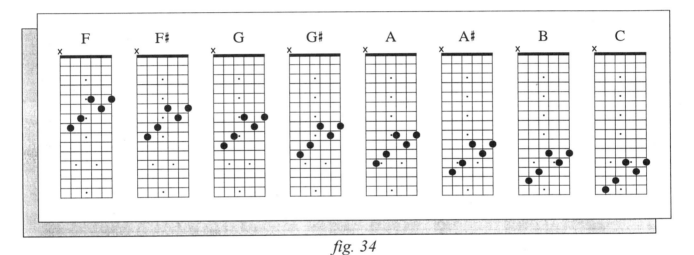

fig. 34

The same F chord voicing decends in figure 35 down to the key of C. Descending all the way we see that any movable chord can become an open chord. The fingers used may change, however, due to the open strings.

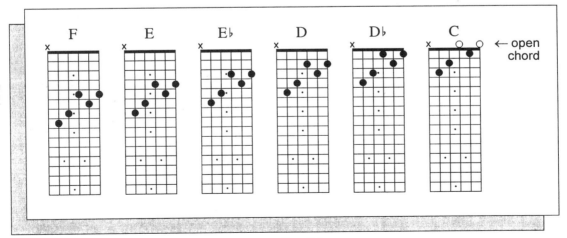

fig. 35

M (MAJOR)

F   F#/G♭ 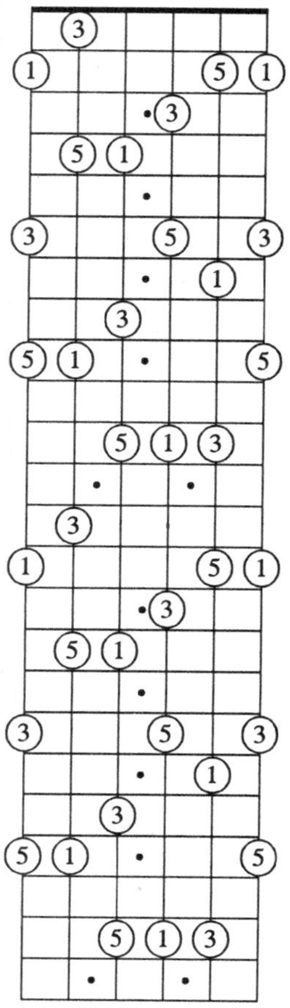   G 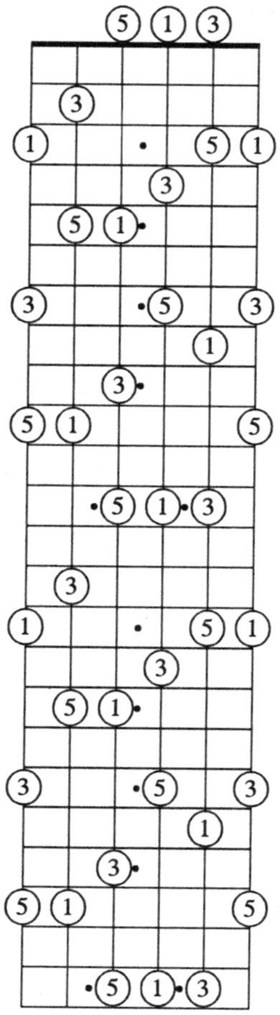   A♭ 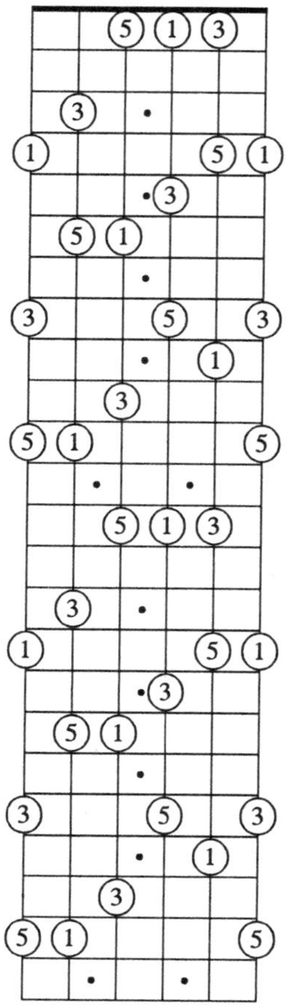   A 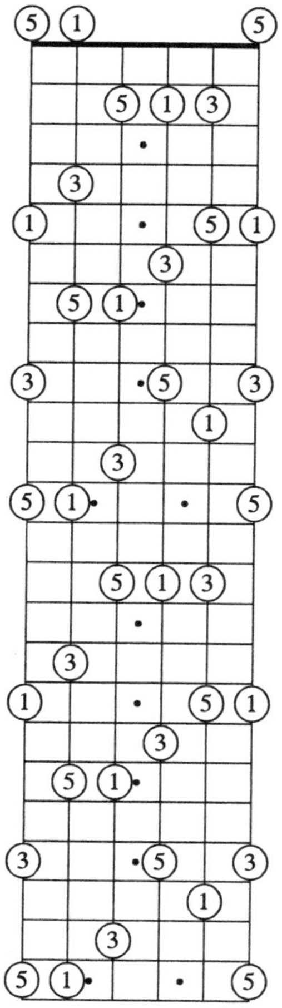   B♭

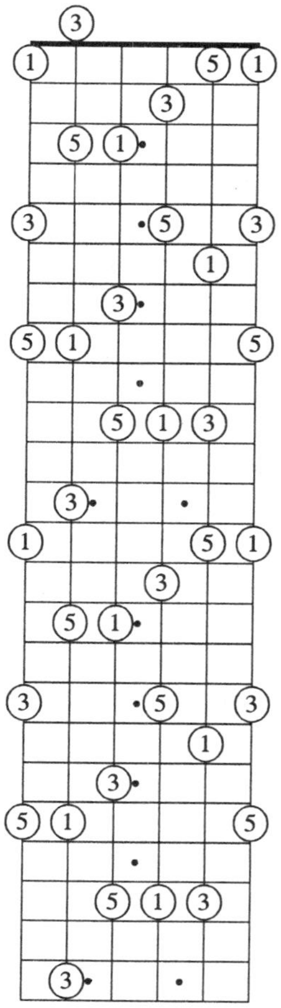

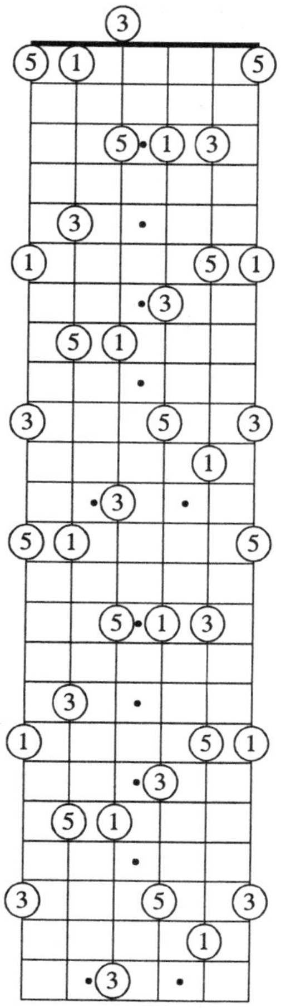

B/C♭ 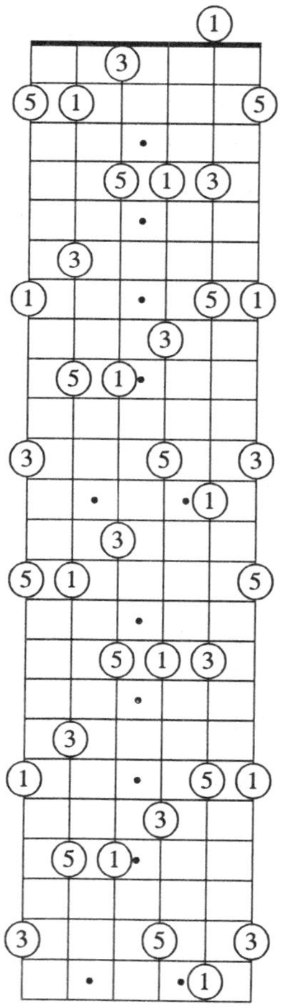   C 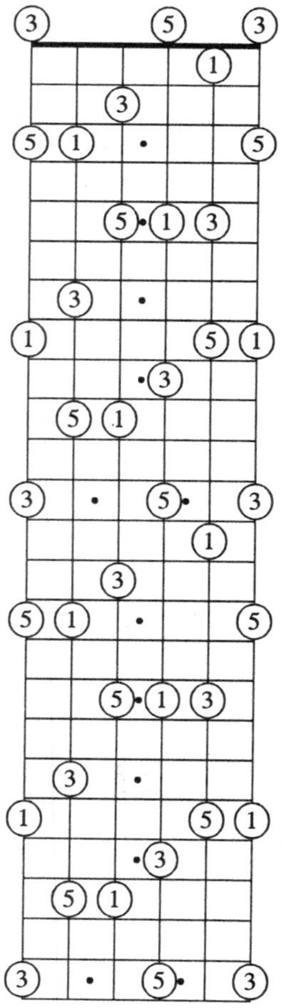   C#/D♭ 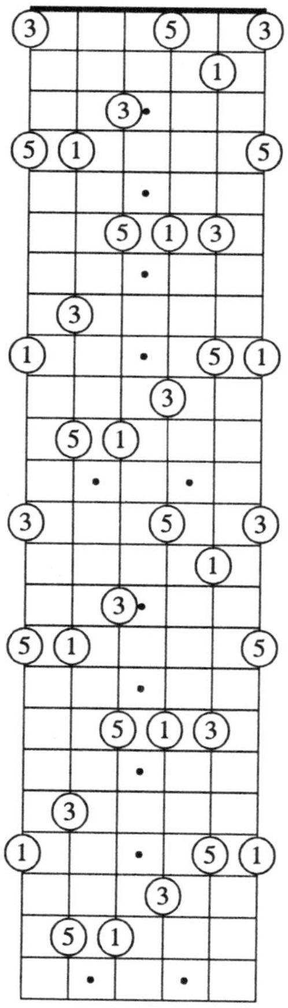   D 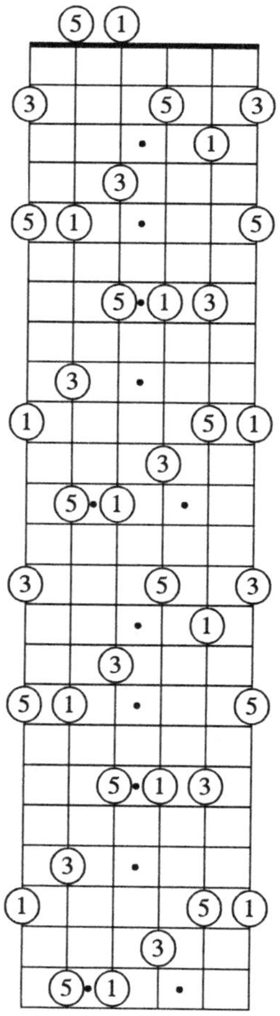   E♭ 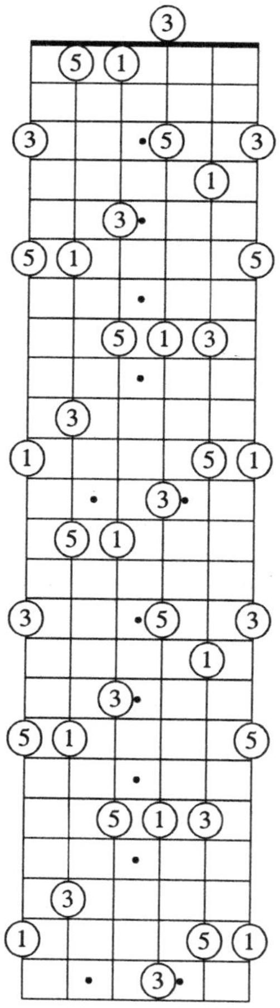   E

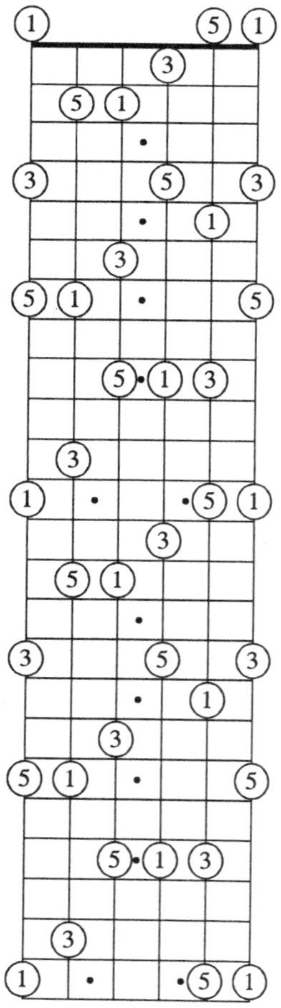

44

M (MAJOR)

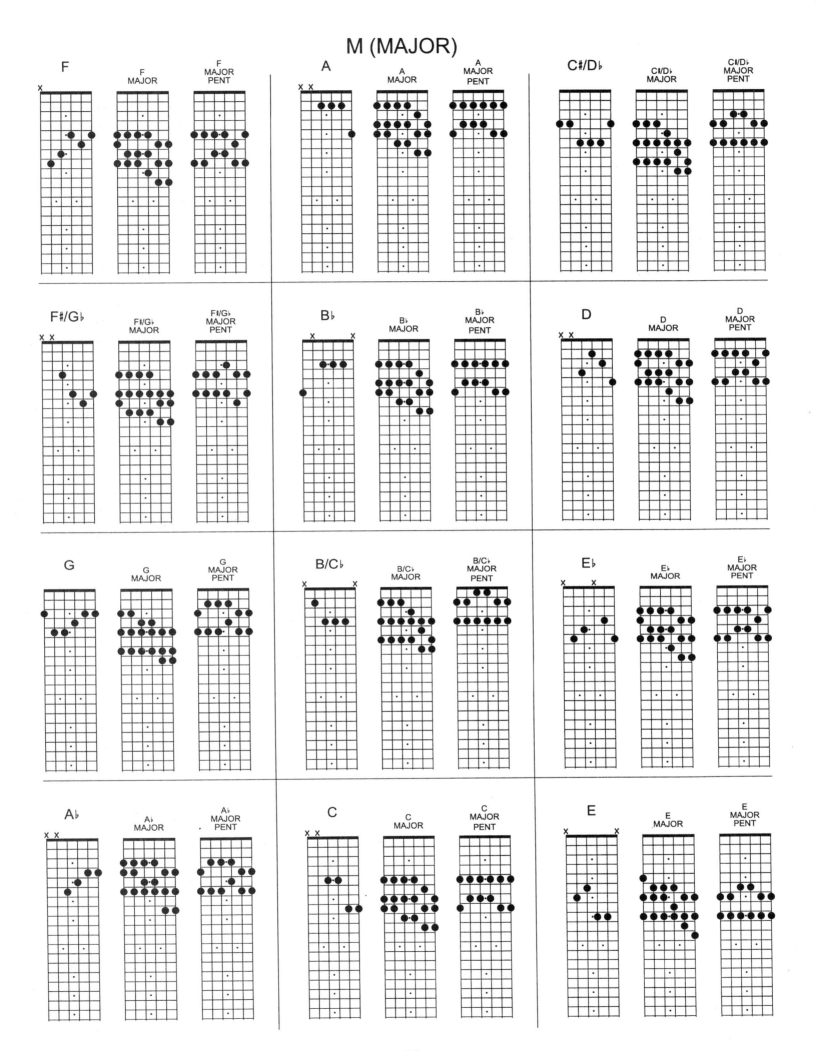

(MINOR)

F

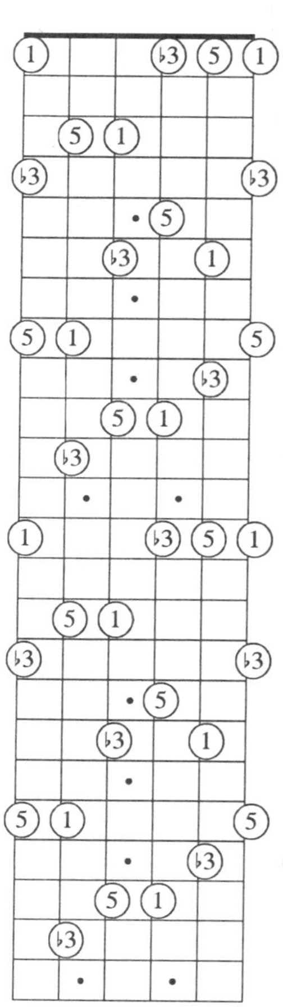

F♯/G♭

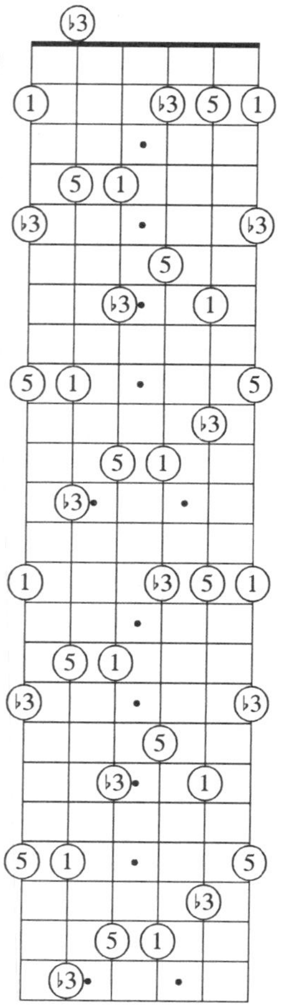

G

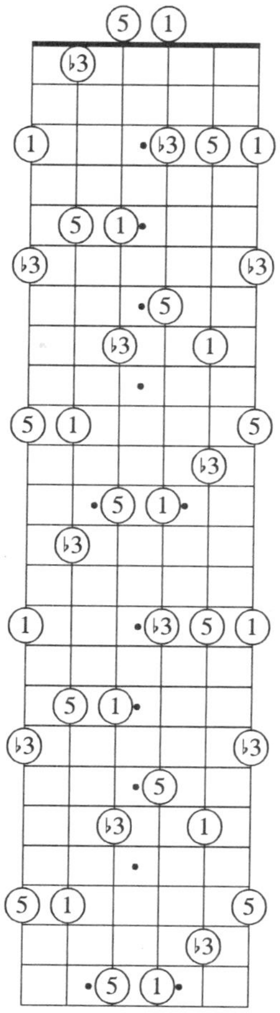

A♭

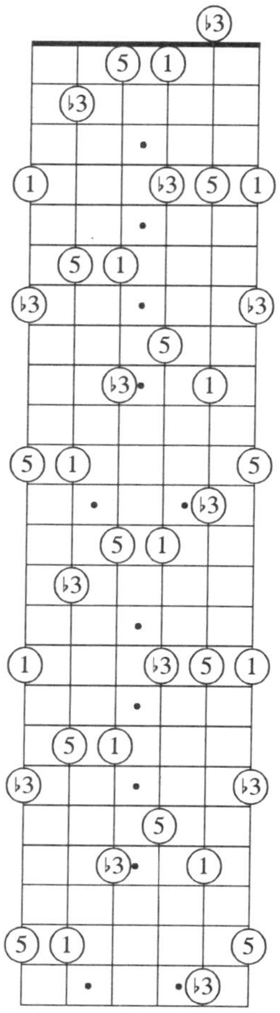

A

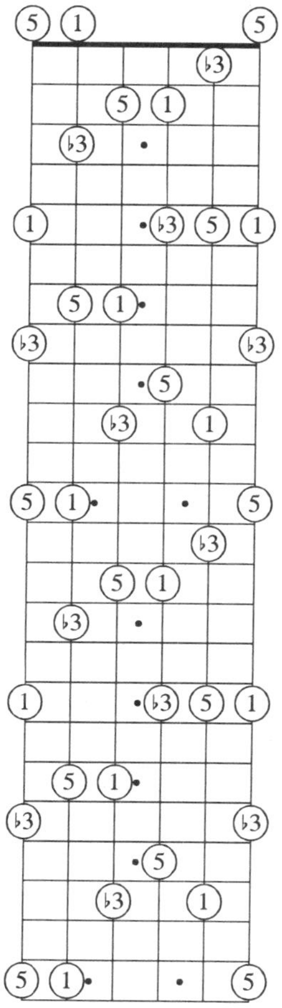

B♭

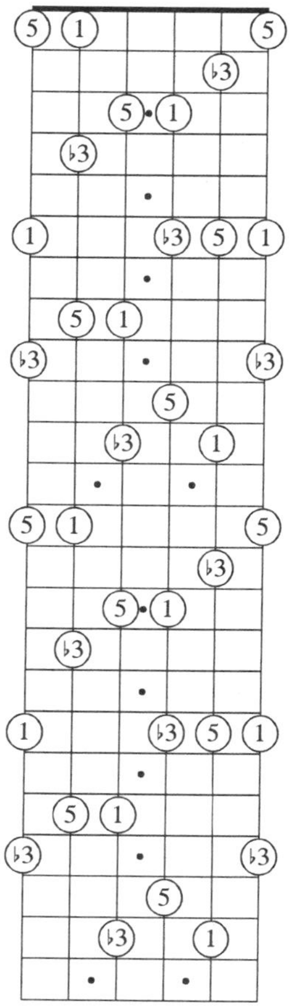

B/C♭

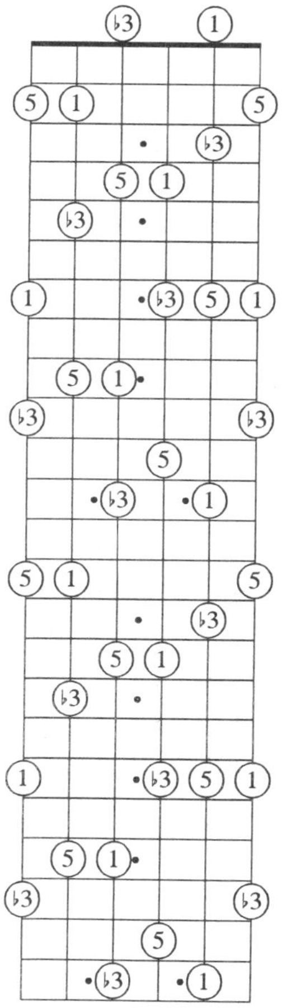

C

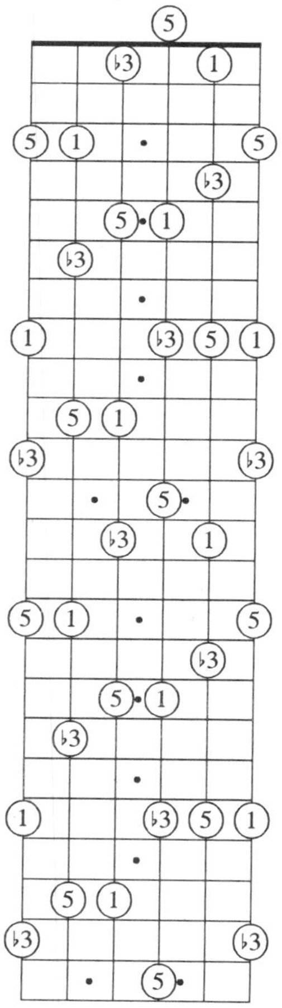

C♯/D♭

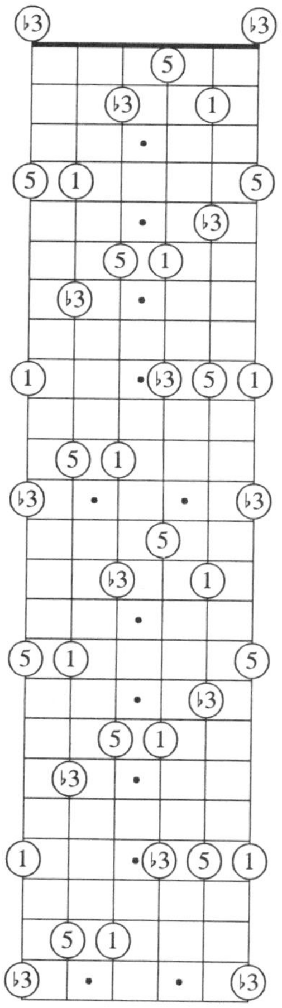

D

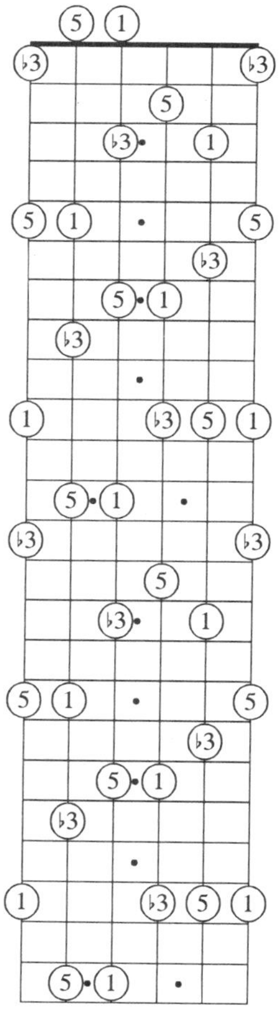

E♭

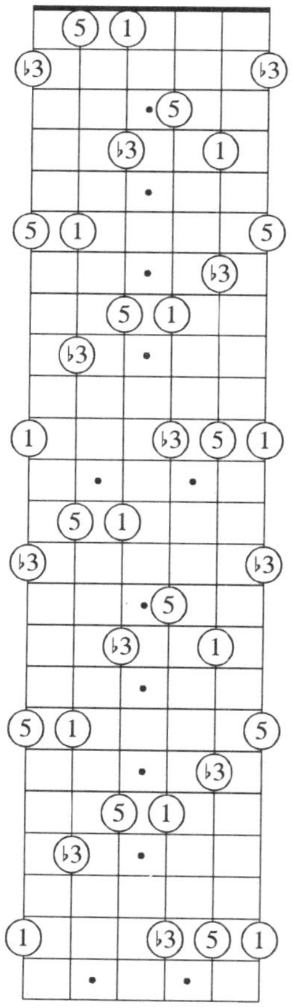

E

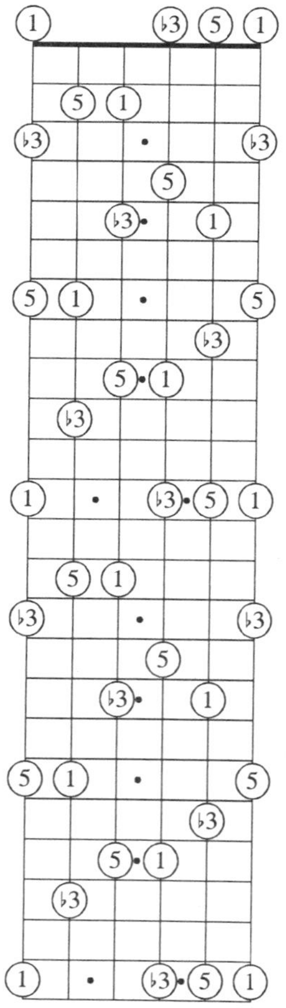

(MINOR)

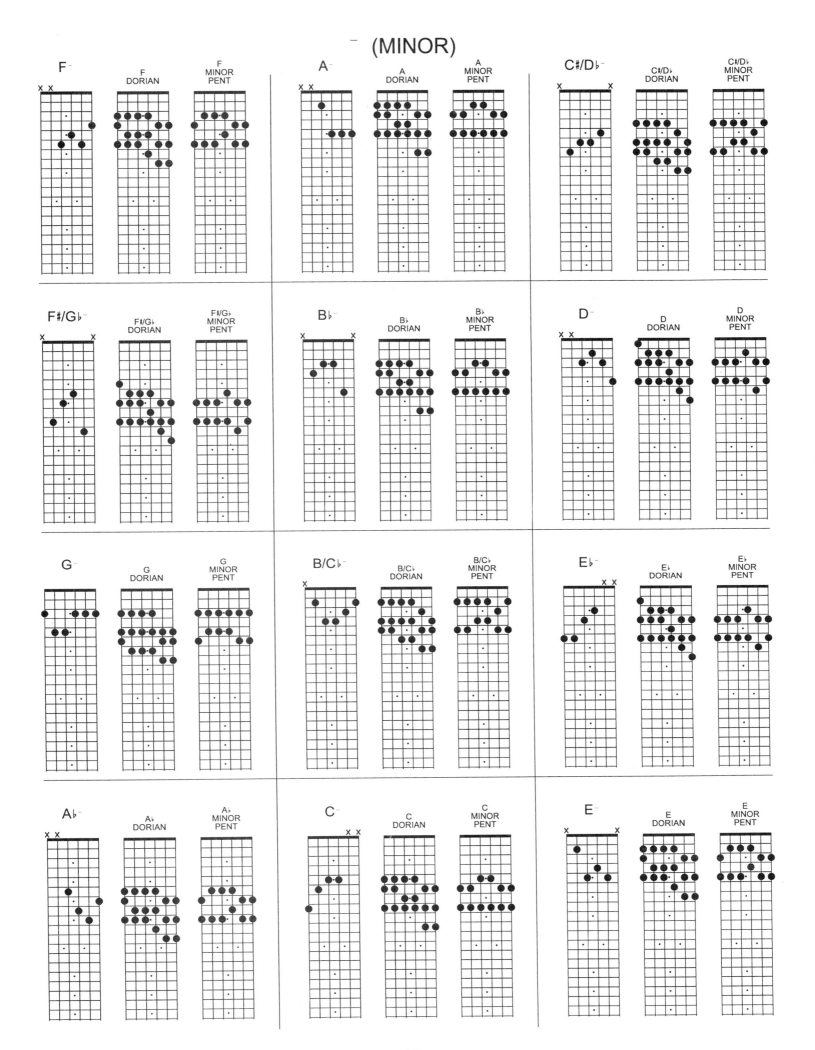

47

sus2 (SUSPENDED SECOND)

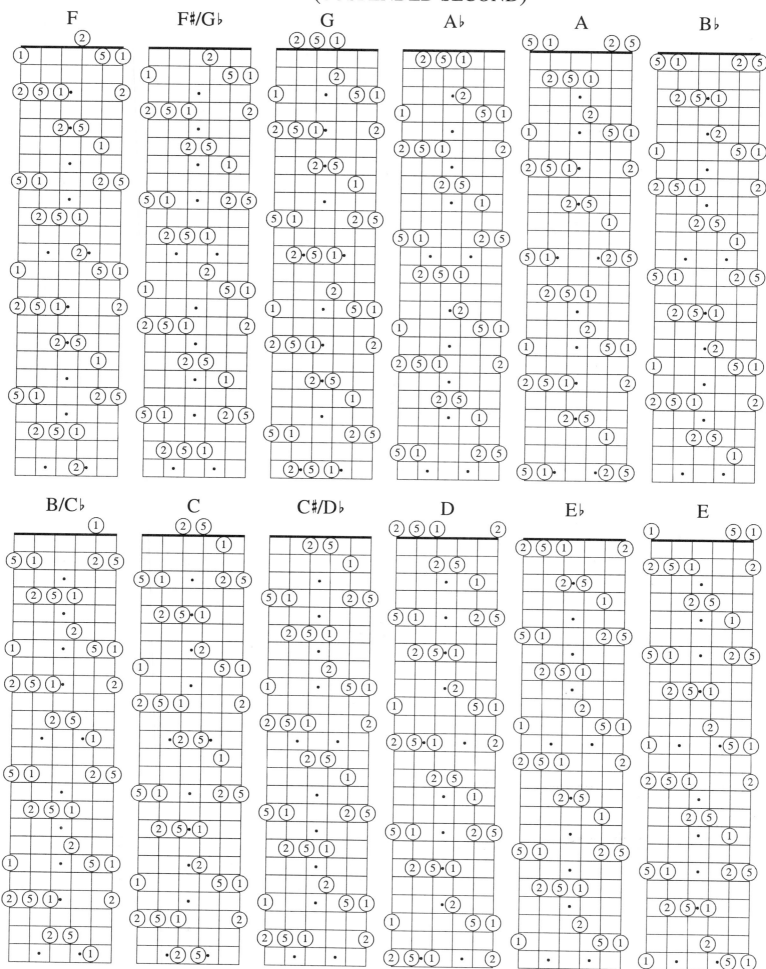

sus2

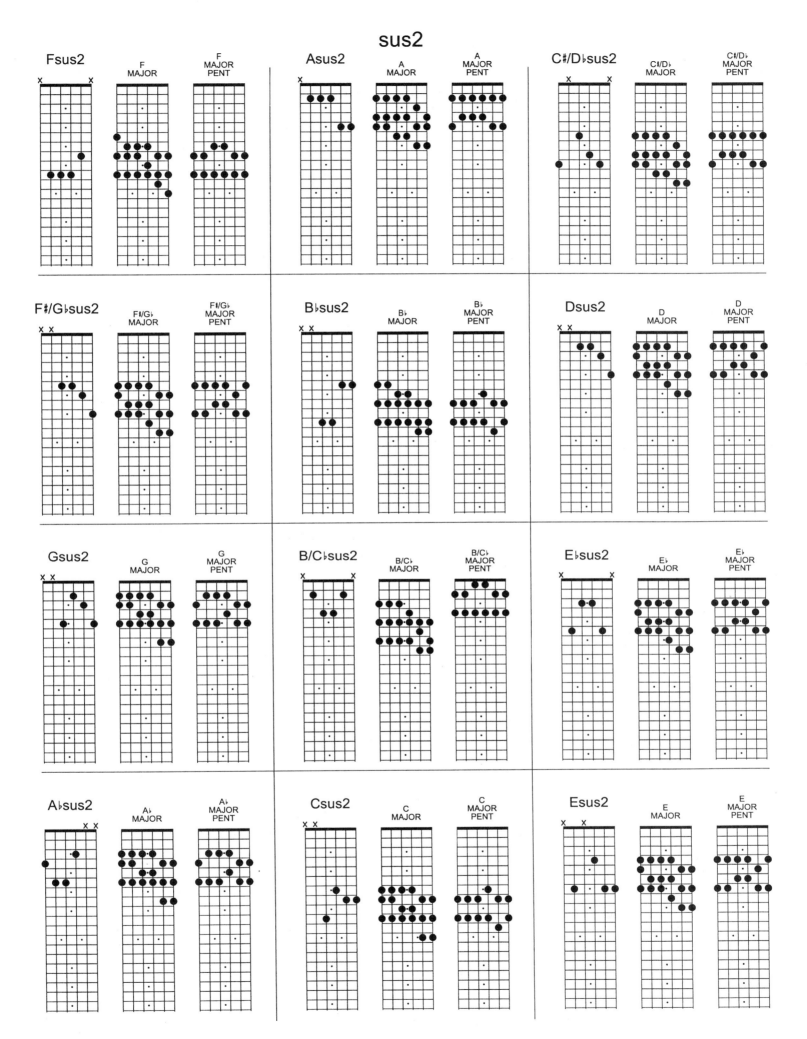

sus (4) (SUSPENDED FOURTH)

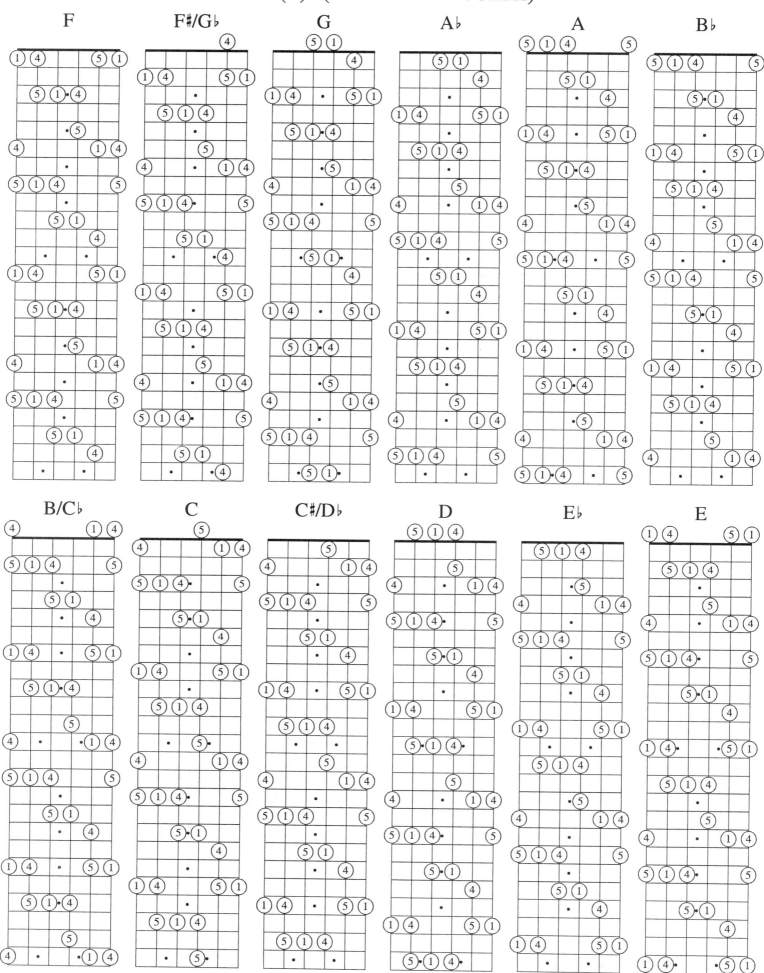

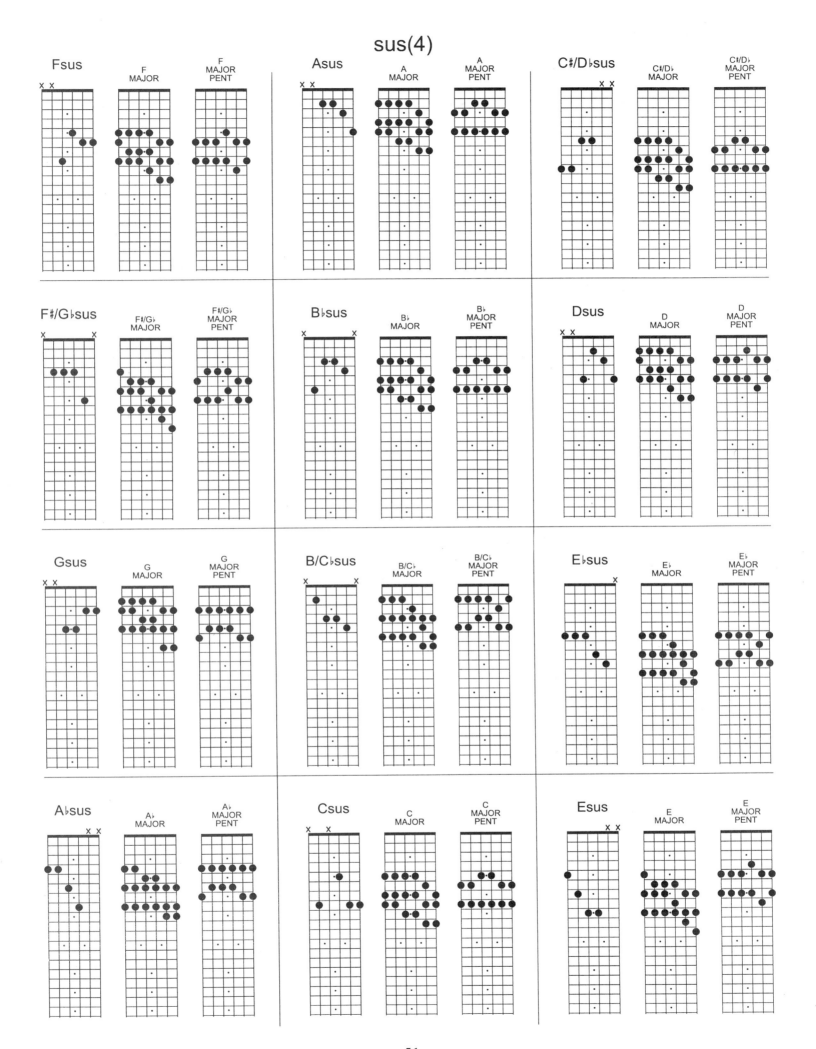

♭5 (FLATTED FIFTH)

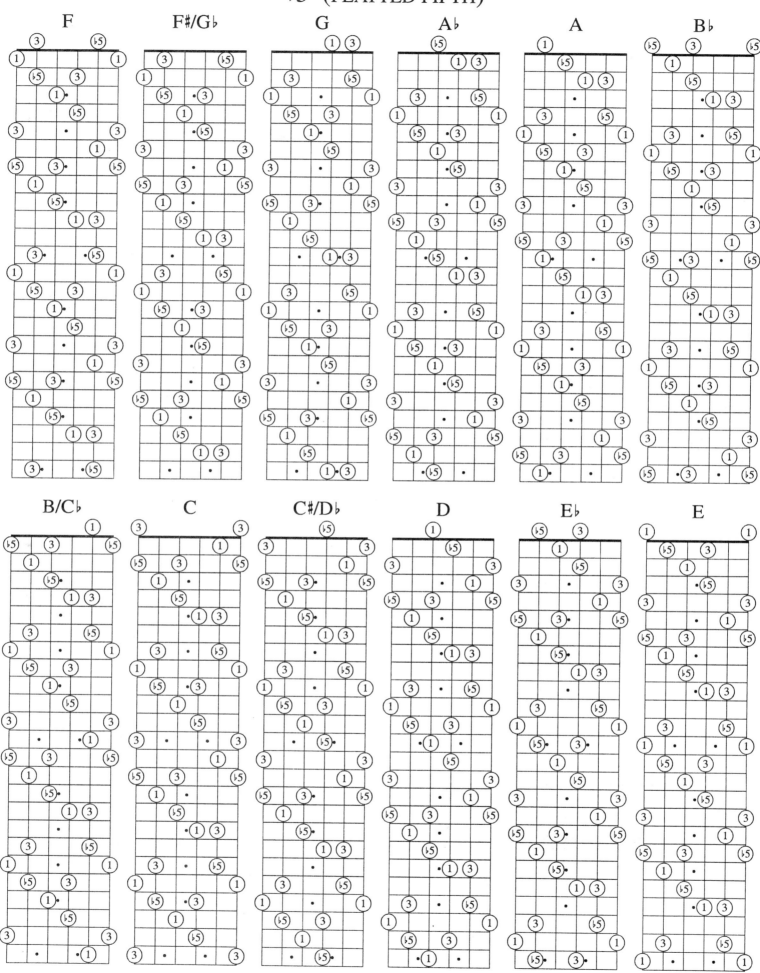

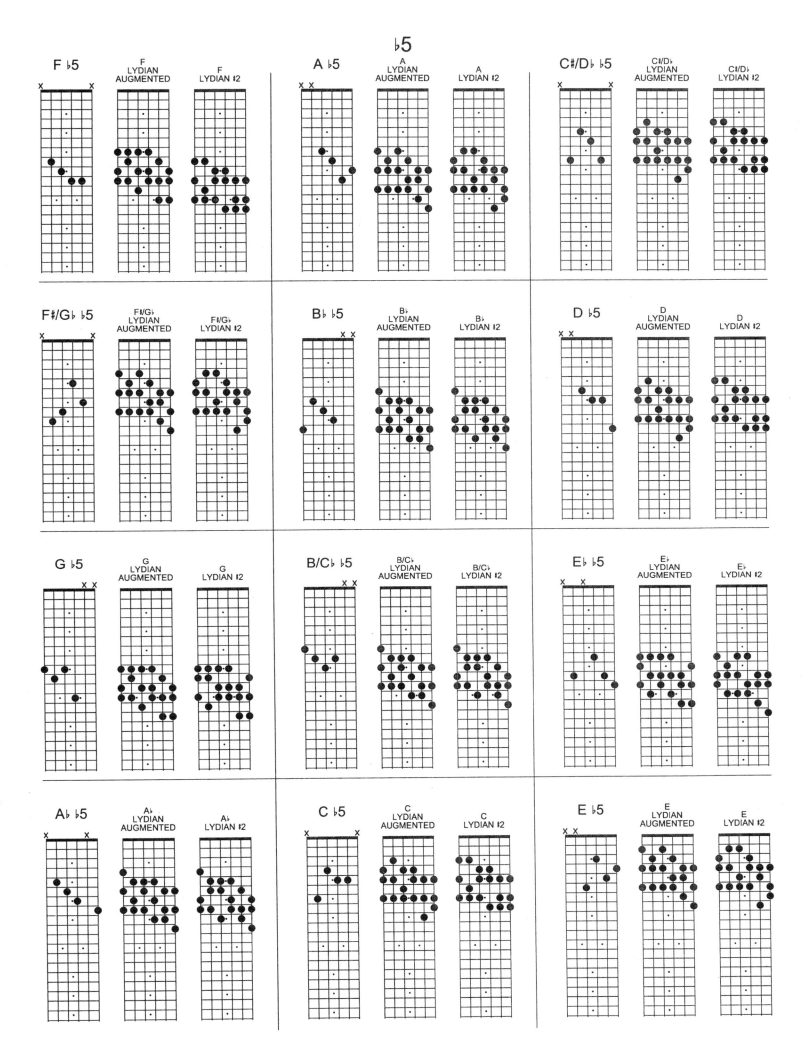

° (DIMINISHED)

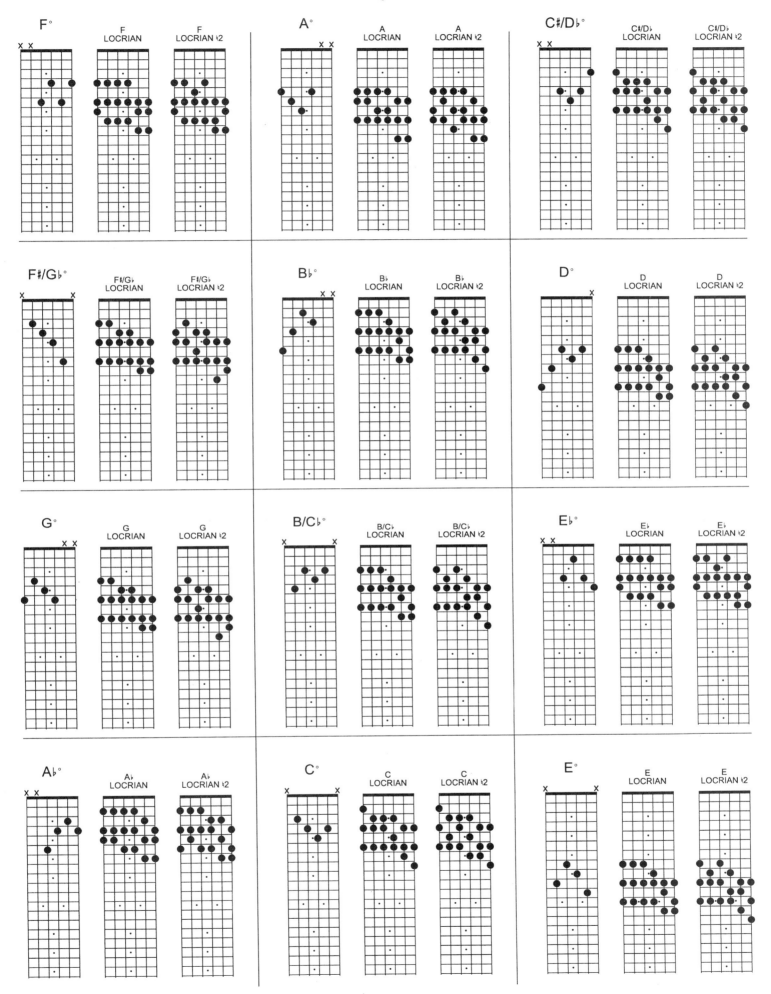

+ (AUGMENTED)

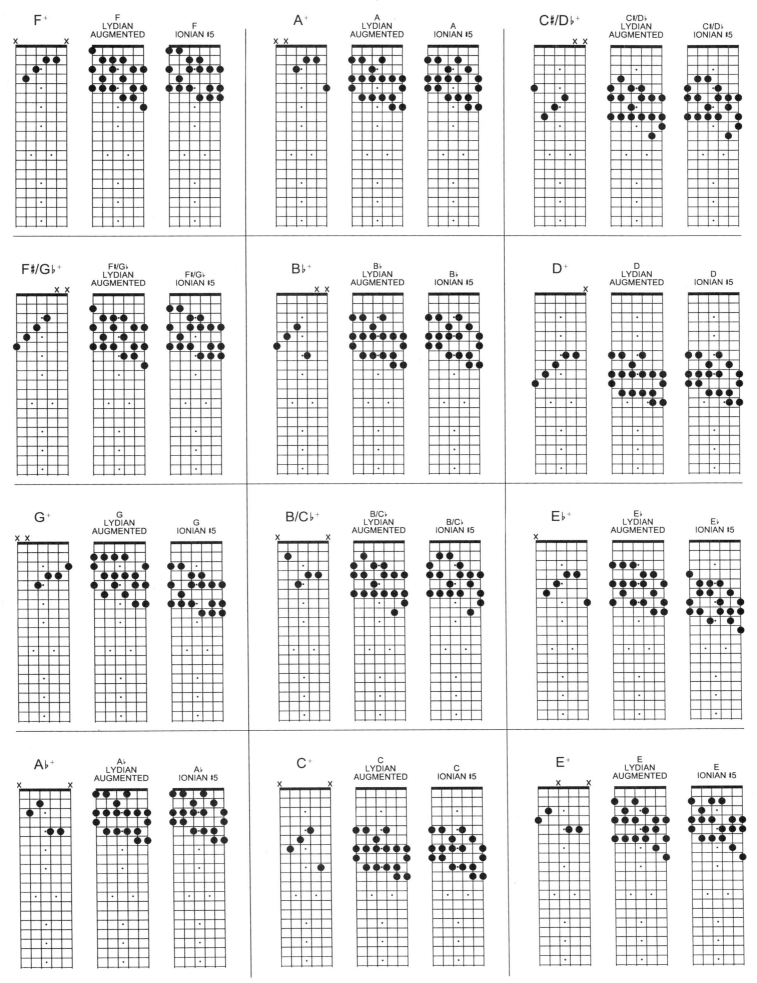

♭6 (FLATTED SIXTH)

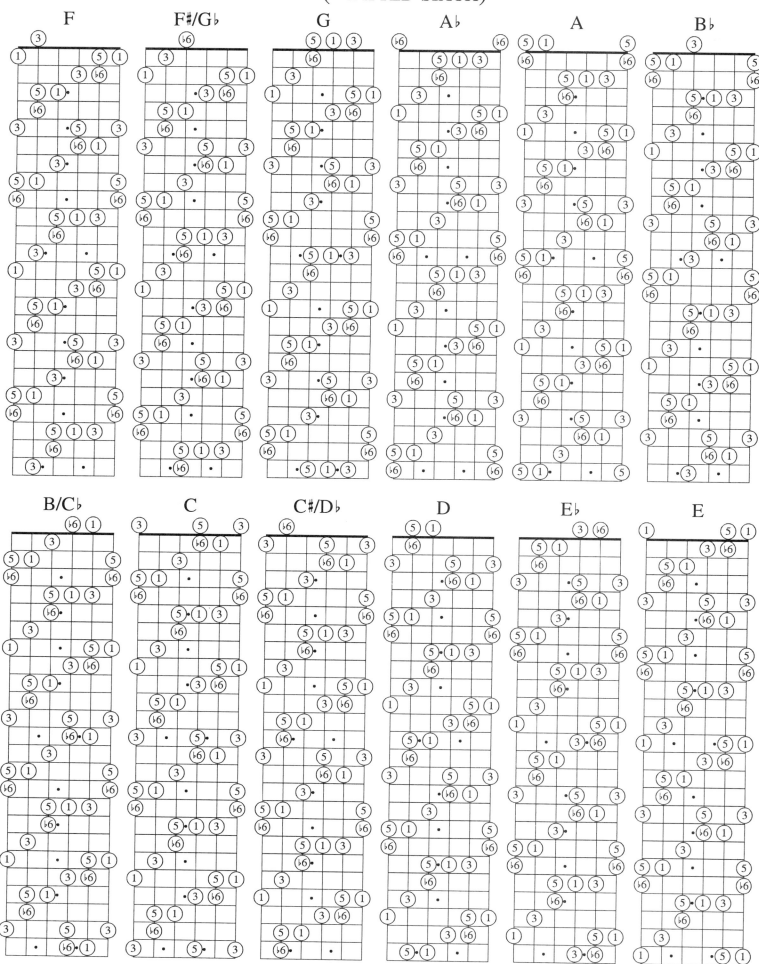

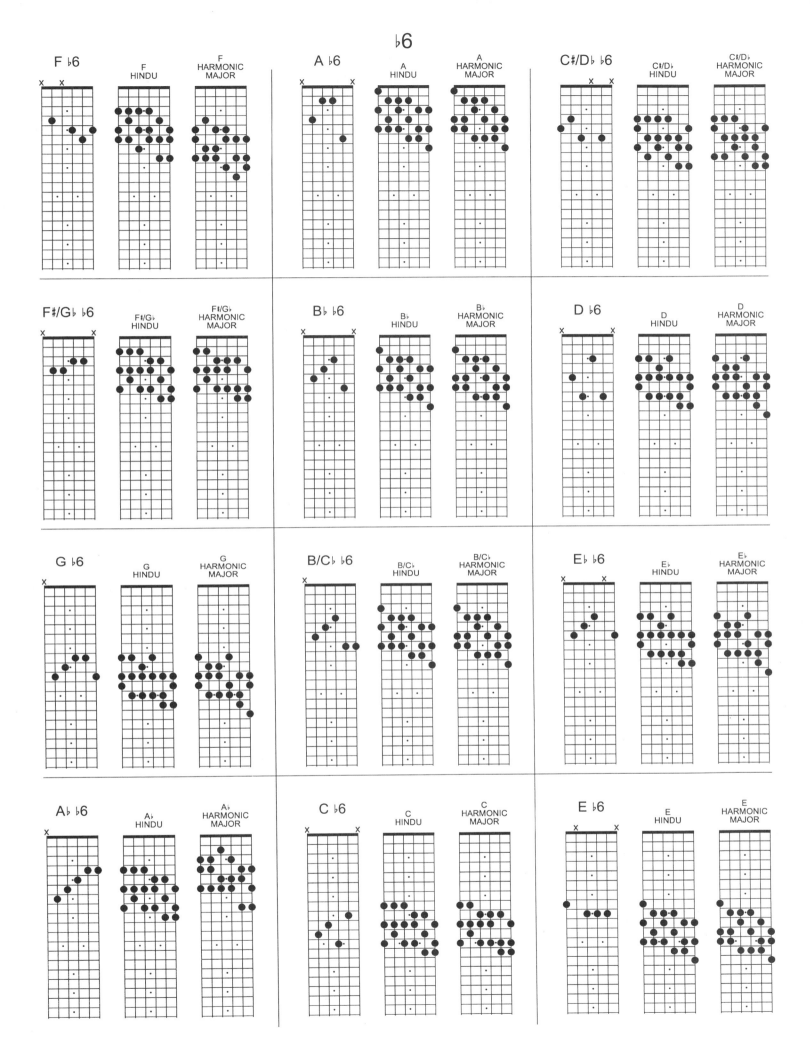

-♭6 (MINOR FLATTED SIXTH)

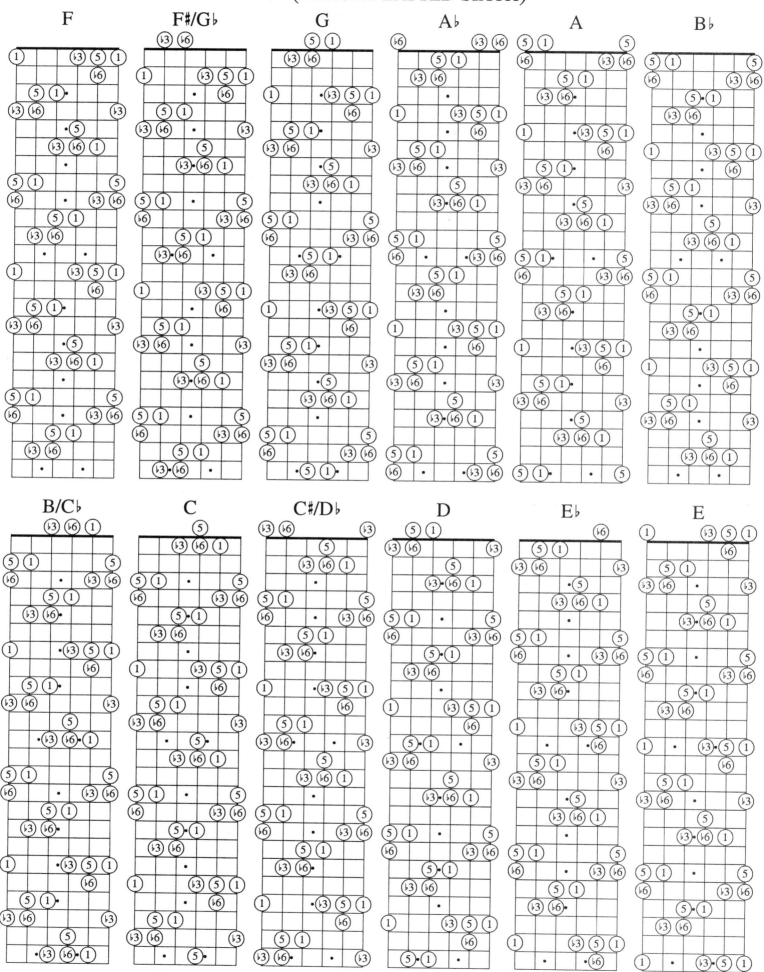

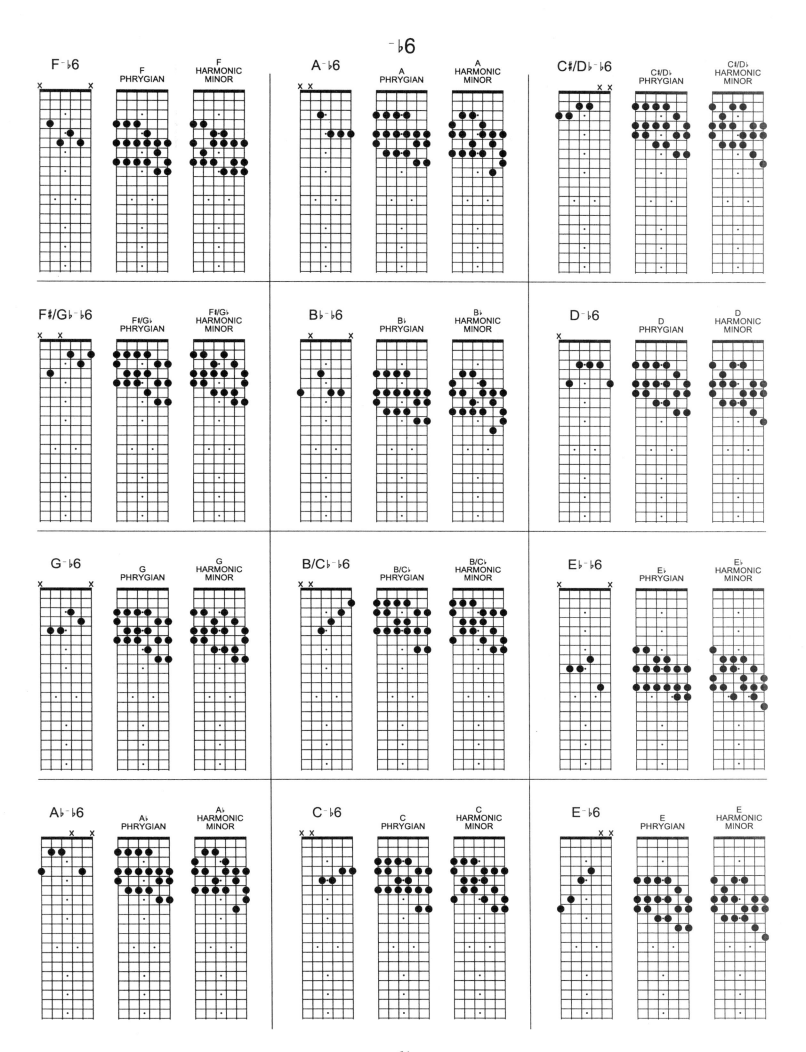

6 (SIXTH)

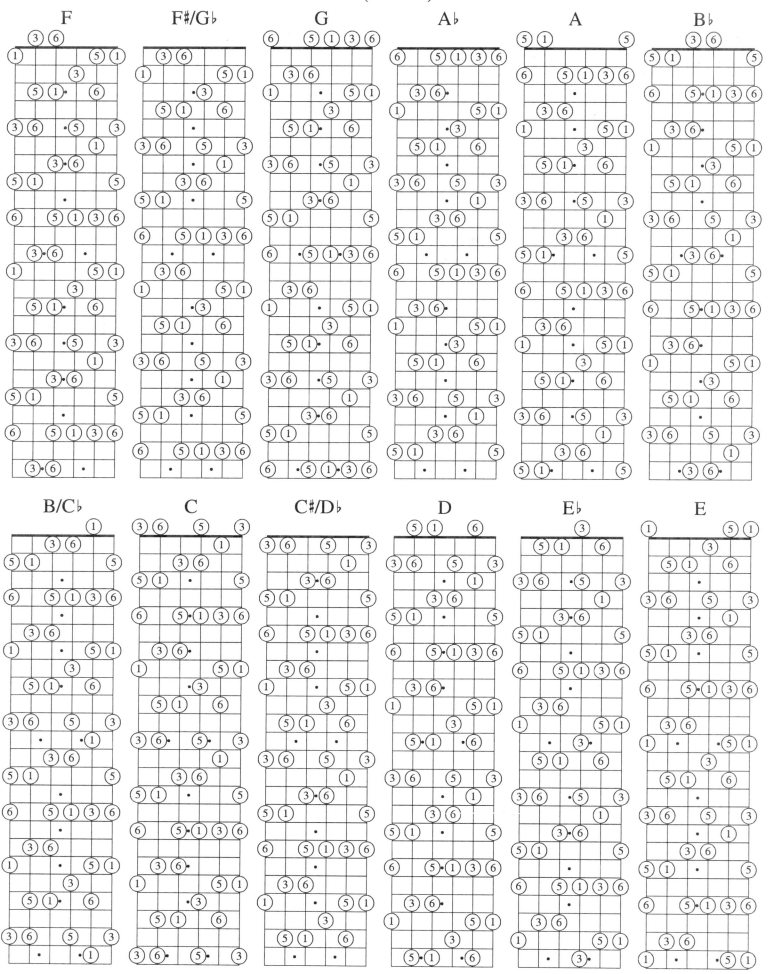

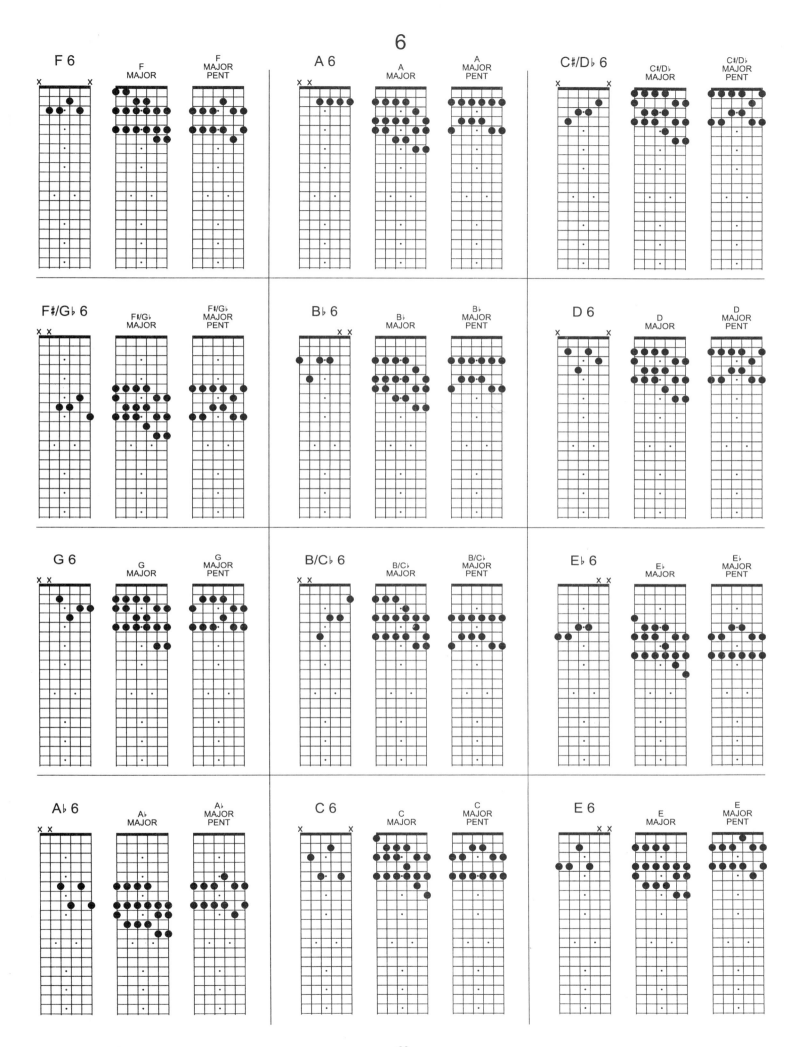

⁻6 (MINOR SIXTH)

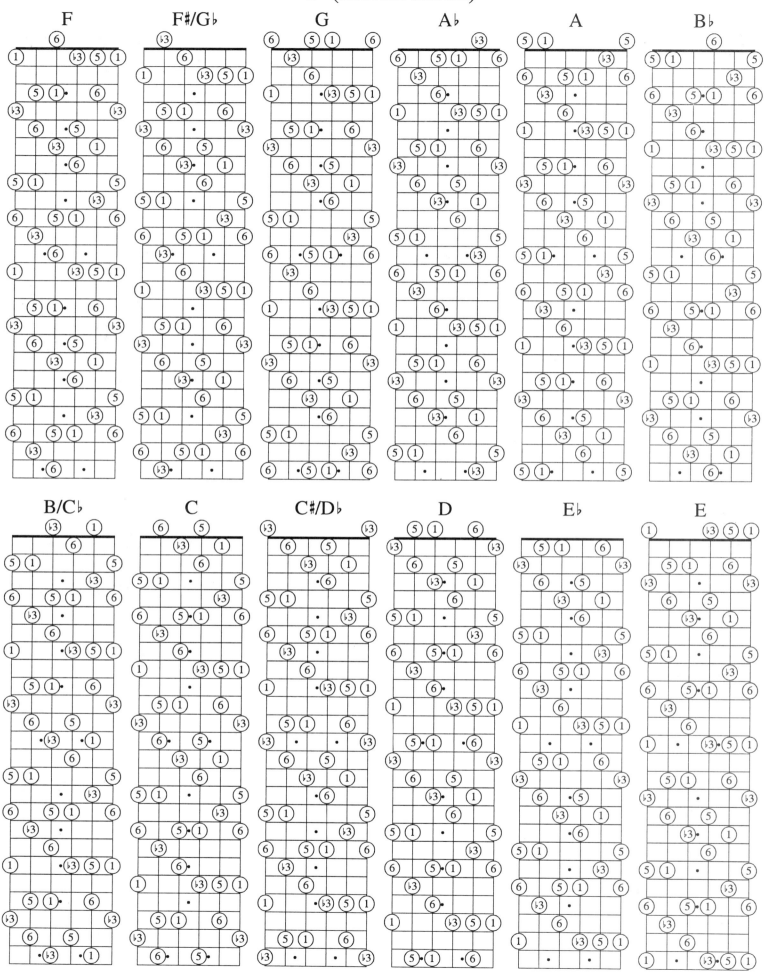

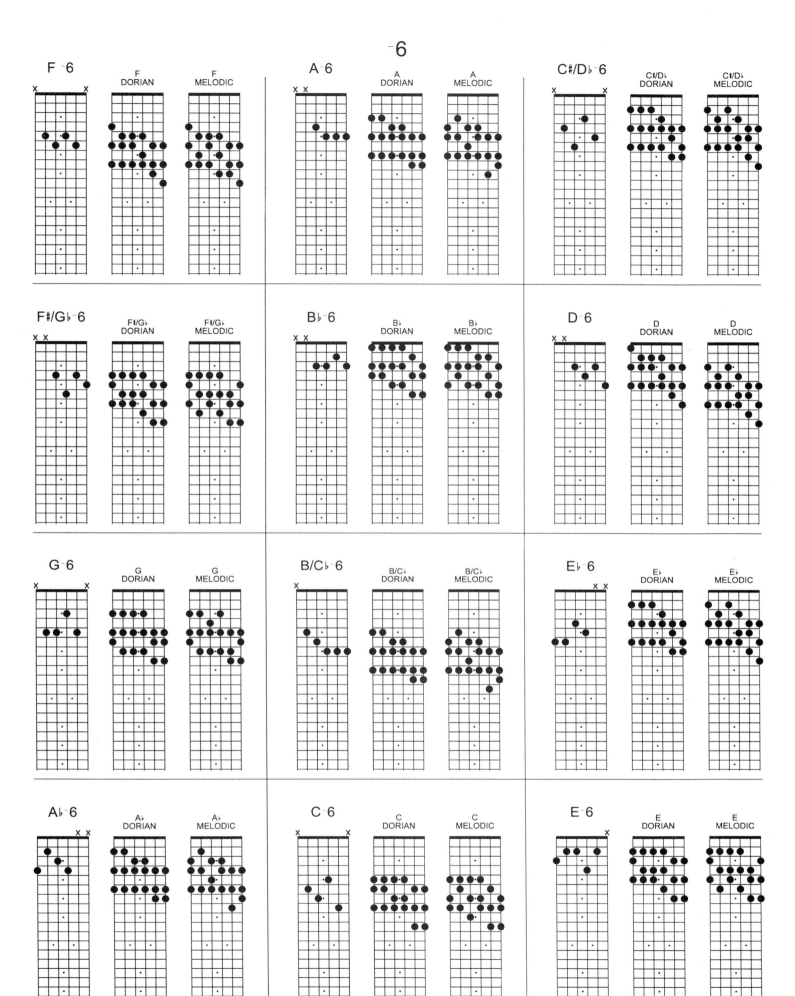

°7 (DIMINISHED SEVENTH)

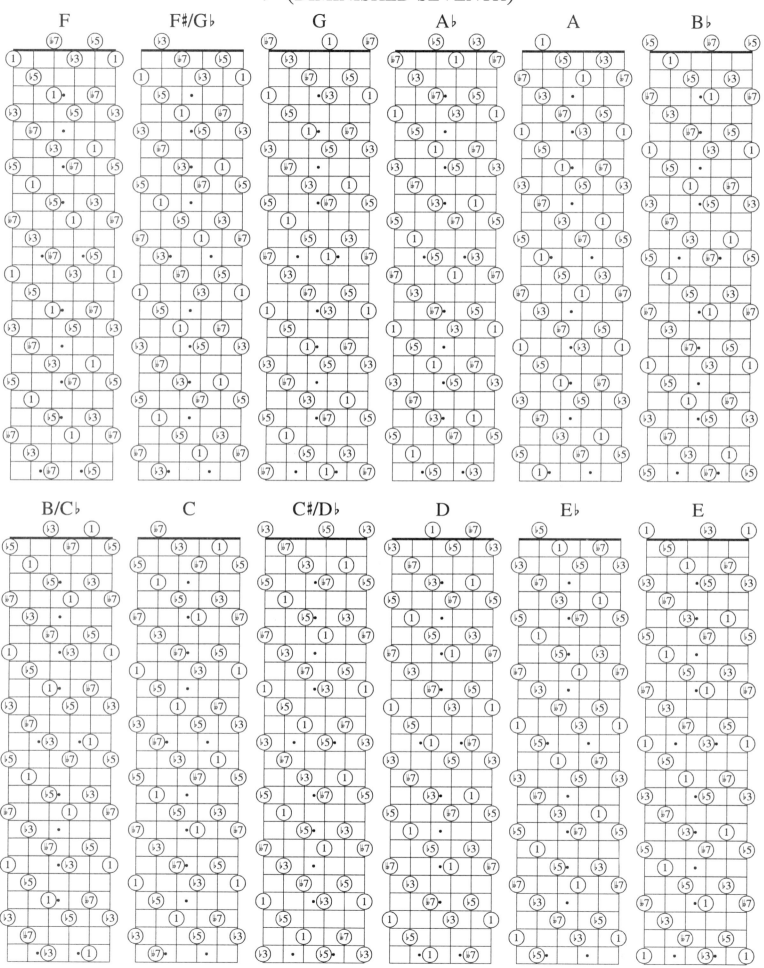

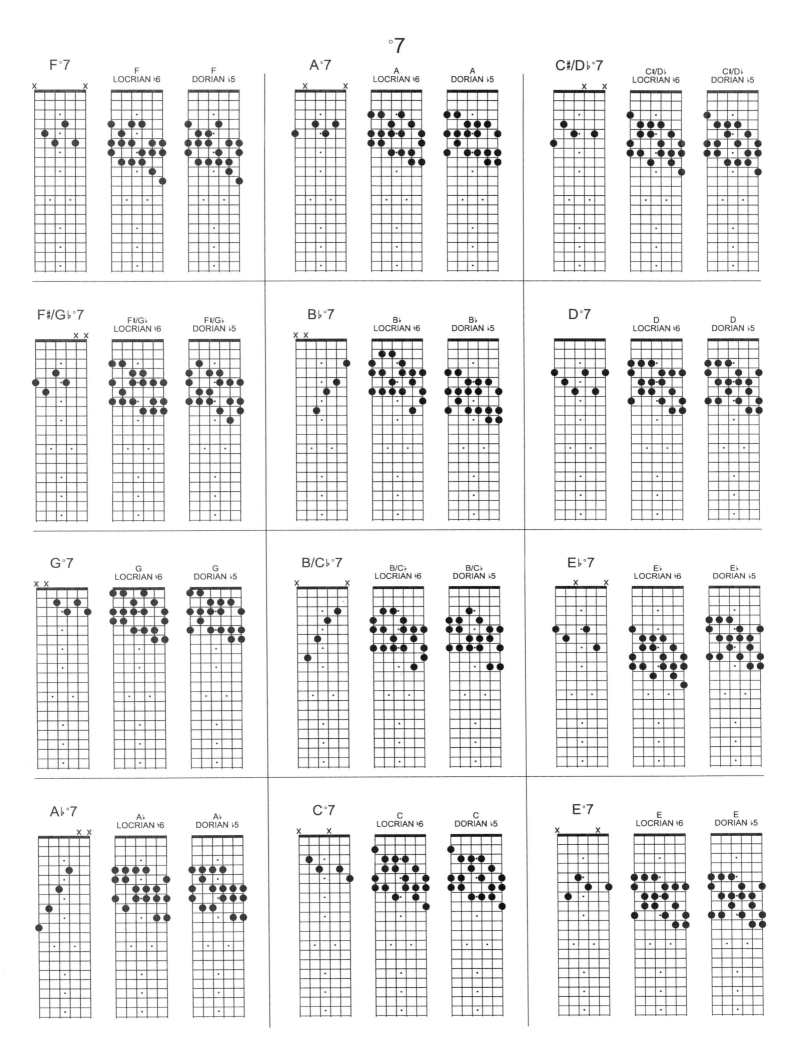

Q(3) (QUARTAL or DOUBLE FOURTH)

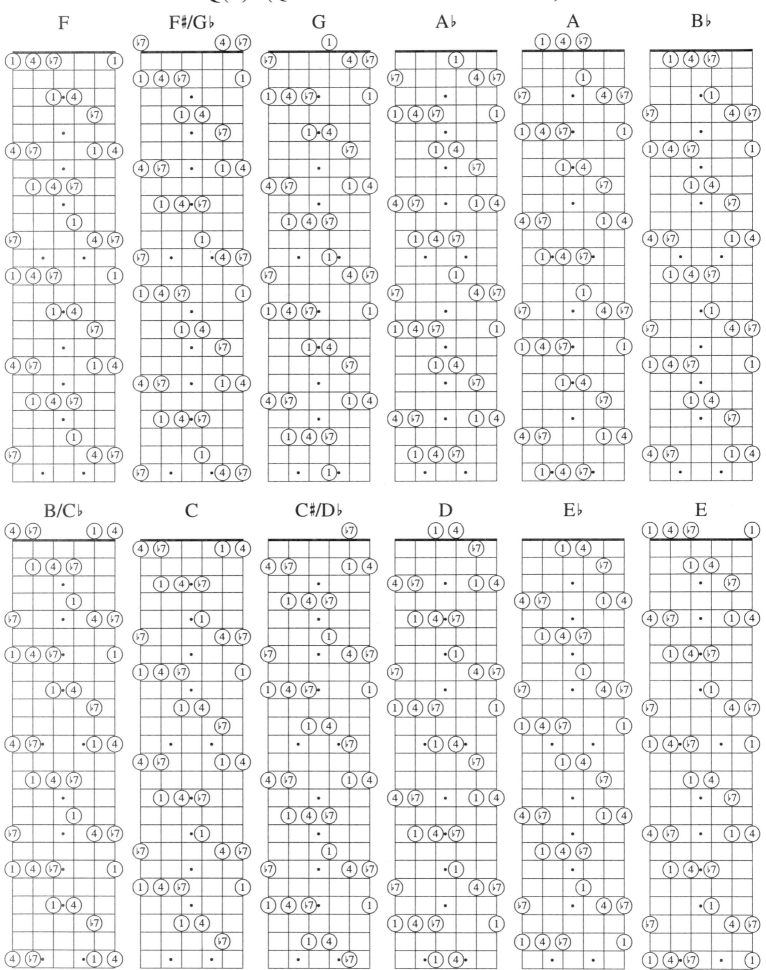

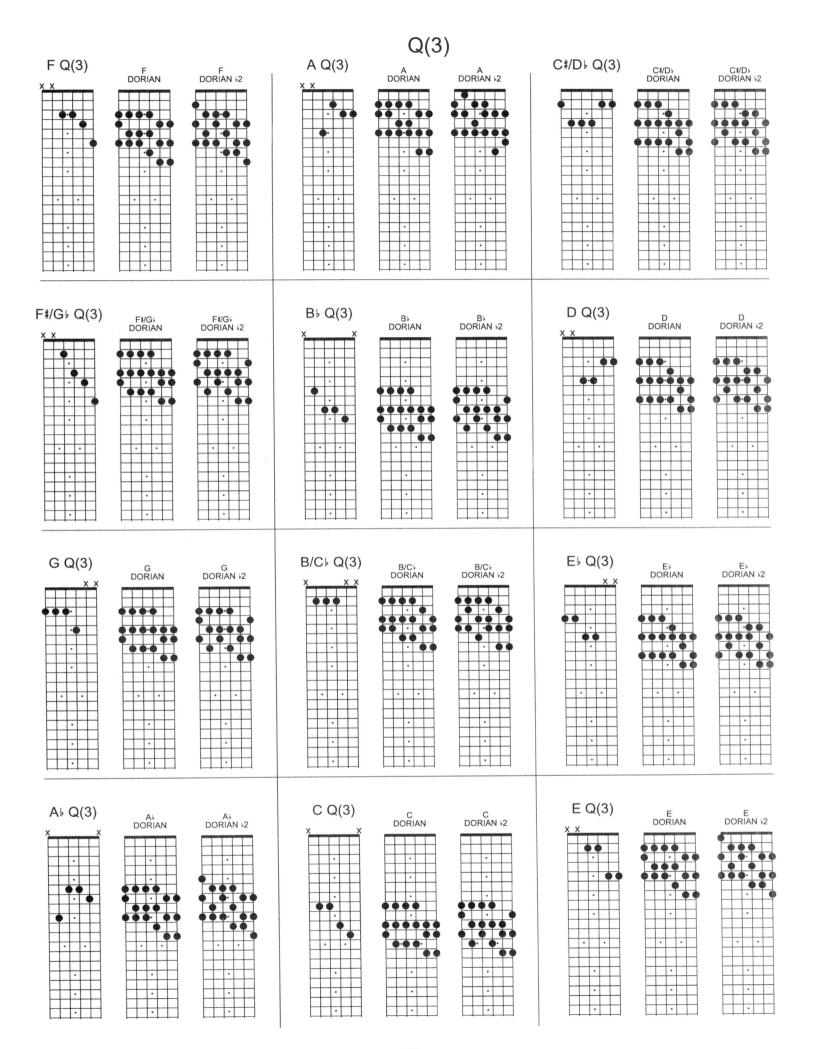

7 (DOMINANT)

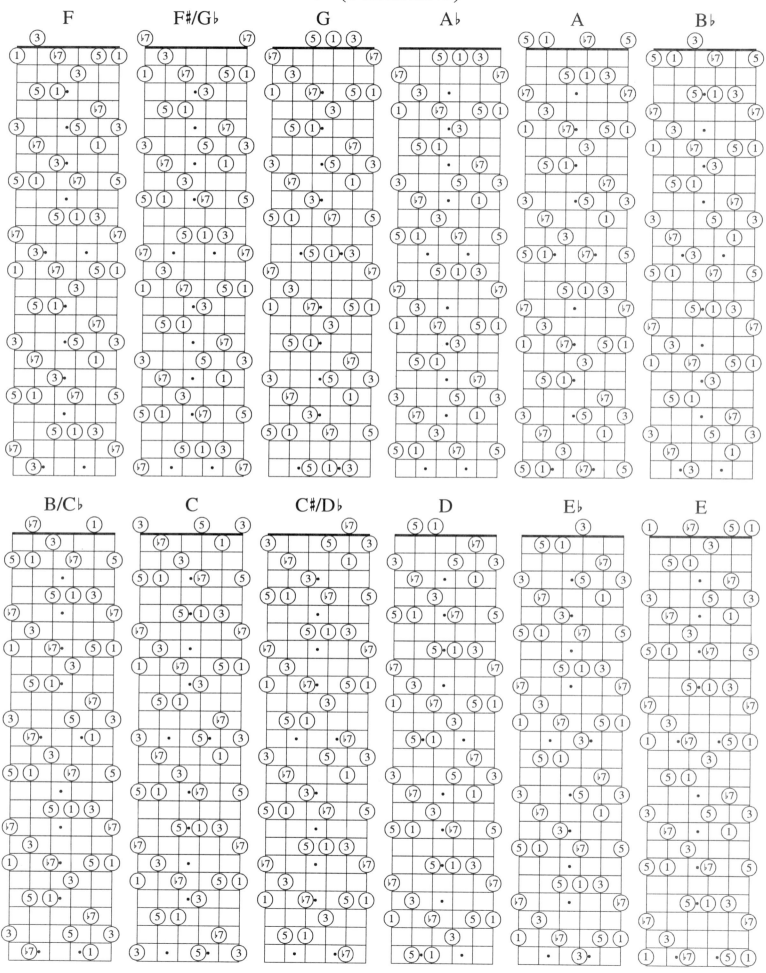

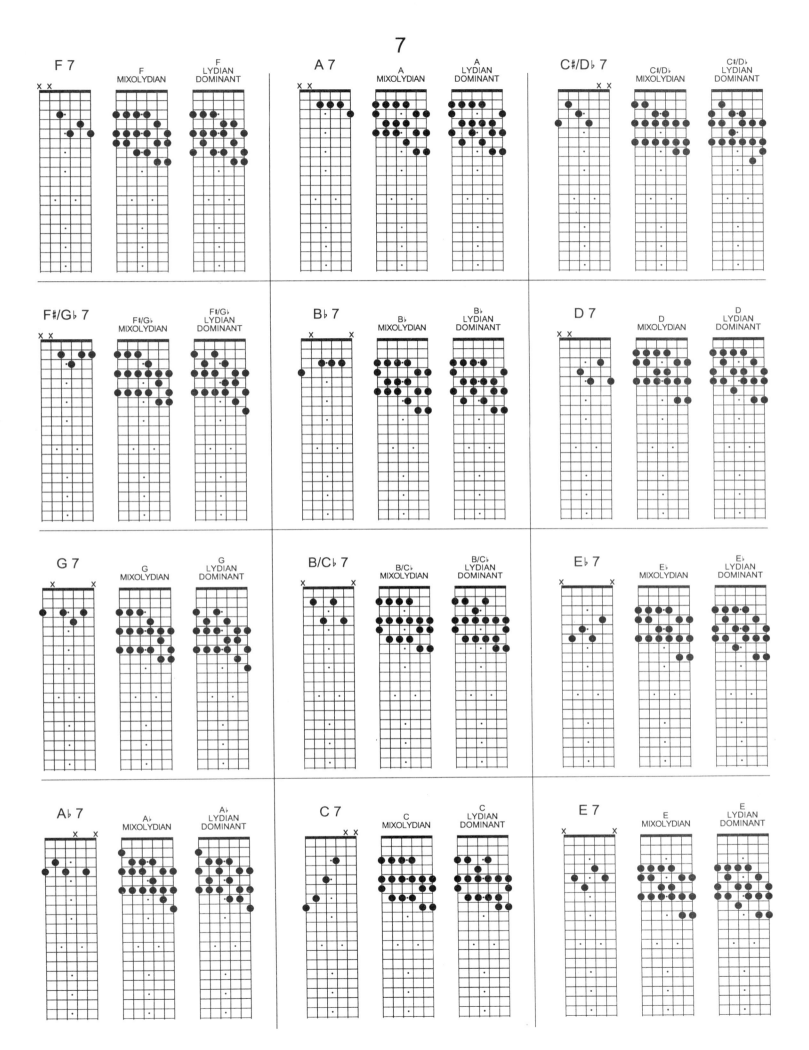

‾7 (MINOR SEVENTH)

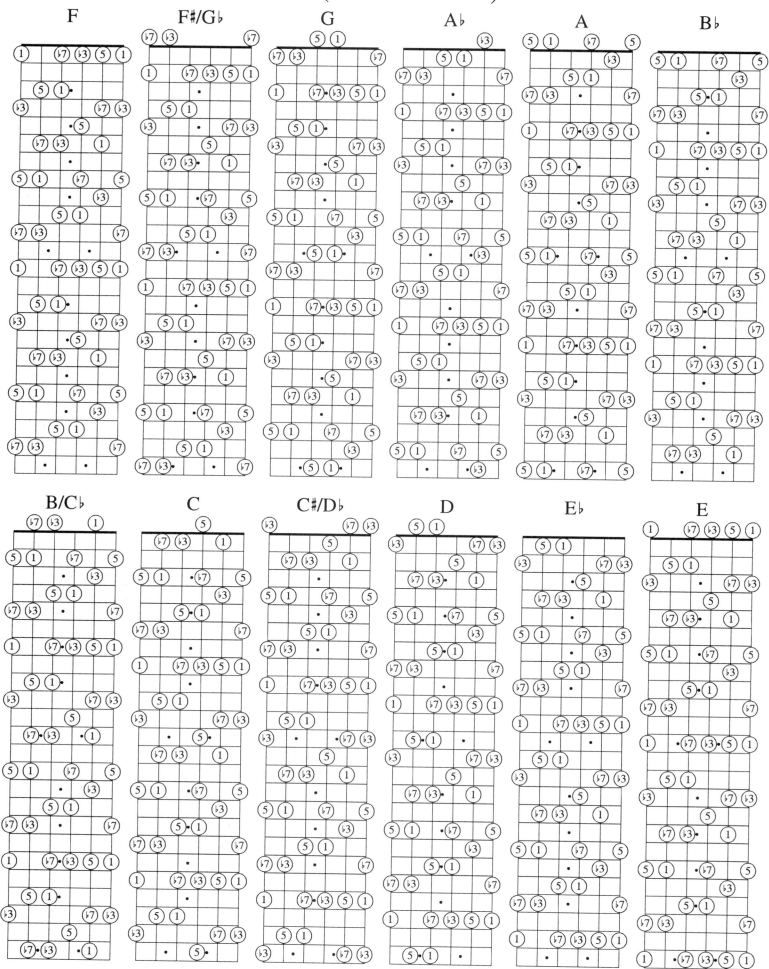

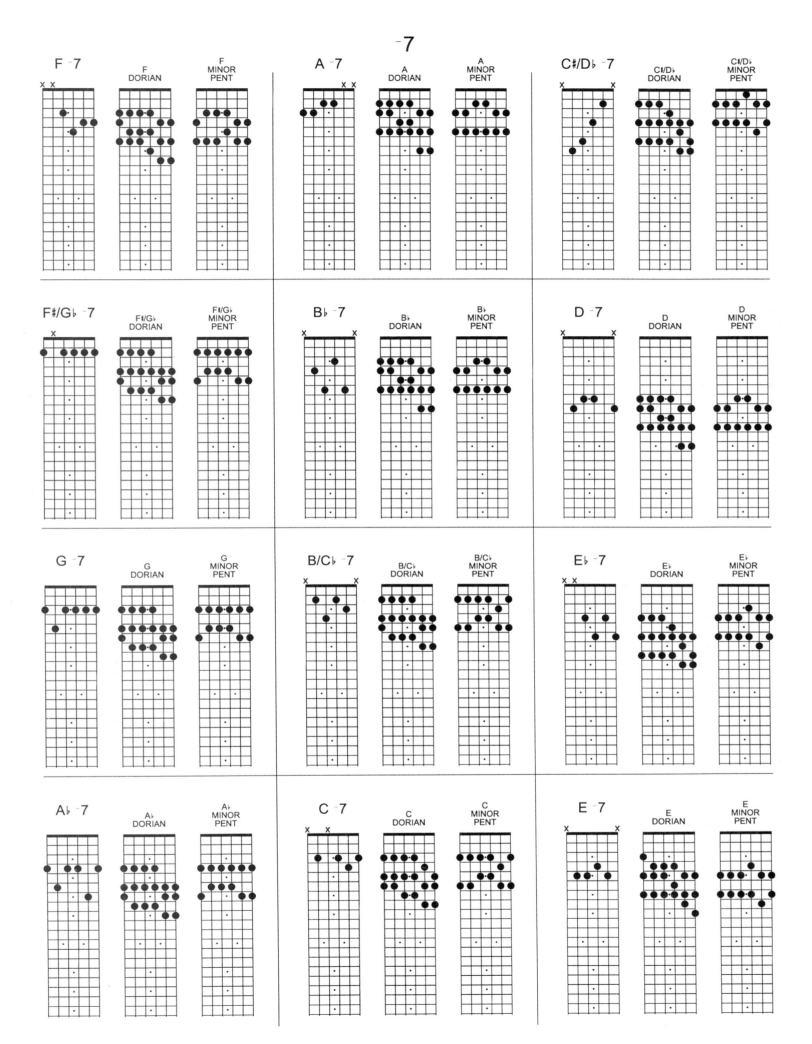

7sus2 (DOMINANT sus2)

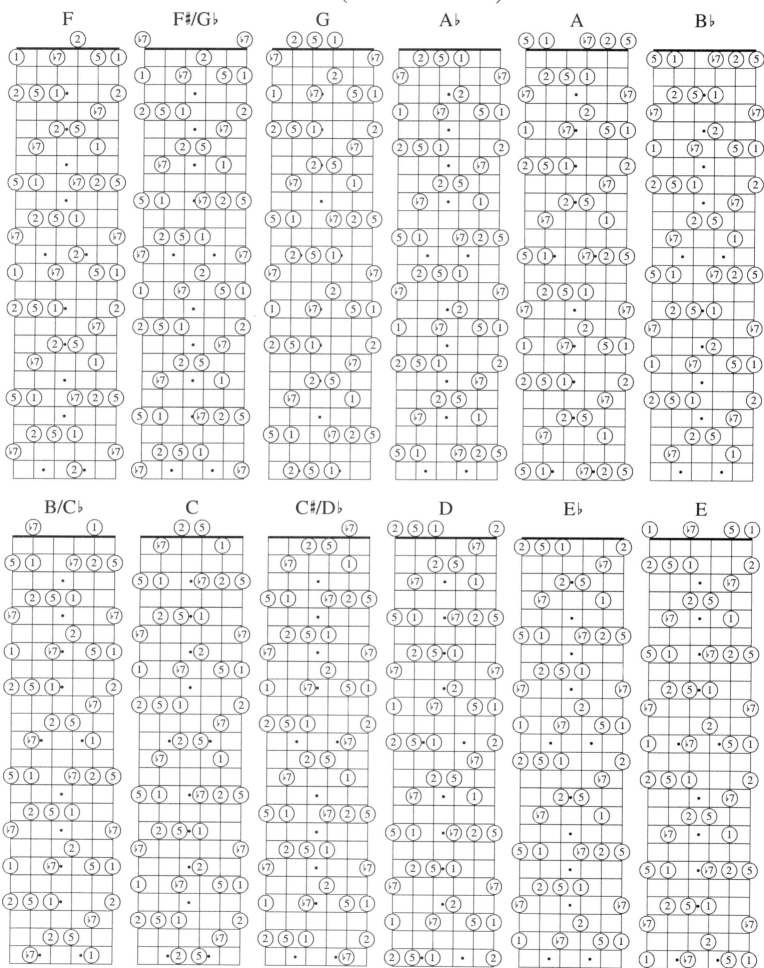

7sus2

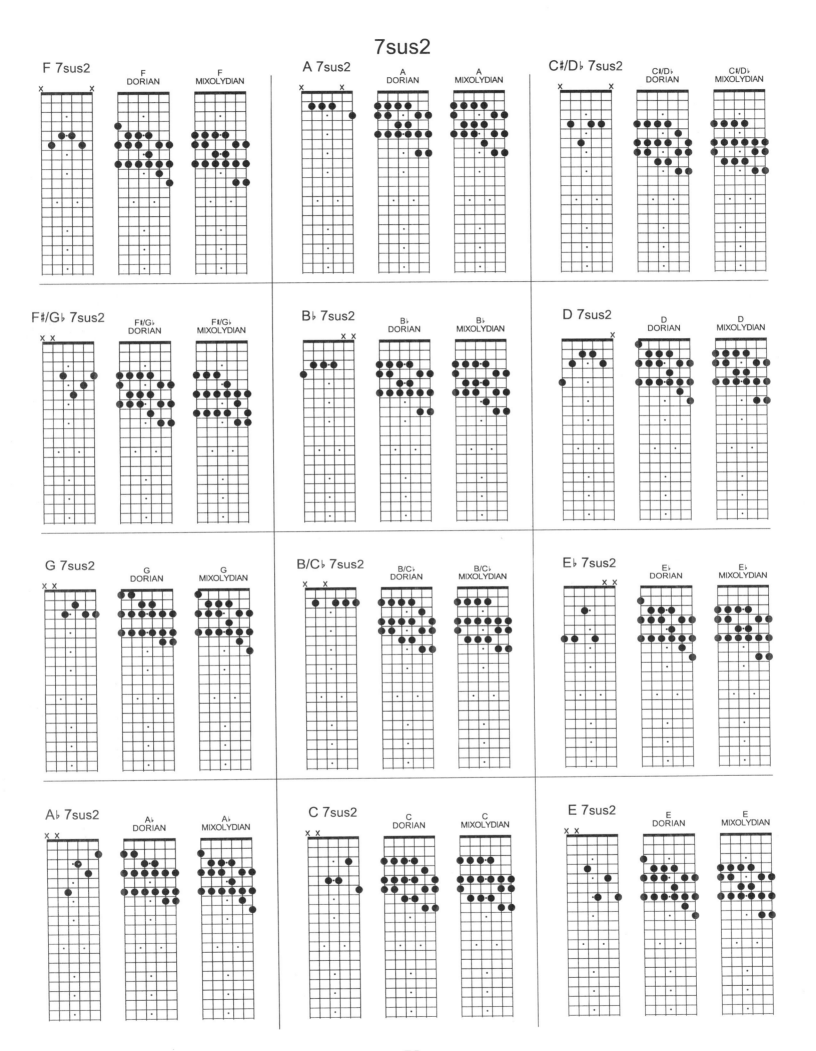

7sus (DOMINANT SUS)

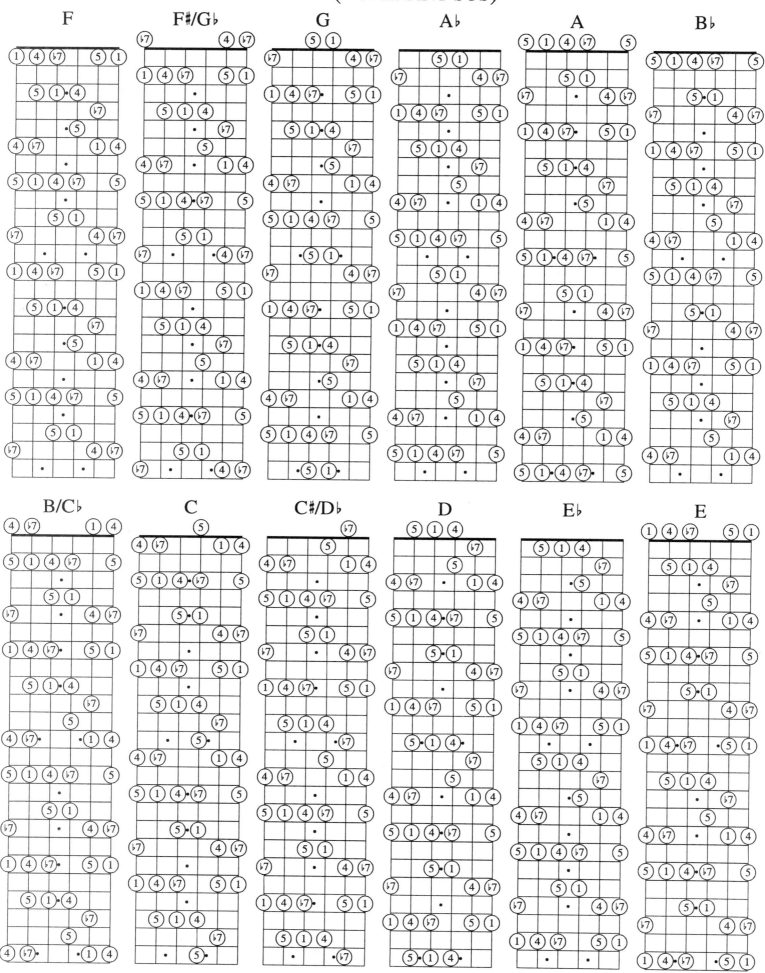

7sus

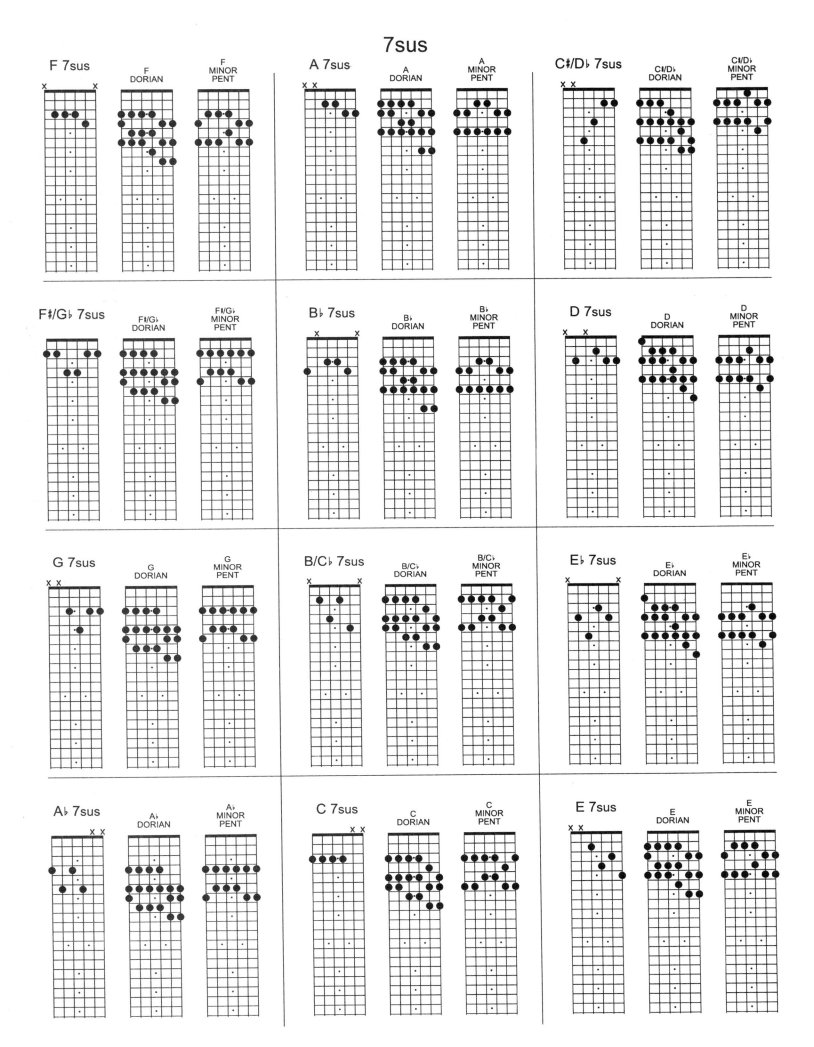

7♭5 (DOMINANT FLAT FIVE)

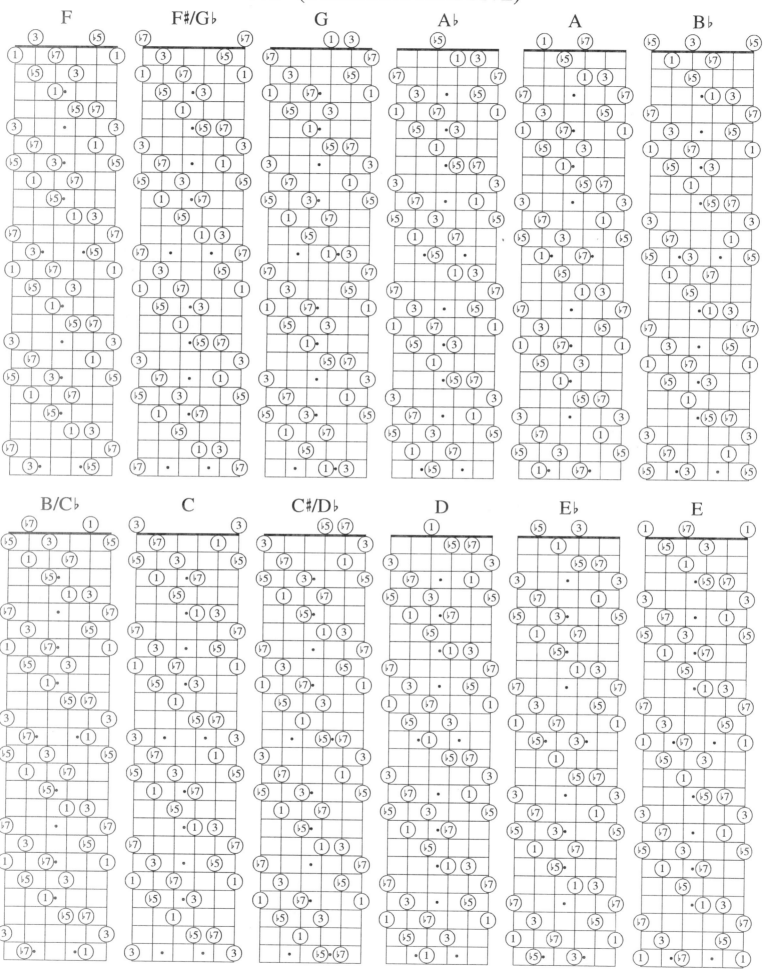

7♭5

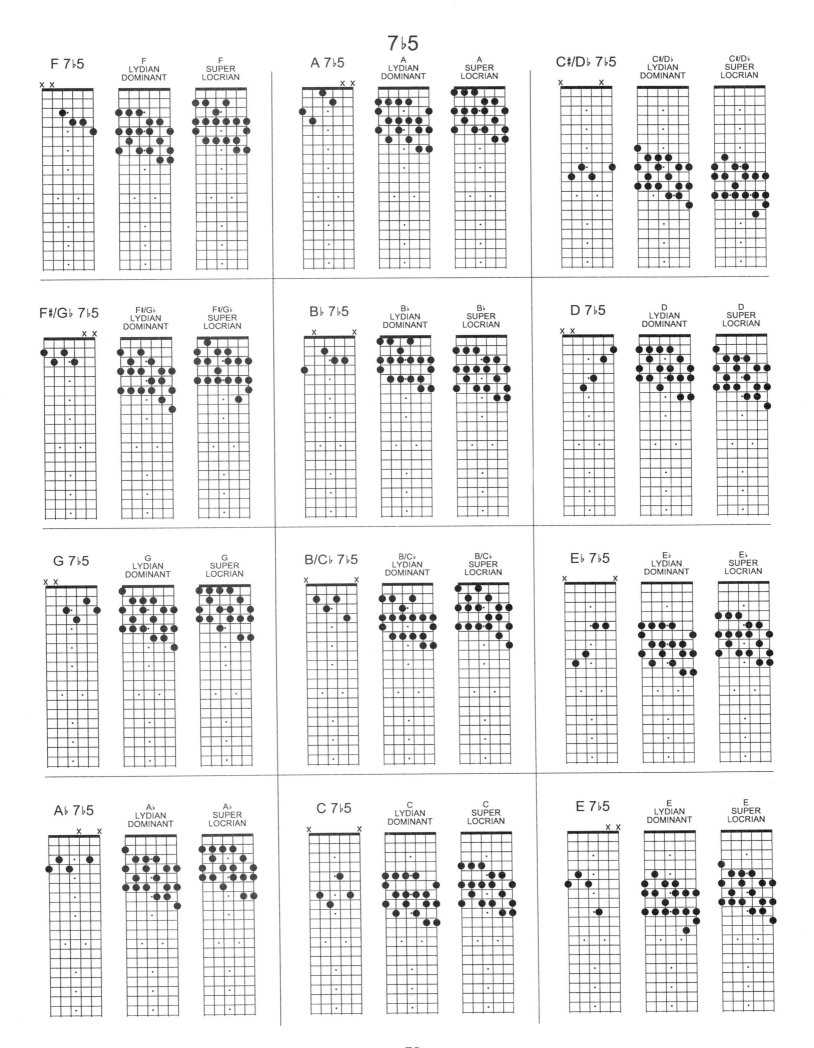

ø (HALF-DIMINISHED)

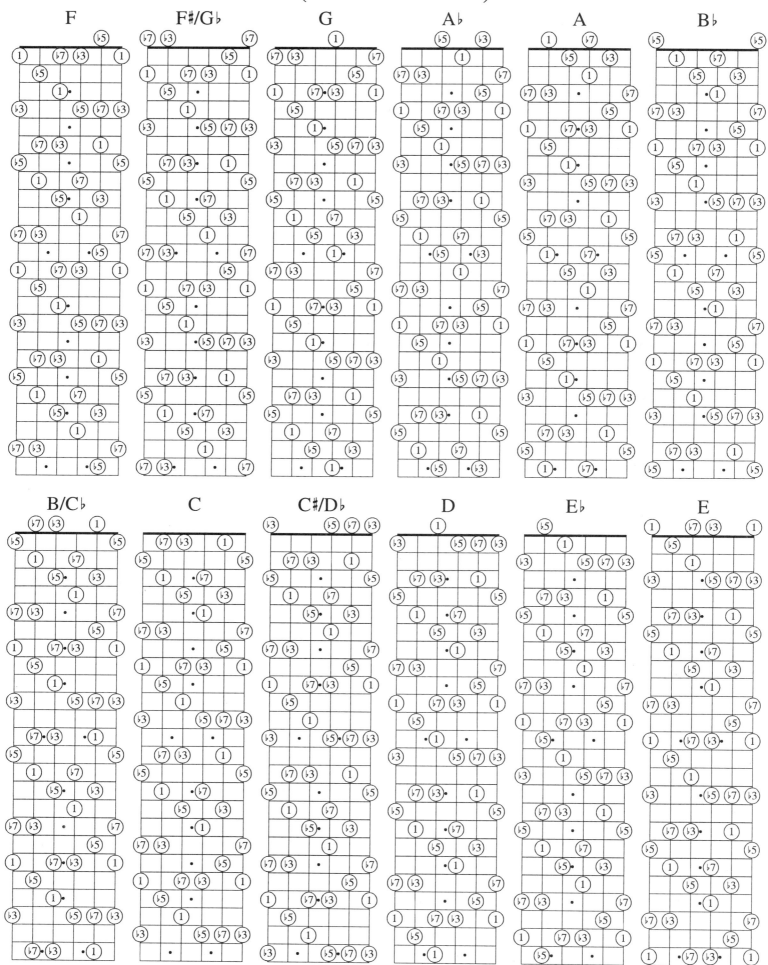

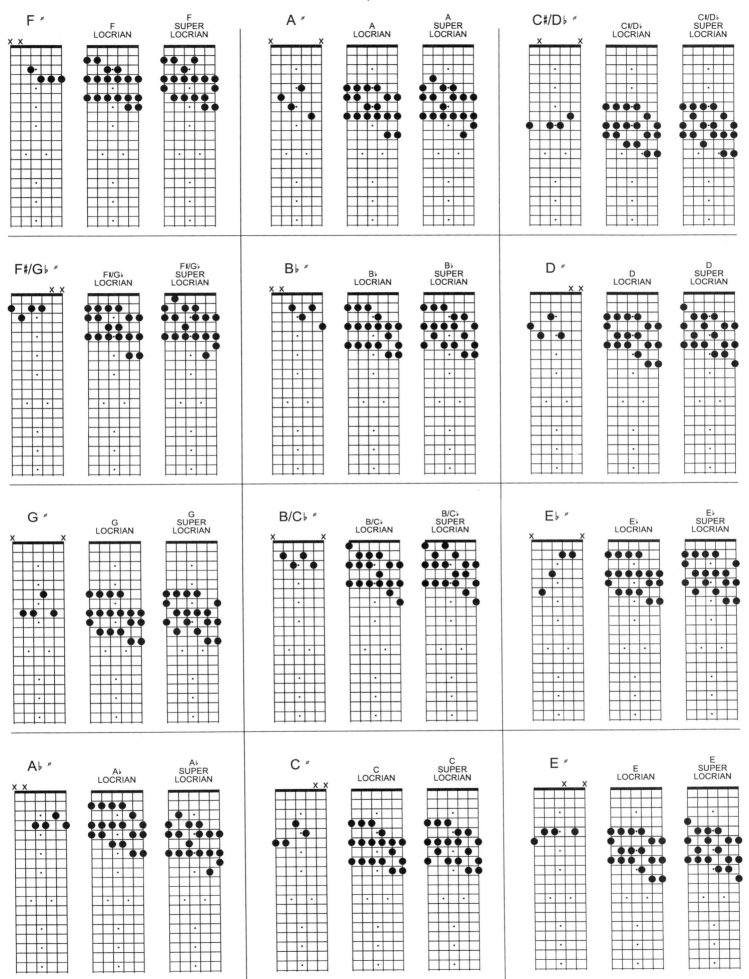

81

7⁺ (DOMINANT AUGMENTED)

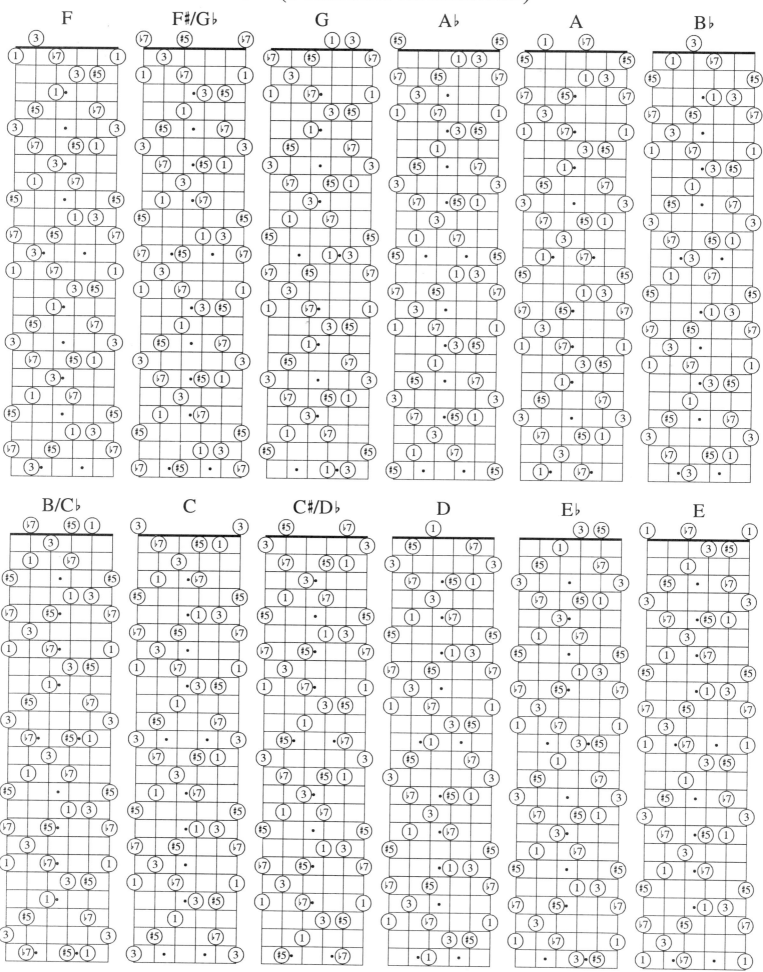

82

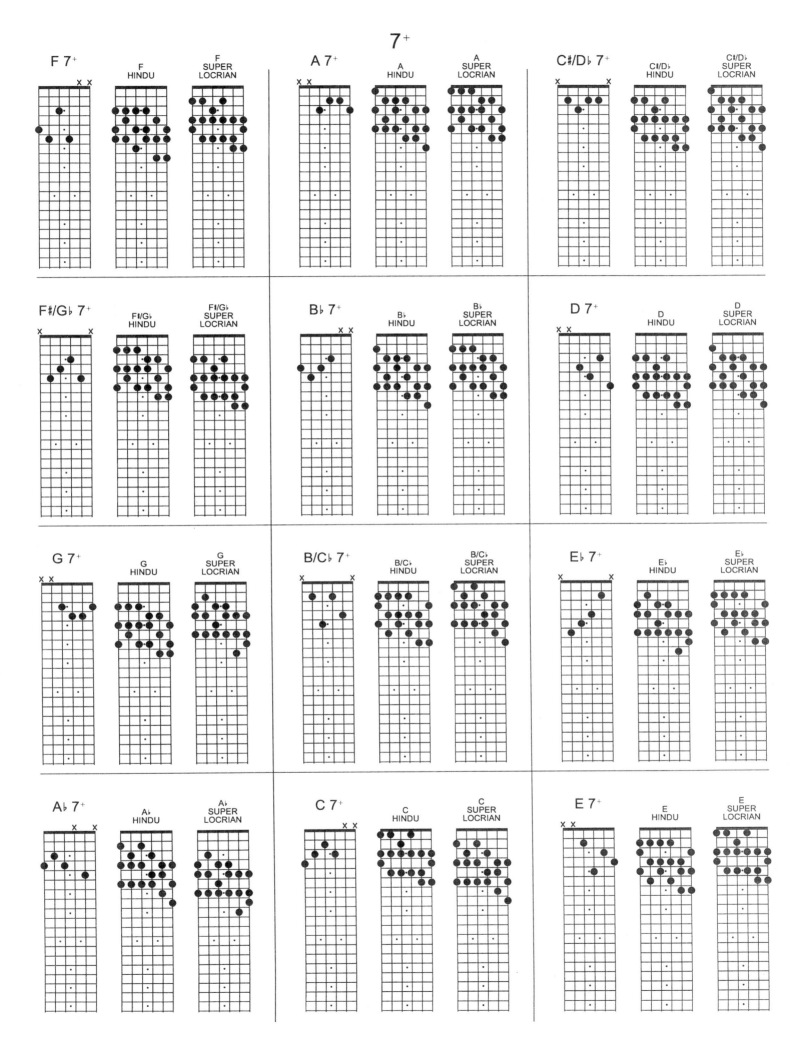

△ (DELTA or Major Seventh)

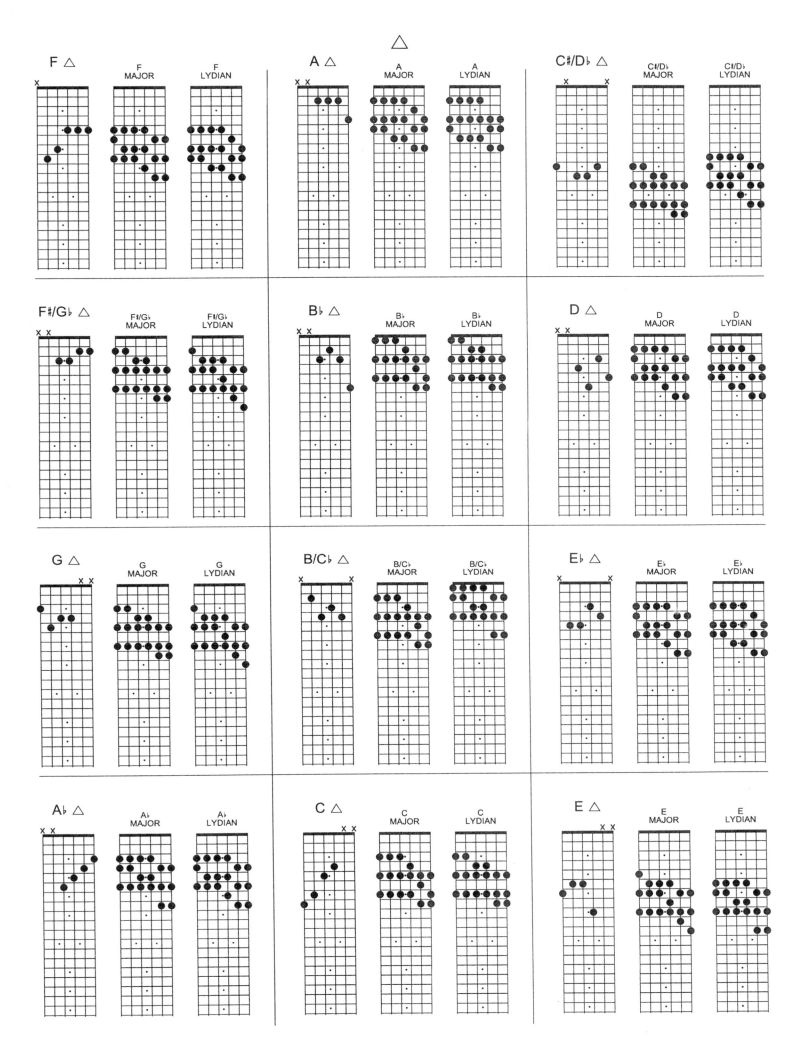

$-\triangle$ (MINOR DELTA or Minor Major)

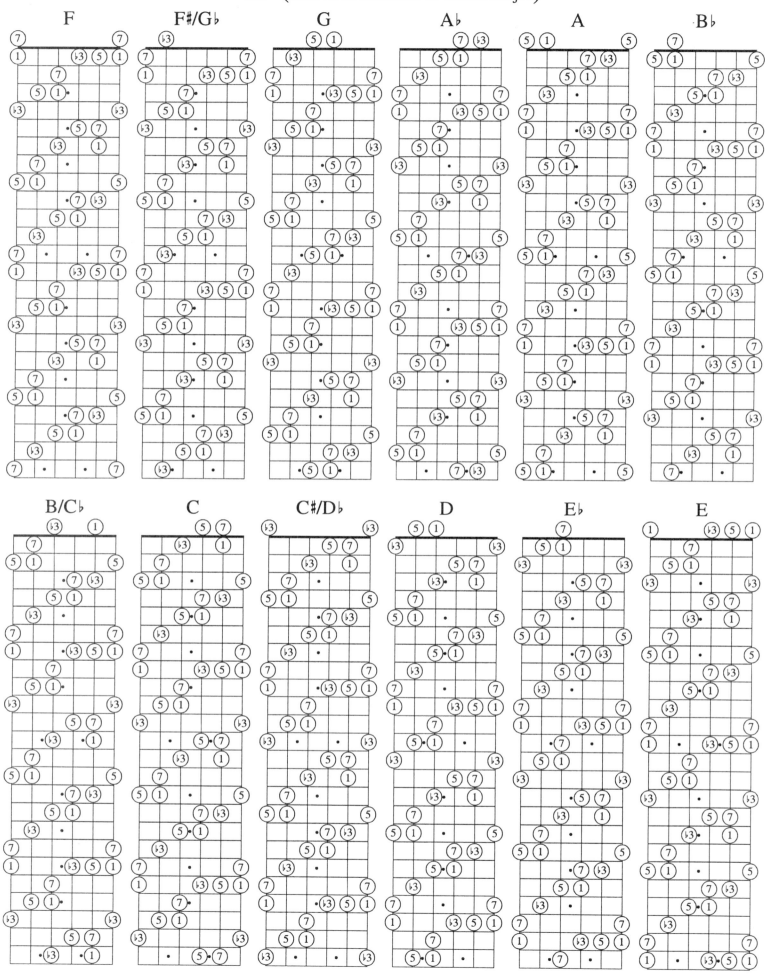

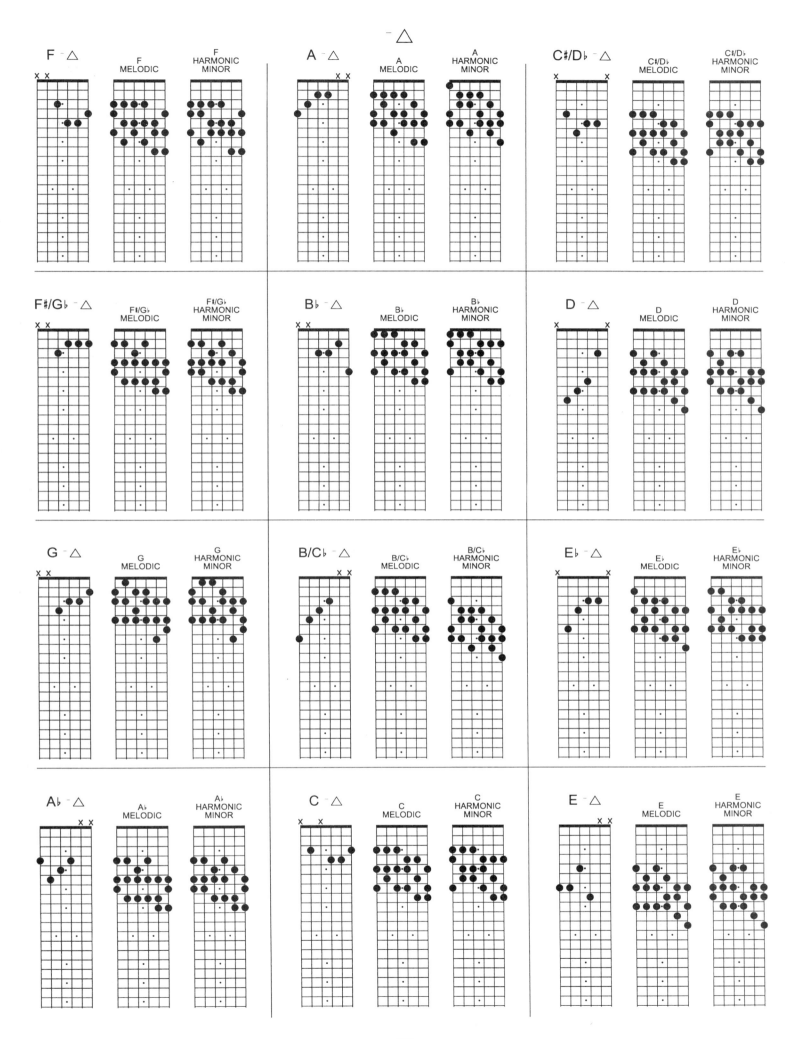

△sus2 (DELTA SUS2 or Major Seventh Suspended Second)

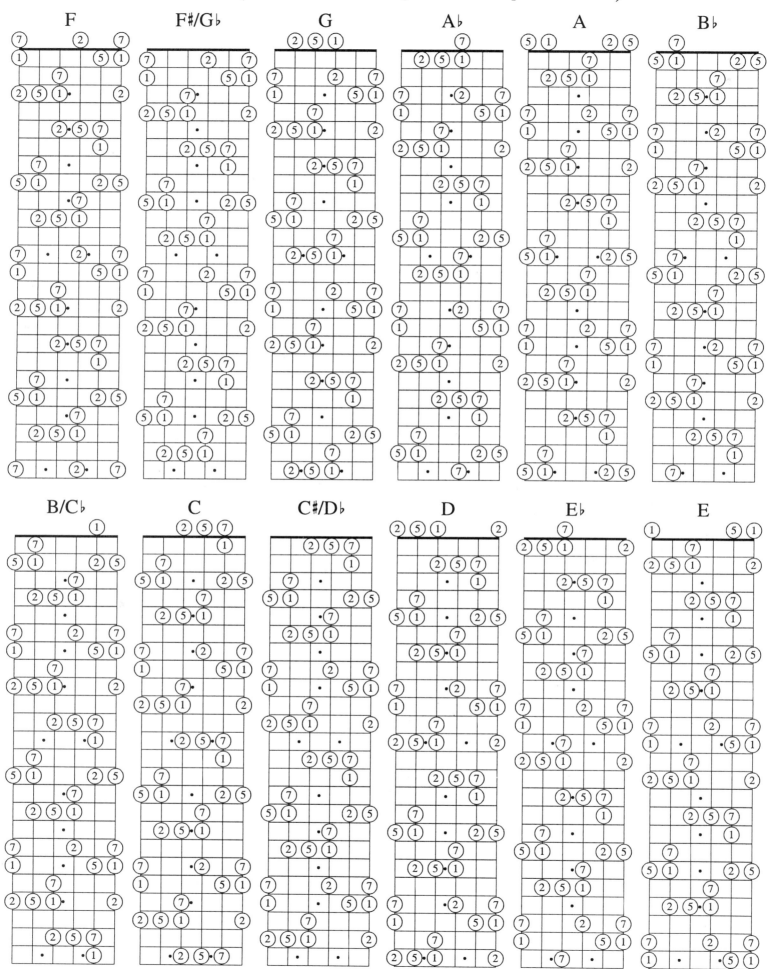

△sus2

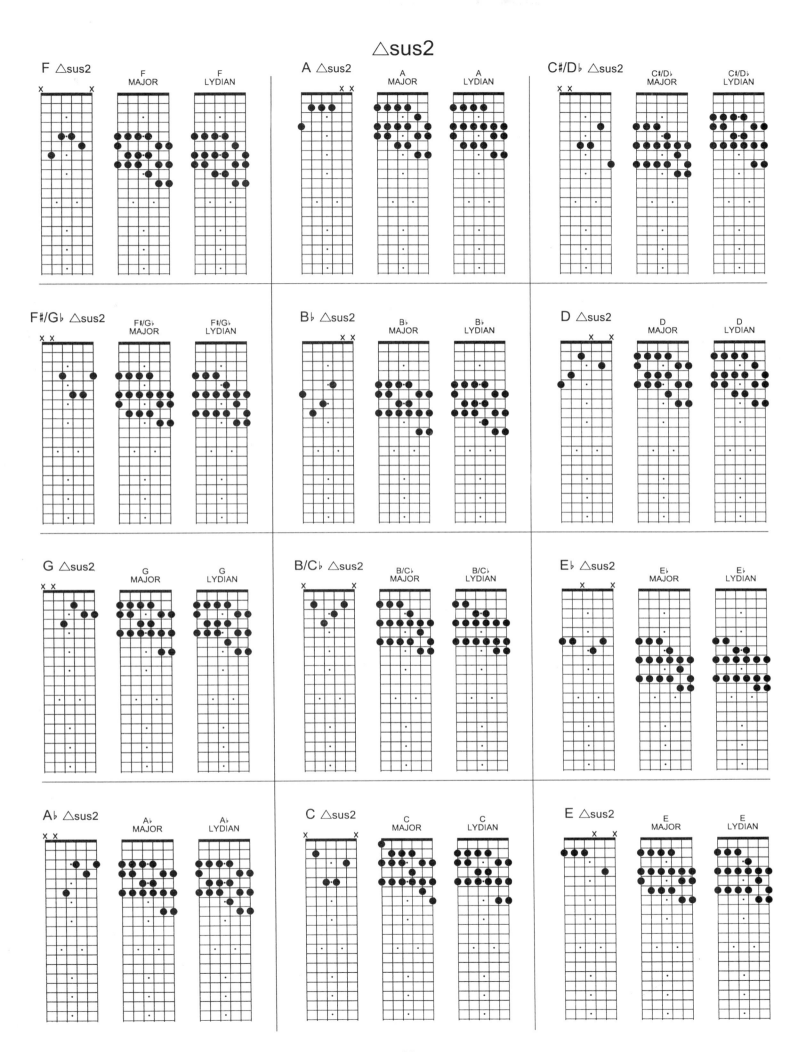

△sus (DELTA SUS or Major Seventh Suspended Fourth)

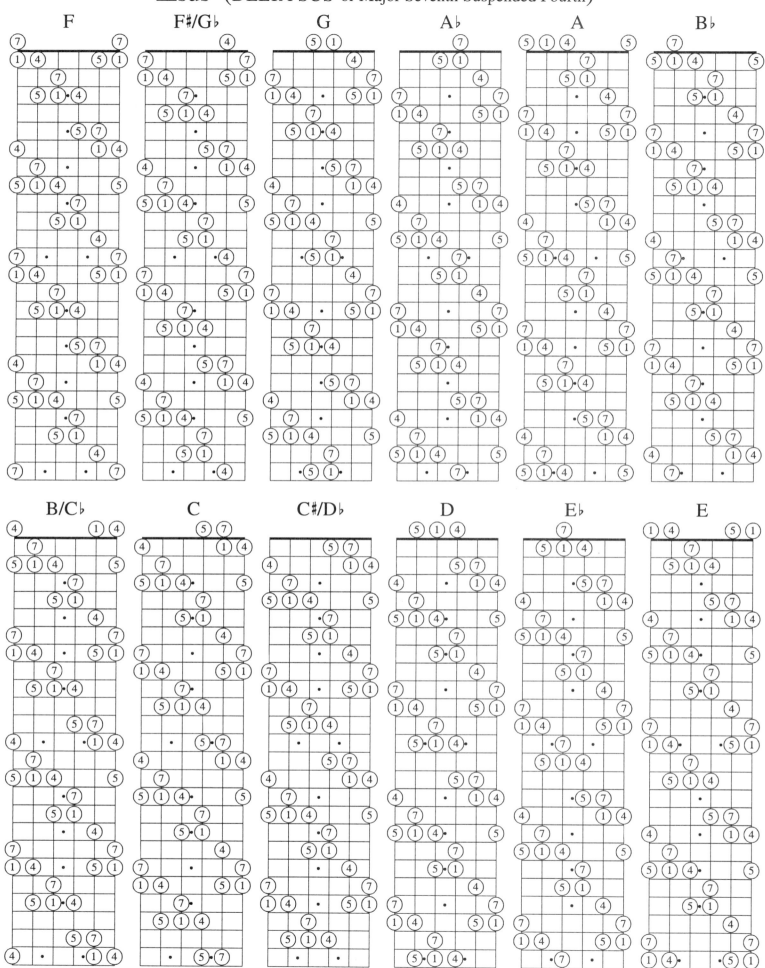

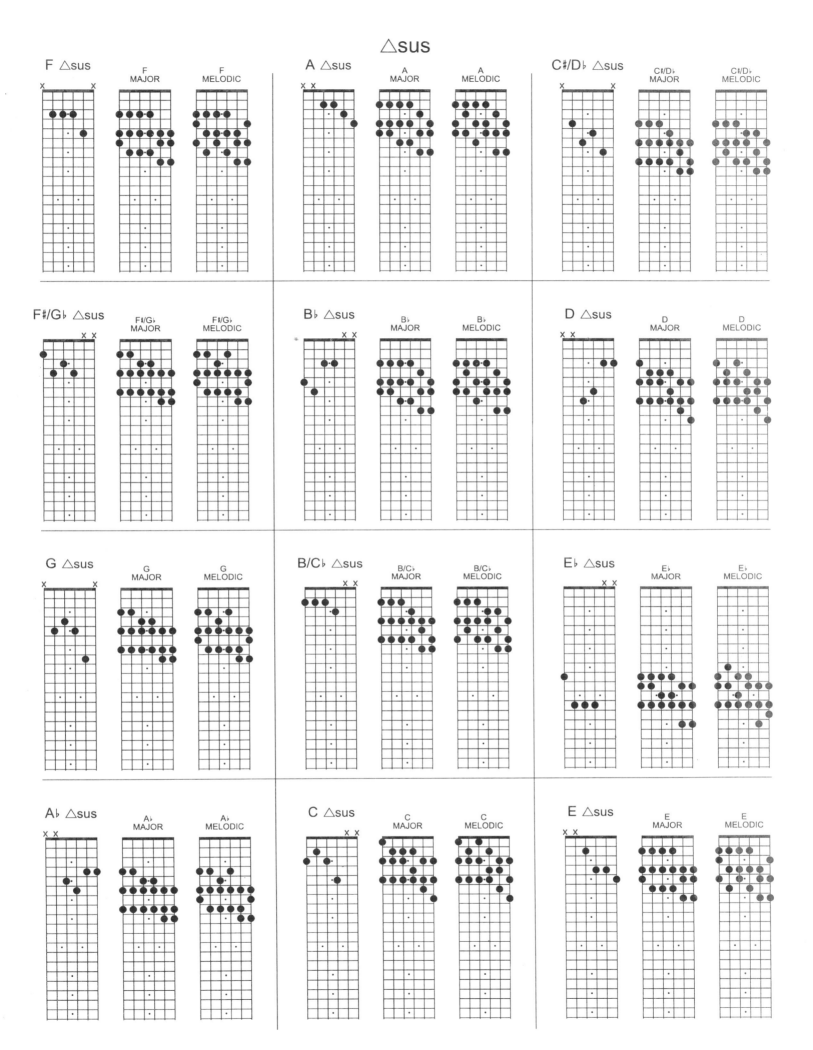

△♭5 (DELTA FLAT FIVE or Major Seventh Flatted Fifth)

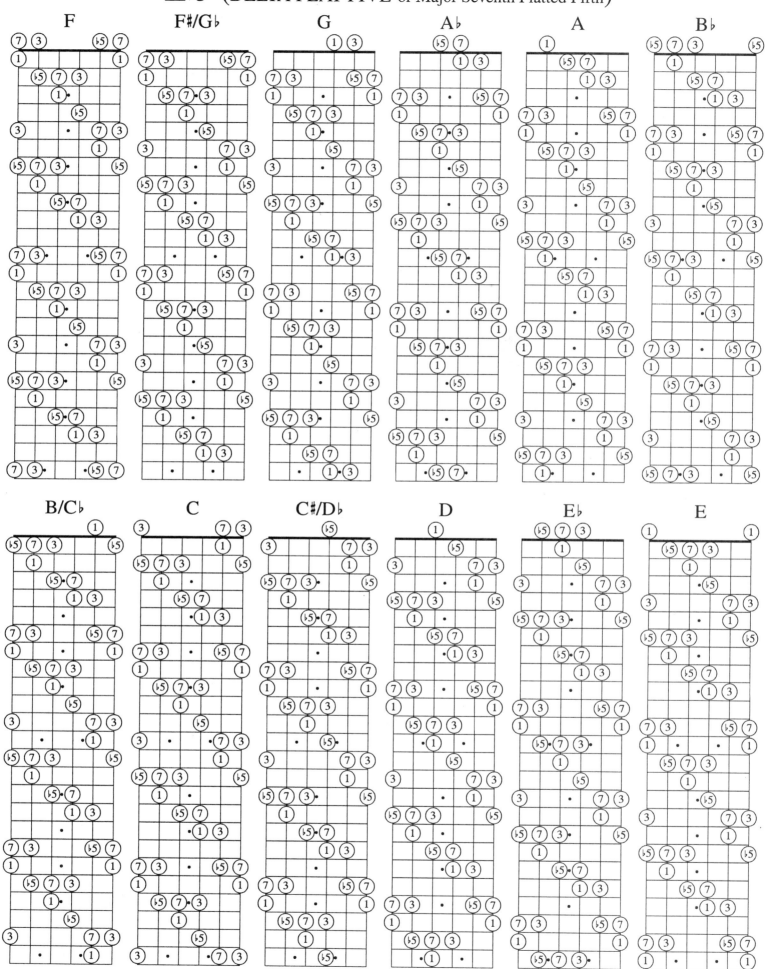

92

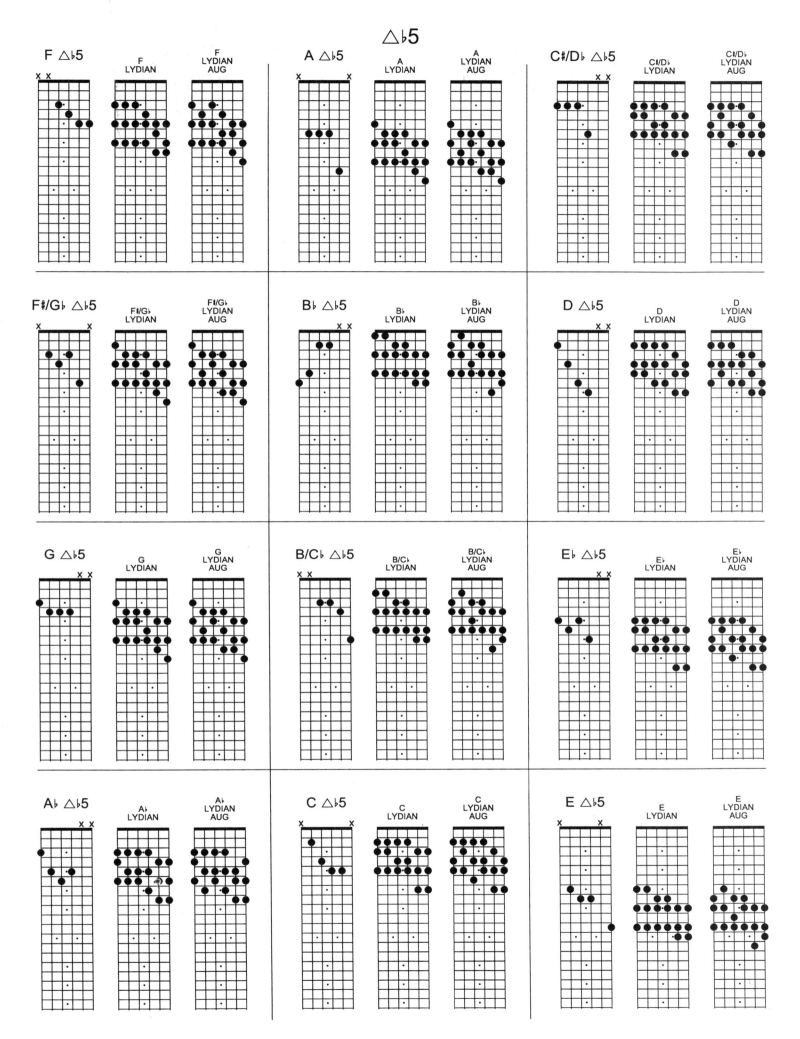

△♭5

93

△° (DELTA DIMINISHED or Major Seventh Diminished)

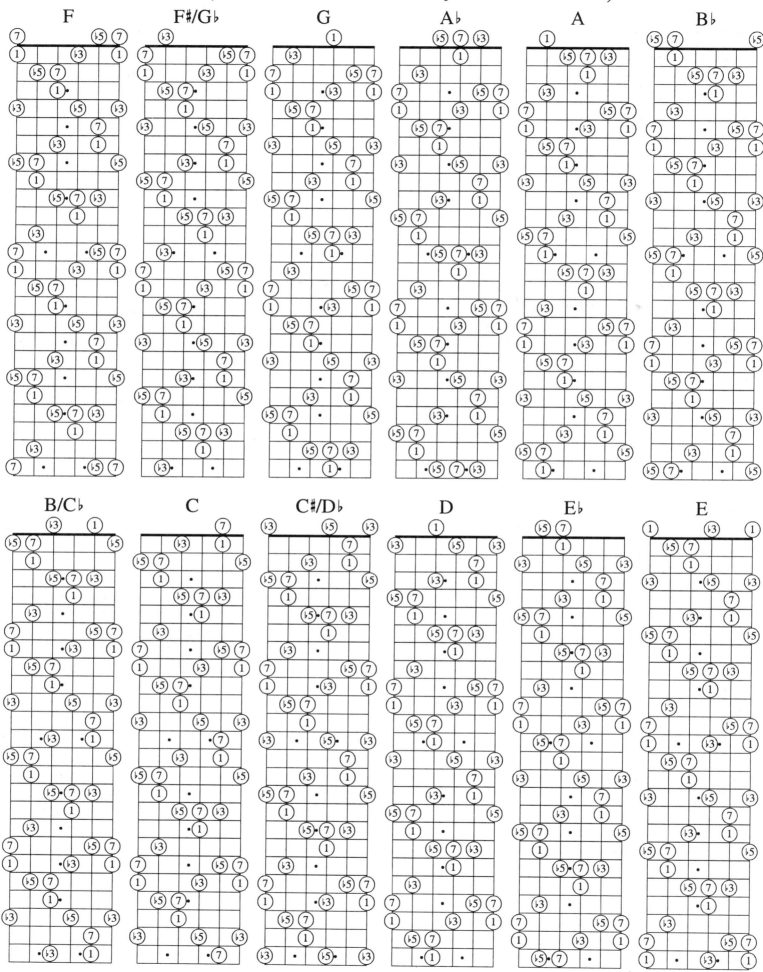

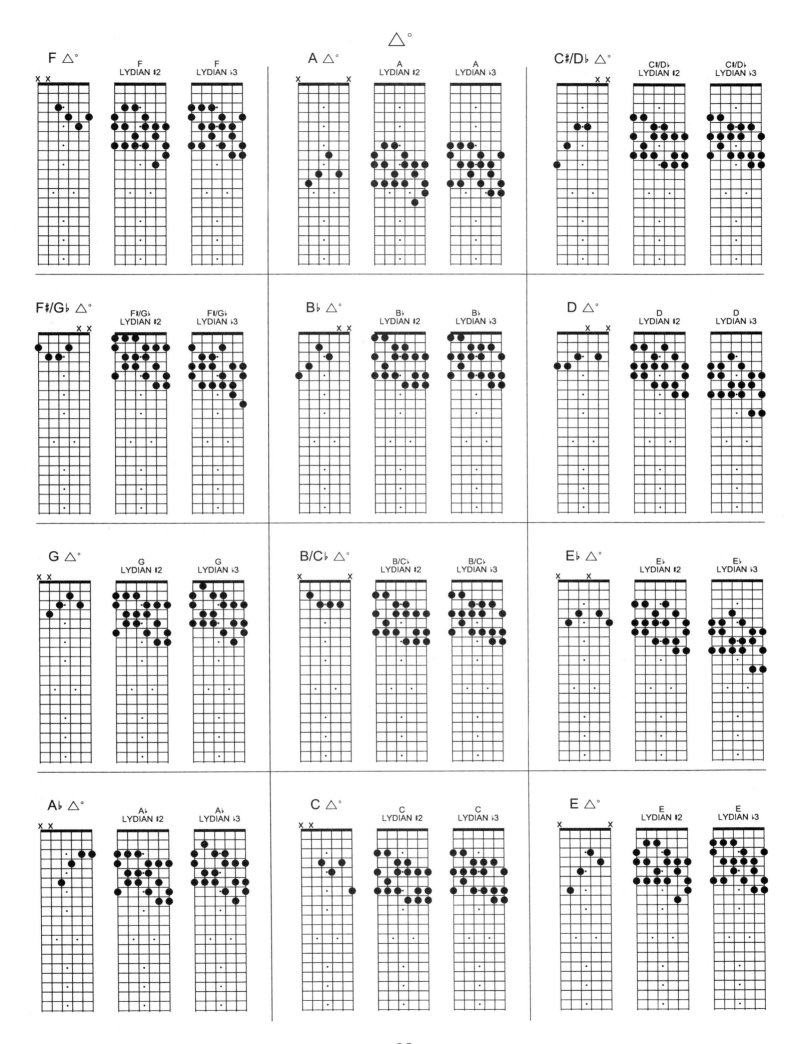

△⁺ (DELTA AUGMENTED or Major Seventh Augmented)

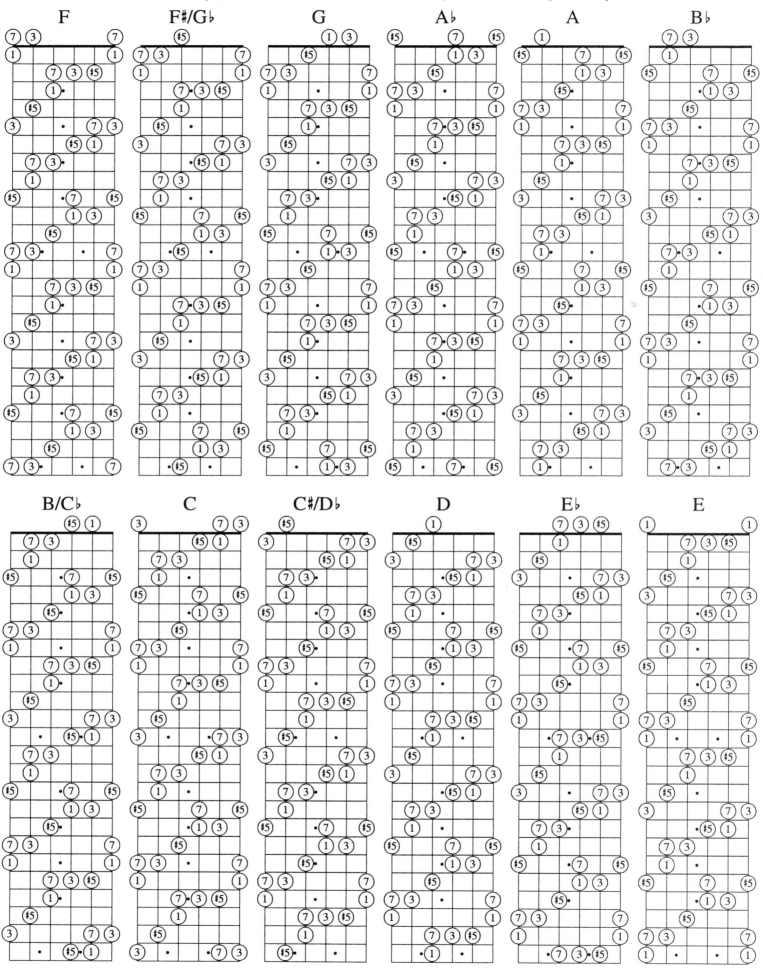

96

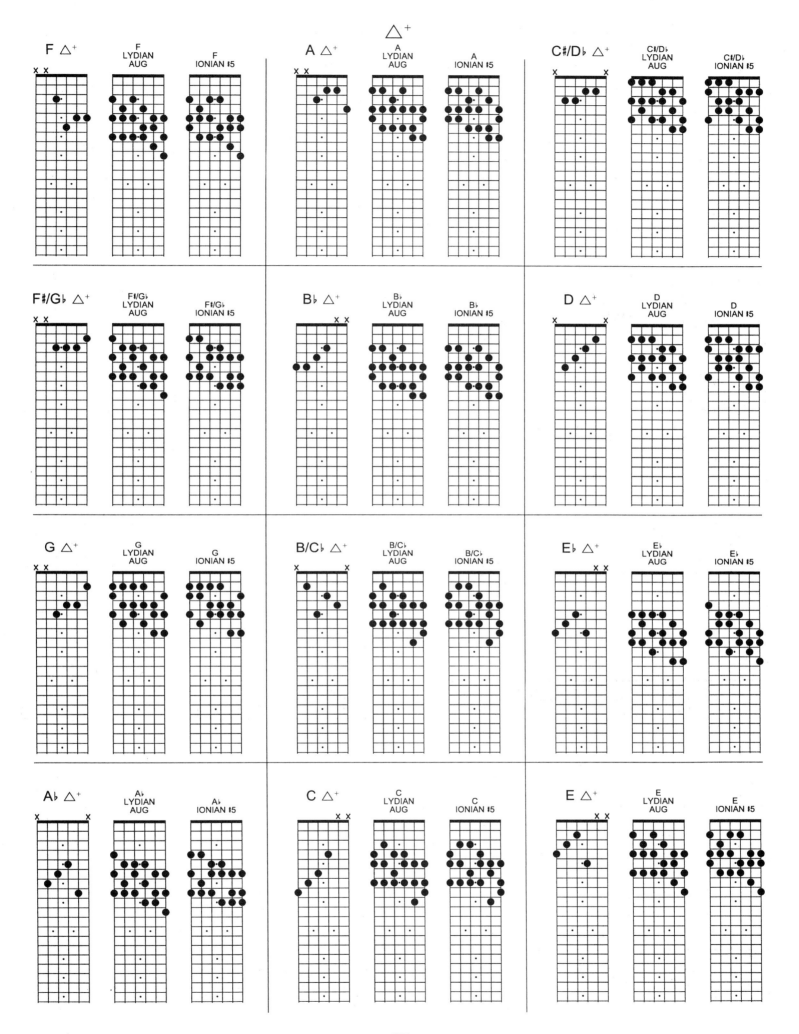

97

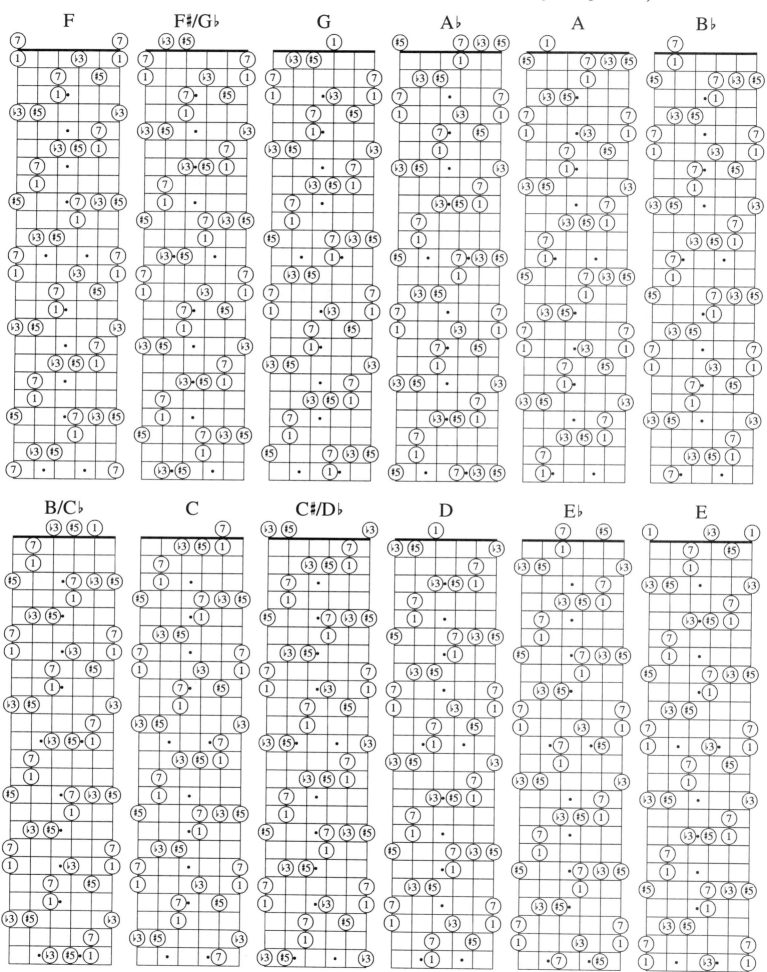

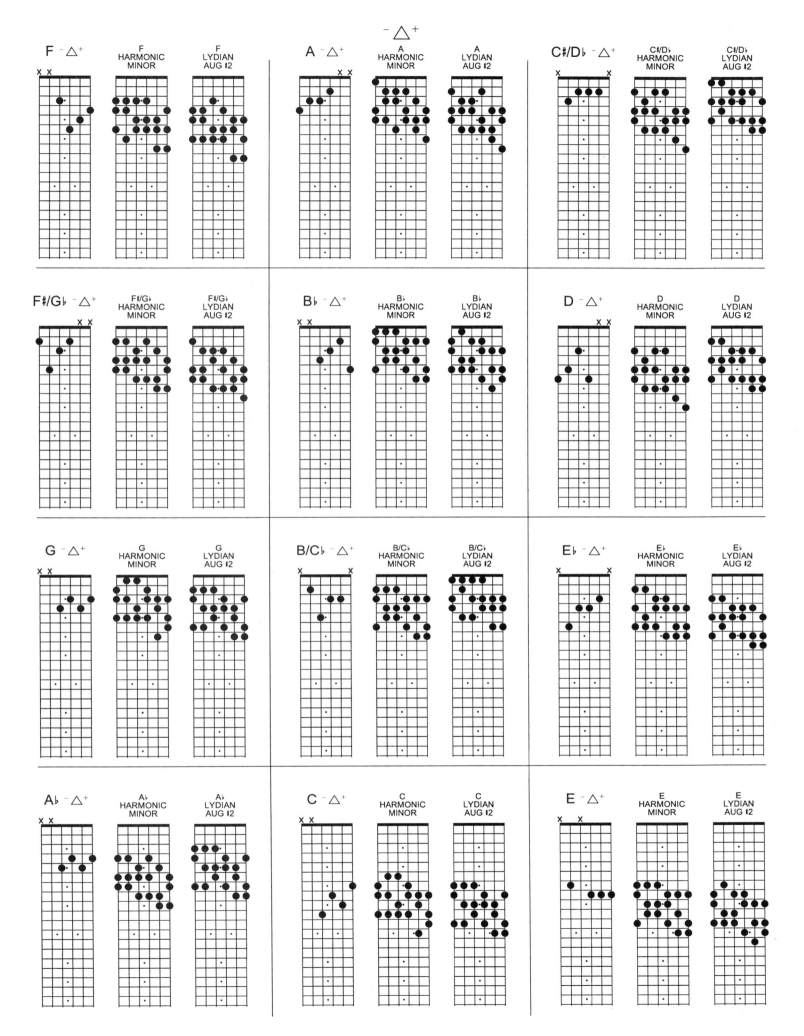

99

PROGRESSIONS

Now that we have set the foundation with a brief study of scales, modes and chords, we are ready to tackle progressions. Let's start with the Major scale and its modes (fig. 36).

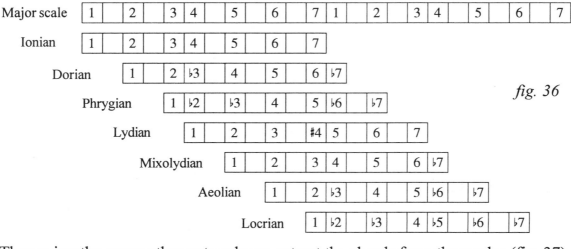

fig. 36

Then using the every other note rule we extract the chords from the modes (fig. 37).

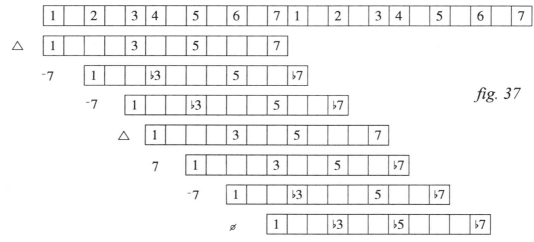

fig. 37

Now we assign pitch to our formula. We will use the key of C for this example (fig. 38).

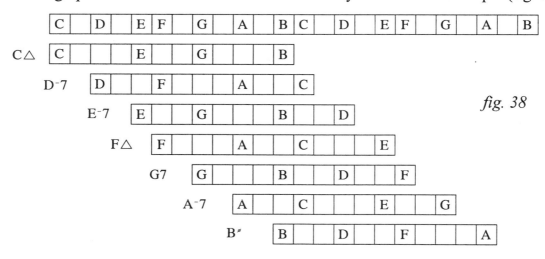

fig. 38

What we have is the first progression type known as the Diatonic Progression. Diatonic means you are using the notes of the scale to derive your chords, in this case the Major scale in the key of C.

In "measure" format the progression looks like this (fig 39):

fig. 39

Now when we extract the chords from the modes of the Major scale for the purpose of creating progressions, the intervallic positions become scale tone degrees and are marked with roman numerals. *fig. 40→*

1	2	3	4	5	6	7
I	II	III	IV	V	VI	VII

Therefore the I position will always be understood to be a major 7, the II position will always be a minor 7, the III position will always be a minor 7 etc. so on and so forth (fig. 41).

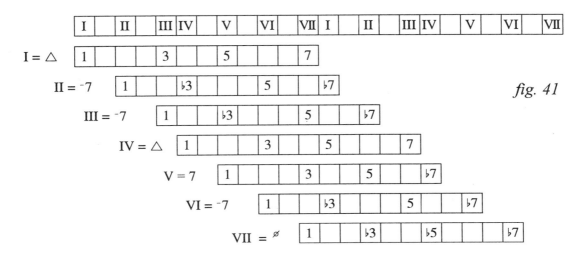

fig. 41

The same diatonic progression from above in scale tone degree "measure" format is demonstrated in fig. 42. This method of scale tone degree format is also known as baseline. Professional musicians most of the time write out their progressions in this way so that the progressions are "generic" allowing them to add pitch on the fly as many times the same tune will have to be played in different keys for different singers.

fig. 42

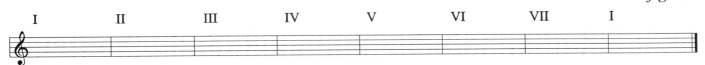

When scale tone degrees have other symbols added then the chord is played accordingly (fig. 43↓).

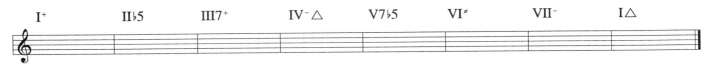

The above baseline progression is demonstrated in the key of "C" so you can see the alterations (fig. 44↓).

Even though the scale tone degrees are standard such as I = △, II = ⁻7 etc., some people will still write them out as I△, II⁻7 etc.

We also use the same method to derive simple diatonic progressions using triads. Starting with the Major scale and its modes again (fig. 45):

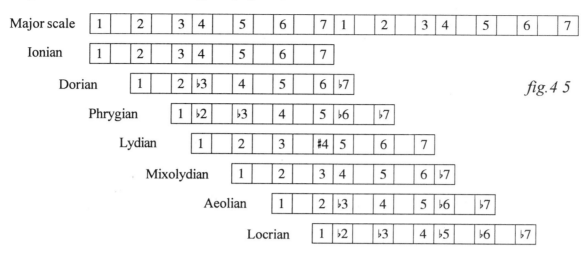

fig. 45

Then using the every other note rule we extract the chords from the modes (fig. 46).

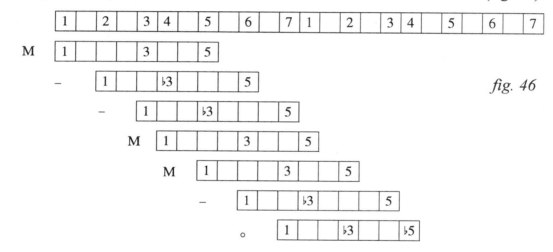

fig. 46

Now we assign pitch to our formula. We will use the key of C for this example (fig. 47).

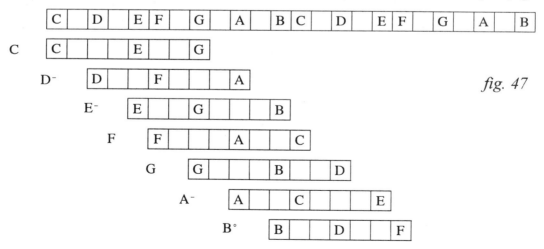

fig. 47

What we have is a diatonic progression using triads in the key of C. Diatonic progressions are graphed out in fretboard format in **The Guitar Grimoire® Progressions** volume.

CIRCLE OF FIFTHS

The next type of progression is known as circle progressions. Before we can understand circle progressions we must be able to understand the circle of fifths (fig. 49).

The "Circle of Fifths" demonstrates the relationship of the scale tone degrees (fig. 48) to each other in fifths (fig. 49).

On the circle of fifths you see 12 positions like the 12 positions of a clock. These 12 positions represent the 12 building blocks of music, the 7 scale tone degrees and the 5 enharmonic degrees. Unlike a clock whose numbers flow consecutively 1, 2, 3, 4, 5 etc. the positions on the circle of fifths are I, V, II, VI, etc. In other words they move in fifths.

To better understand the Circle of Fifths, let's string several octaves of building blocks together as in the figure below. Space allows for three octaves only (fig. 50).

Notice that one fifth is made up of 8 blocks. The numbers in bold below appear in the circle of fifths diagram above (start at I on top and follow clockwise).

COUNTING FIFTHS:
STEP 1: start at the " I "
STEP 2: count one 5th (8 blocks)
STEP 3: continue counting where left off

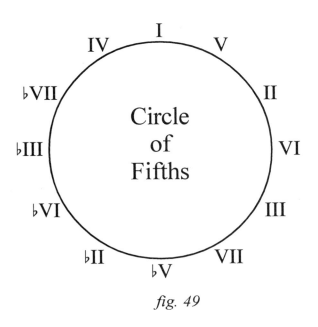

fig. 48

fig. 49

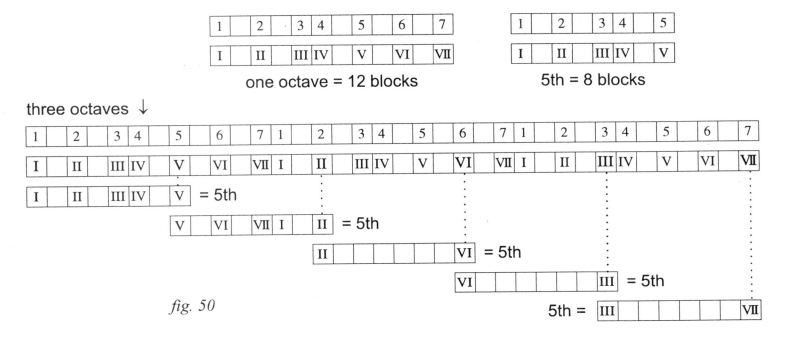

one octave = 12 blocks

5th = 8 blocks

three octaves ↓

fig. 50

103

We ran out of space in the previous example by putting the octaves in a straight line. We can loop seven octaves end to end, to form a complete circle. In the diagram below (fig. 51) the emphasized tones are the fifths. This is another way of demonstrating a "Circle of Fifths".

The Circle of Fifths gets its name from moving in a clockwise direction around the circle from the top or the I starting point. In a counterclockwise direction, the emphasized tones become fourths, which also contain 8 building blocks starting from the I descending to the IV. This is an *inverted* fifth.

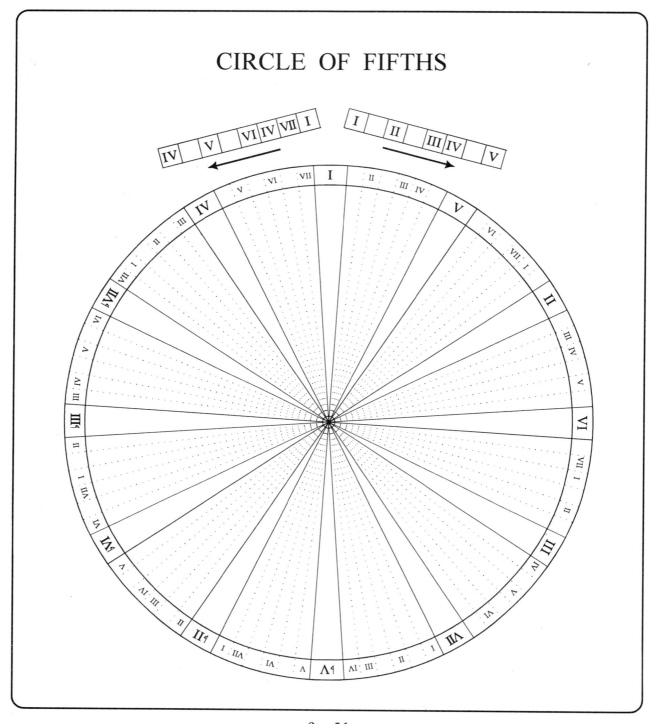

fig. 51

Now that you know that each position is a fifth, what about the relationship to other positions. For example, if you take any position as a starting point then skip a position, that is a whole tone or step. This holds true for any position on the circle of fifths. Fig 52 demonstrates this. This works in both directions.

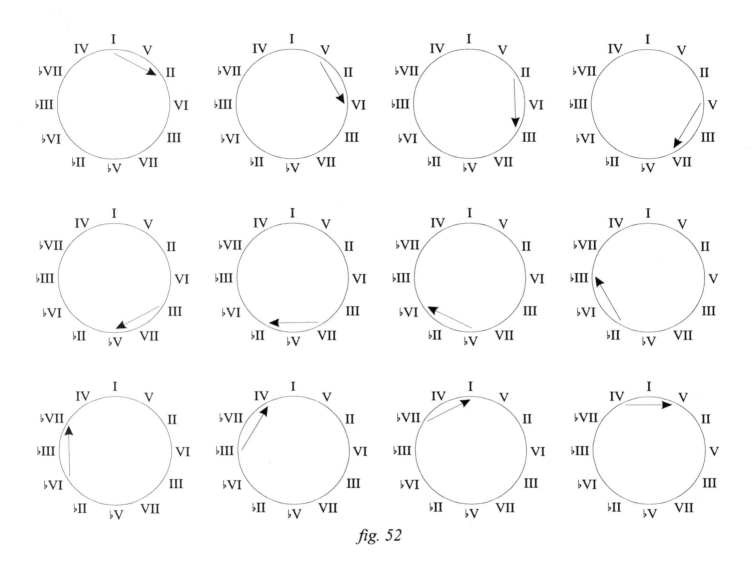

fig. 52

If we take any position as our starting point and skip two positions clockwise we have a sixth. This holds true regardless of which position you start on (fig. 53).

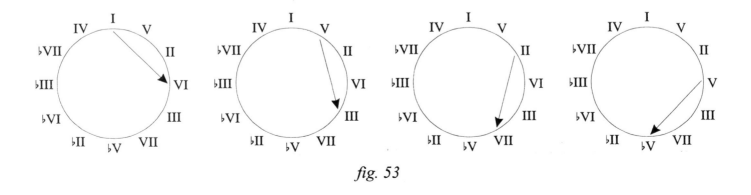

fig. 53

105

This works in reverse as well, however, you get a minor third. Bear in mind, though, that a minor third is an inverted sixth (fig. 54).

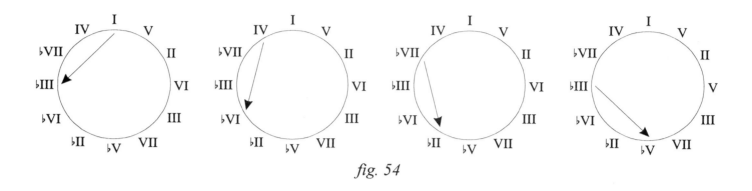

fig. 54

Now if you take any starting position and skip three positions clockwise, what you have is a major third or two whole tones or steps. Again this works whatever position you start from (fig. 55).

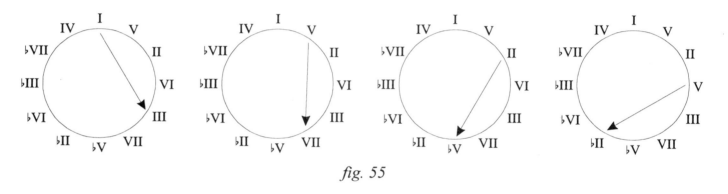

fig. 55

This works in reverse too. If you skip three positions from your starting point counterclockwise you get a minor sixth. A minor sixth is an inverted third (fig. 56).

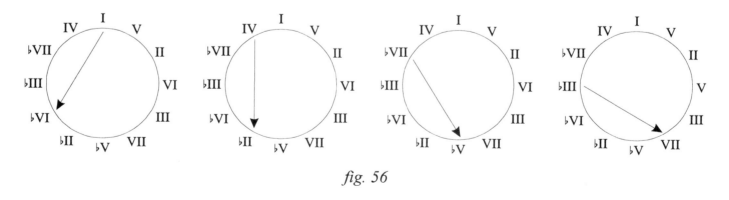

fig. 56

If we skip four positions clockwise from our starting point we have a seventh or five and a half steps. Again this holds true regardless of where you start (fig 57).

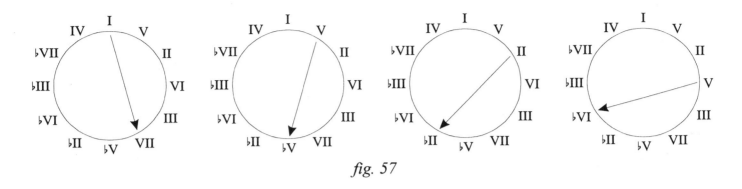

fig. 57

If we skip four positions counterclockwise we get a minor second or a half-step. A minor second is an inverted seventh (fig.58).

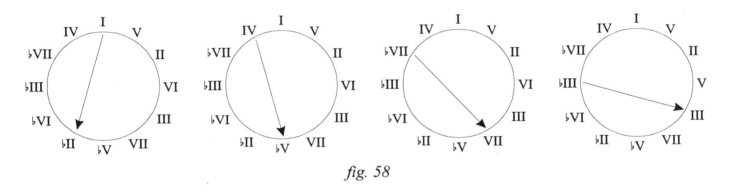

fig. 58

And if we shoot directly across from our starting point we get a flatted fifth (fig. 59).

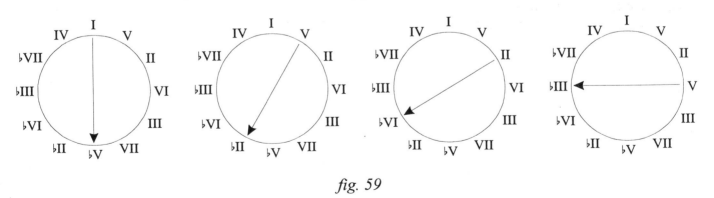

fig. 59

CIRCLE PROGRESSIONS

Now that we understand the circle of fifths we can start on the next type of progression known as circle progressions. In jazz and popular music you hear musicians talking about the II, V, I. The II, V, I is the first basic circle progression derived from the circle of fifths. Observe the diagram on the right, we start at the II position on the circle and move counterclockwise to the V position then to the I position (fig. 60).

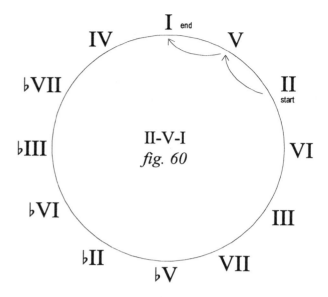

II-V-I
fig. 60

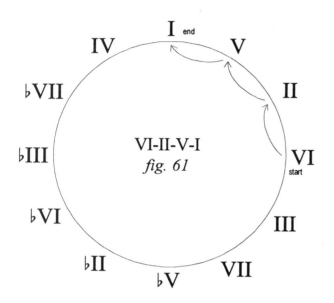

VI-II-V-I
fig. 61

Now we move to the next basic circle progression which is the VI, II, V, I. The same principal applies here. We start at the VI position and move counter-clockwise to the II position then to the V position and end up at the I position (fig. 61).

Once again the next in line for the basic circle progressions is the III, VI, II, V, I. We start at the III position and move counter-clockwise to the VI position then to the II position then to the V position then we end up at the I position (fig. 62).

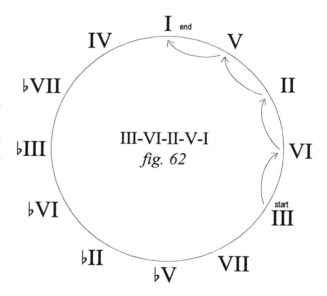

III-VI-II-V-I
fig. 62

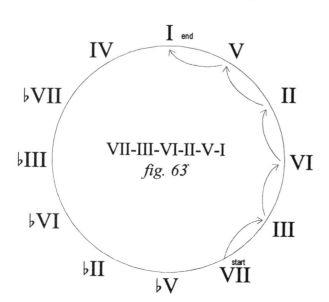

VII-III-VI-II-V-I
fig. 63

The next basic circle progression is the VII, III, VI, II, V, I. We start at the VII position and just like the other progression move counterclockwise to the III position then to the VI position then to the II postition then to the V position and end up at the I position (fig. 63). See a pattern taking place? Good.

The last of the basic circle progressions throws us a curve ball. Instead of starting at the ♭V position and continuing counterclockwise, it starts at the IV position then shoots across to the VII position and from the VII continues counterclockwise along the circle of fifths as the other progressions on the previous page. This is the IV, VII, III, VI, II, V, I (fig. 64).

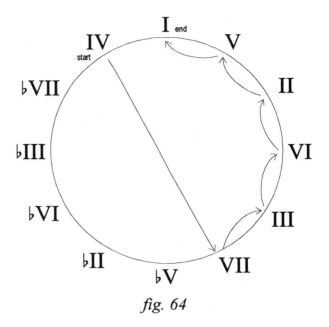

fig. 64

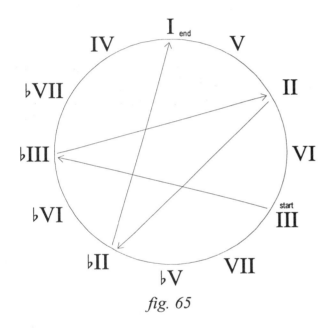

fig. 65

The next type of progression is the chromatic progression. But as far as I'm concerned, the chromatic progression comes from the circle of fifths too (fig. 65).

Circle progressions can be combined with chromatic progessions in creating songs as figure 66 demonstrates.

In fact, you can combine circle, diatonic, and chromatic progessions when creating songs.

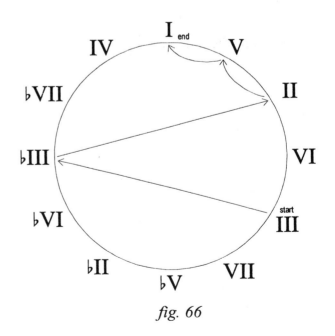

fig. 66

INSTANT SONG CREATOR - THE A A B A METHOD

In this section are some of the many four measure progressions from **The Guitar Grimoire®** **Progressions** volume. They are voiced in straight Major & Minor open voicings.

Here's how it works. There is a method of creating songs known as the A A B A method. "A" represents a short progression, usually four measures, and "B" represents a short progression.

What this means is, you play the progression, repeat it, play the next progression and return to the first progression (fig.67).

But you are not limited to A A B A combinations.

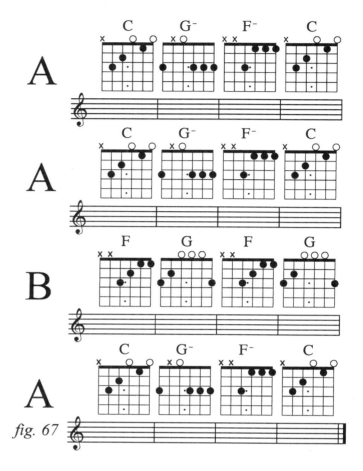

fig. 67

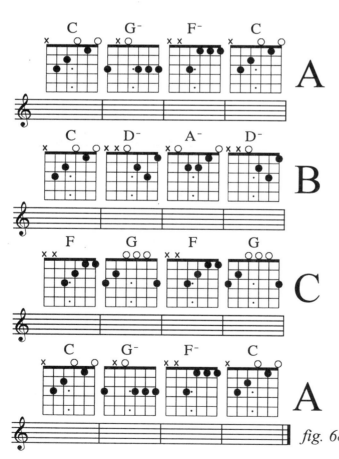

fig. 68

The example to the left (fig. 68) demonstrates an A B C A combination. Observe that the second line is different from the A A B A example above.

You can do A B B A combinations, or A B A B combinations, or A B C D combinations, or A B A C combinations. Get the picture?

The only limitations are those that you place upon yourself.

Remember, the "A", the "B", the "C", the "D", of the A A B A etc., represent progressions and not pitch.

In essence, the A A B A means, little progressions strung together to make a big progression. In other words, a song.

110

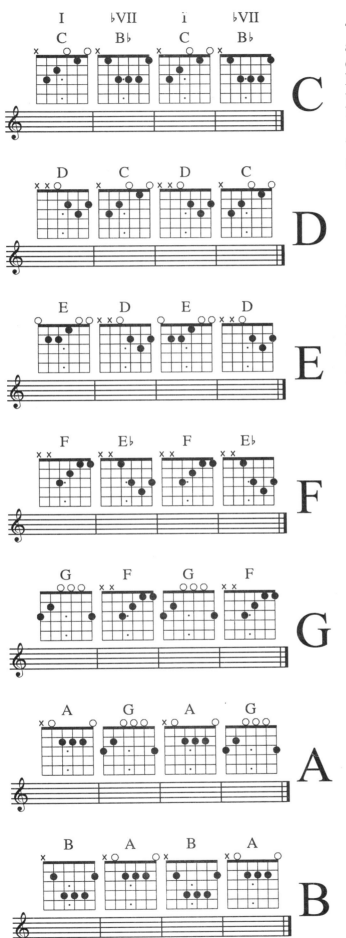

The four measure progressions in this section are graphed out in two columns per page. Each column is one progression graphed out in the keys of C,D,E,F,G,A,B, using open chord voicings. At the very top of each column is the baseline or root motion. See figure 69.

This section is then divided into sub-sections, as in,

> progressions that start on the I chord
> progressions that start on the II chord
> progressions that start on the III chord
> progressions that start on the IV chord
> progressions that start on the V chord
> progressions that start on the VI chord
> progressions that start on the ♭VII chord

In case you are wondering why it's the ♭VII and not the VII chord, the ♭VII chord for this type of progression sounds better.

Notice that progressions starting on the II thru ♭VII chord sub-sections, are still listed as C,D,E,F,G,A,B.

When you are creating a song with these progressions, all sub-section choices, I, II, III, etc. (in other words A A B A combinations), must be from the same key in order to stay in key, unless you are changing the key of the song for the last verse and chorus.

As you get more familiar with these progressions you can revoice them or extend them. A major can become a major seventh or you can use a dominant seventh or sixth or augmented etc. Whatever alteration you make depends upon your creativity. You will be the judge as to whether it sounds good or not. Of course, if you think it sounds good and people start throwing rotten fruit at you, you might have to reconsider the alterations you have made.

fig. 69

111

CHORDS USED IN 4 MEASURE PROGRESSIONS

The chord voicings in this section are open chord voicings, which means they are played in the open position, by the nut, and incorporate open strings. A few of the voicings, however, do not have open strings.

For your convenience, the chart below shows all the chords used in the four measure progressions (fig. 70).

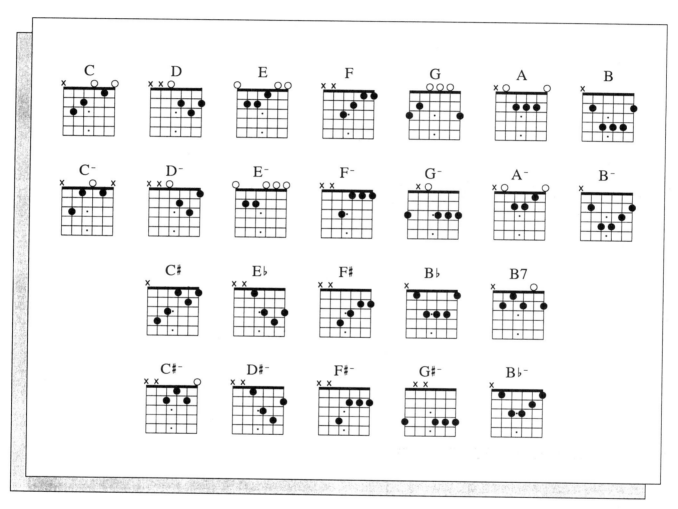

fig. 70

4 MEASURE PROGRESSIONS STARTING AT I

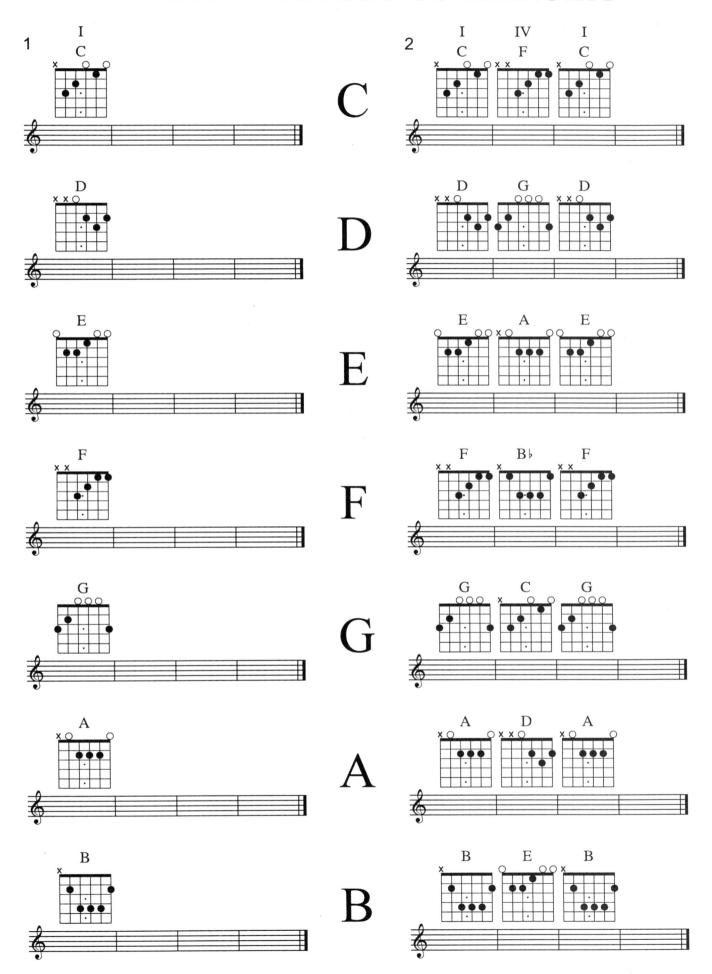

4 MEASURE PROGRESSIONS STARTING AT I

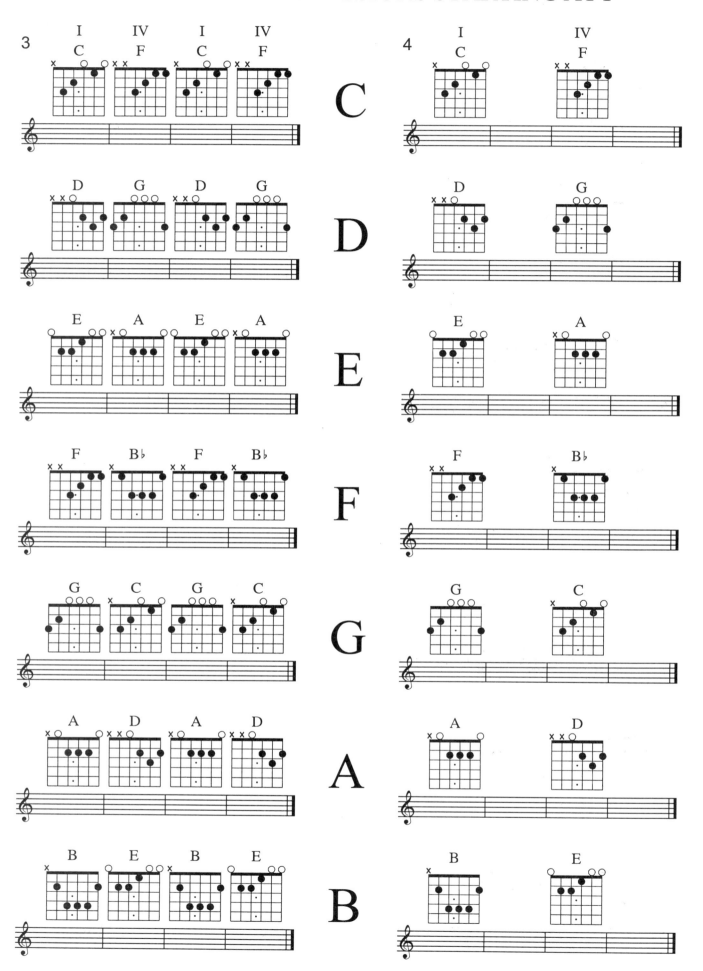

4 MEASURE PROGRESSIONS STARTING AT I

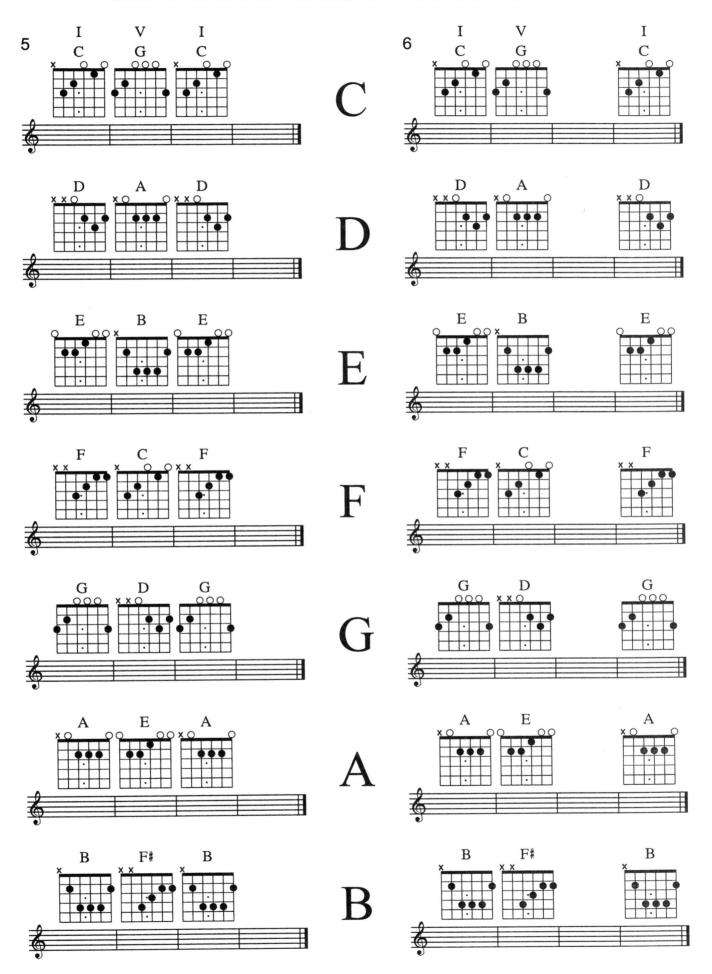

4 MEASURE PROGRESSIONS STARTING AT I

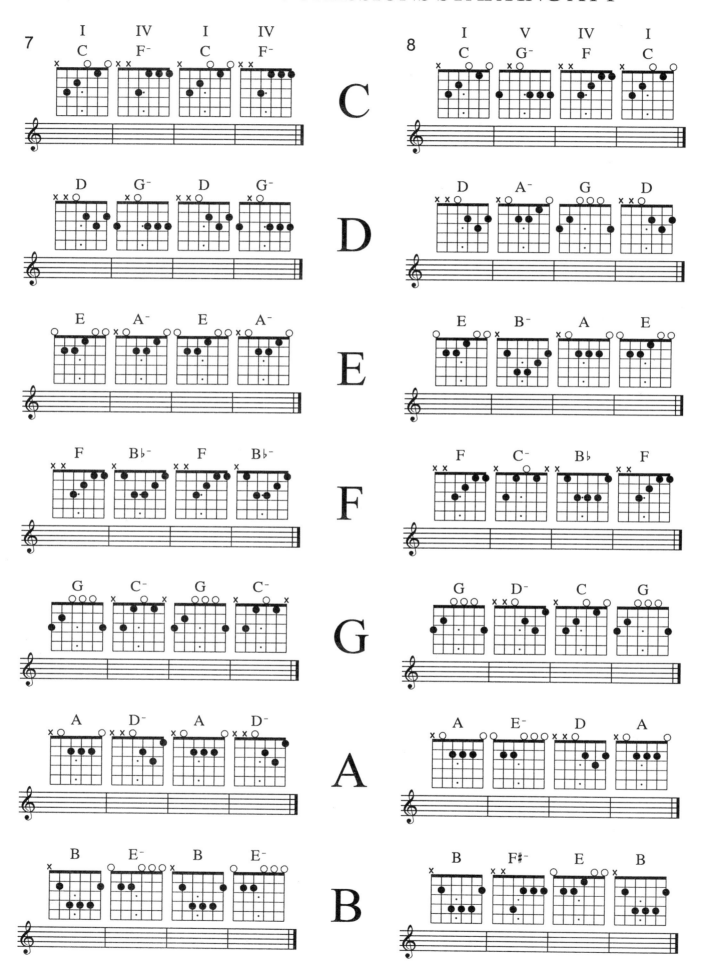

4 MEASURE PROGRESSIONS STARTING AT I

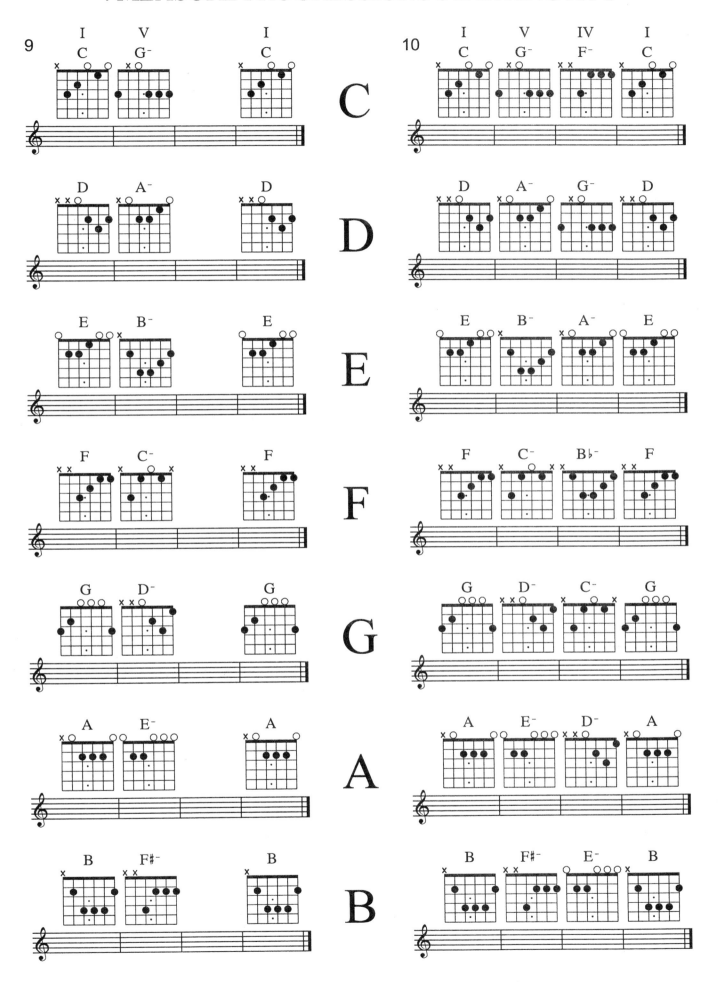

4 MEASURE PROGRESSIONS STARTING AT I

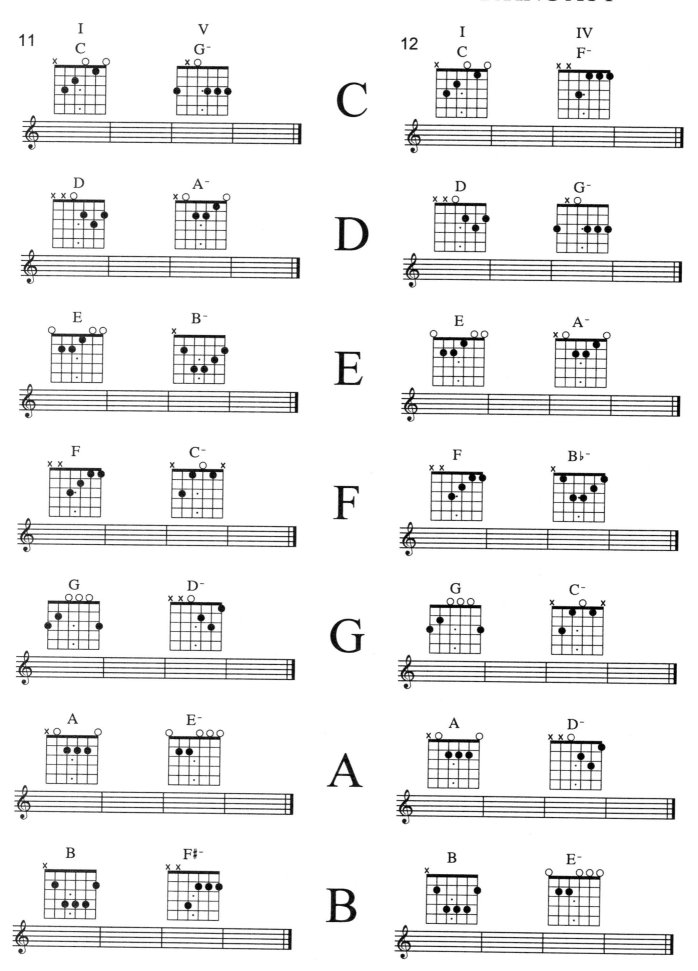

4 MEASURE PROGRESSIONS STARTING AT II

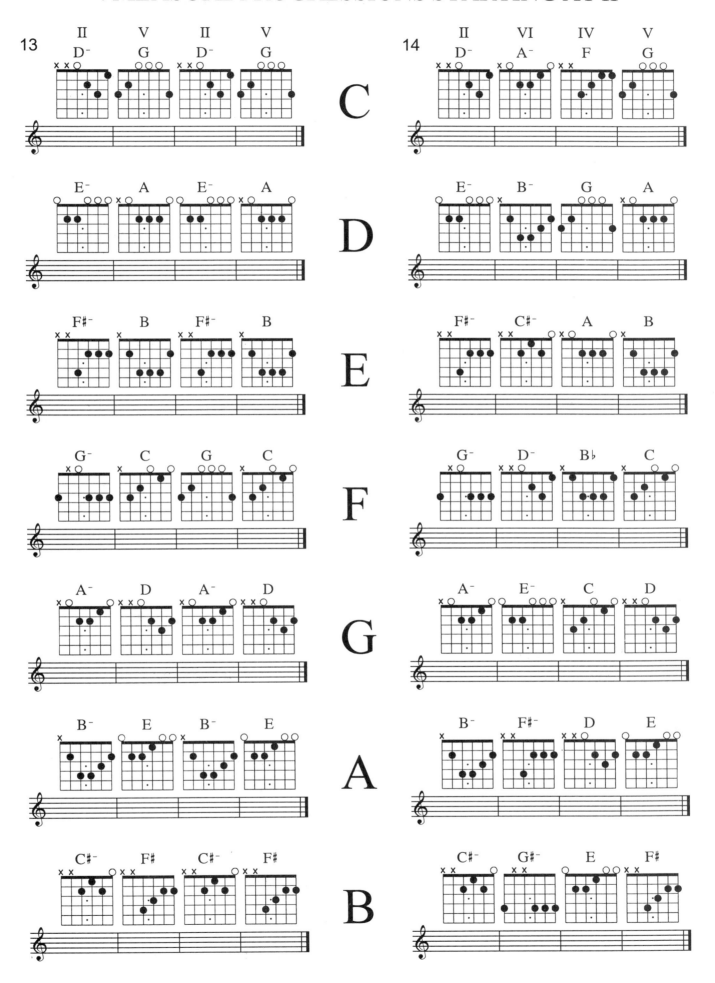

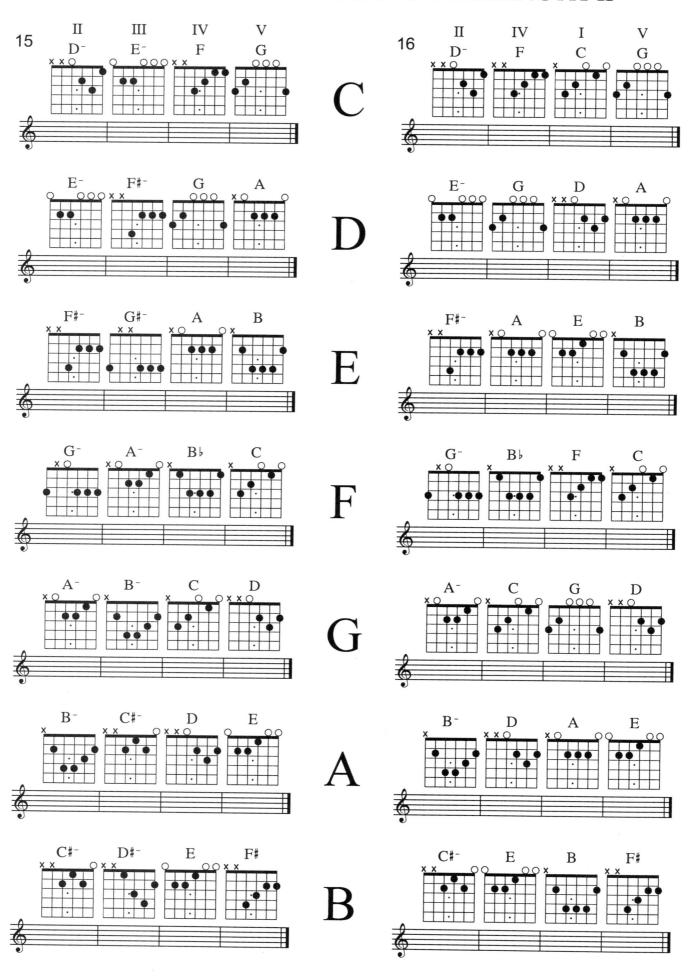

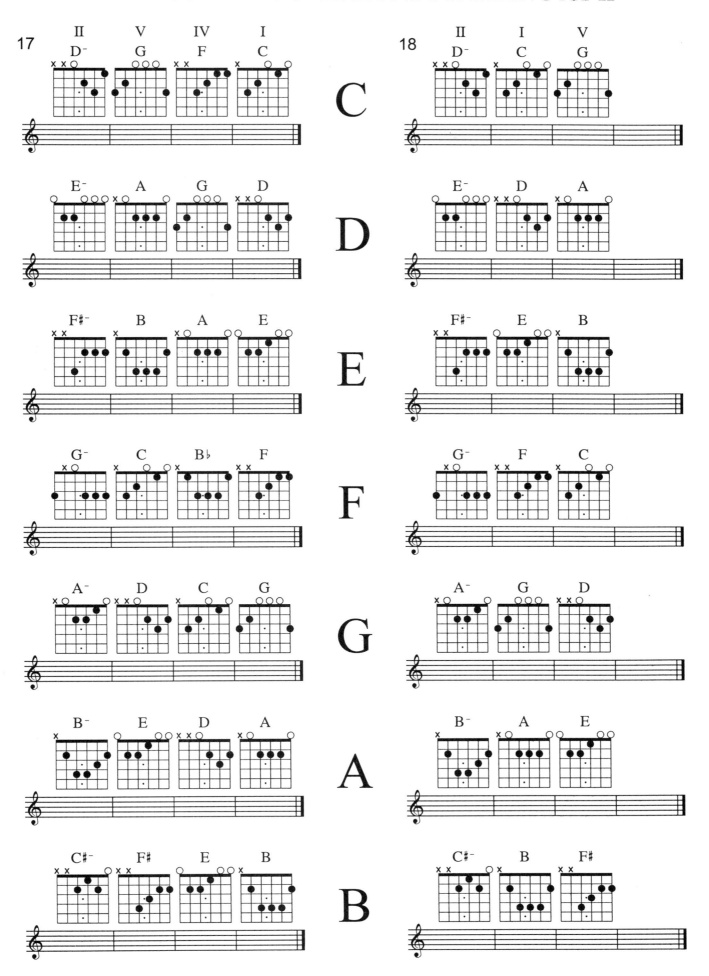

4 MEASURE PROGRESSIONS STARTING AT III

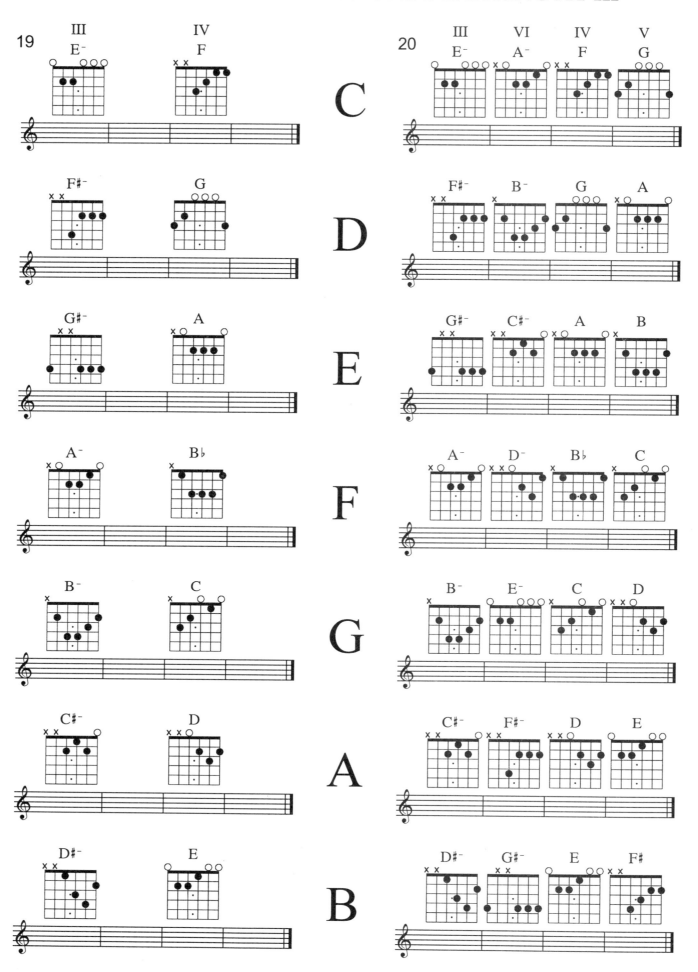

4 MEASURE PROGRESSIONS STARTING AT III

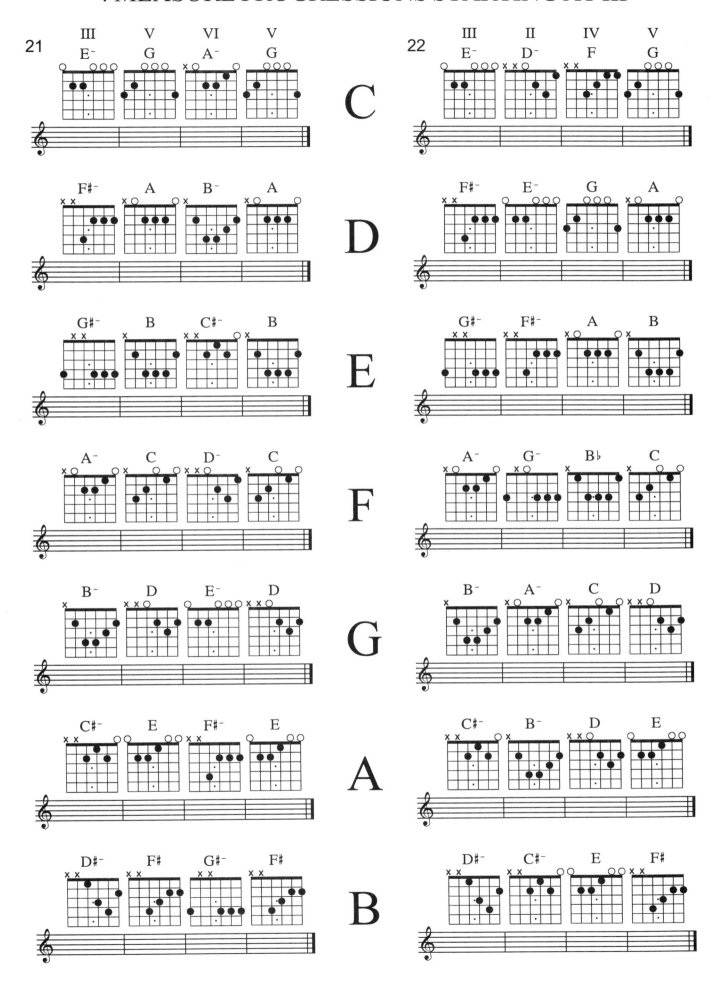

4 MEASURE PROGRESSIONS STARTING AT III

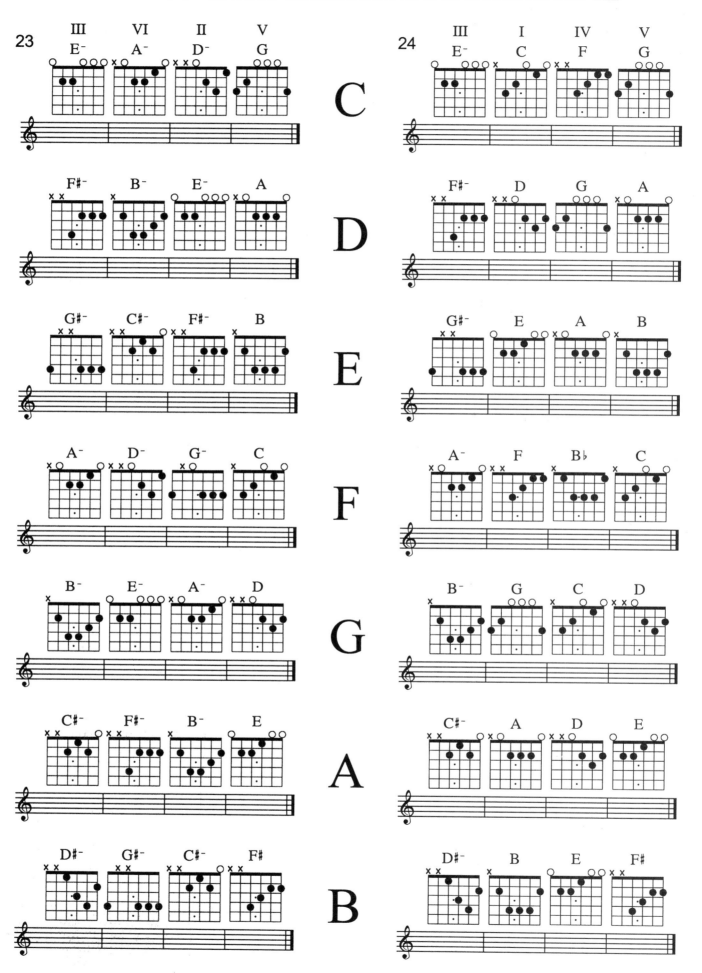

124

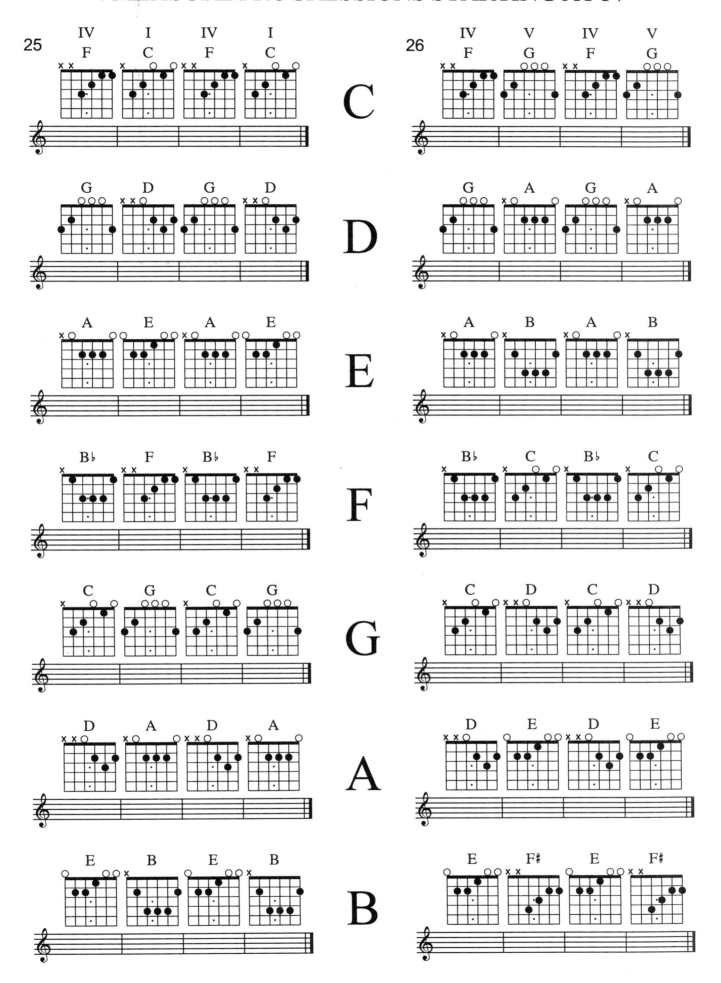

4 MEASURE PROGRESSIONS STARTING AT IV

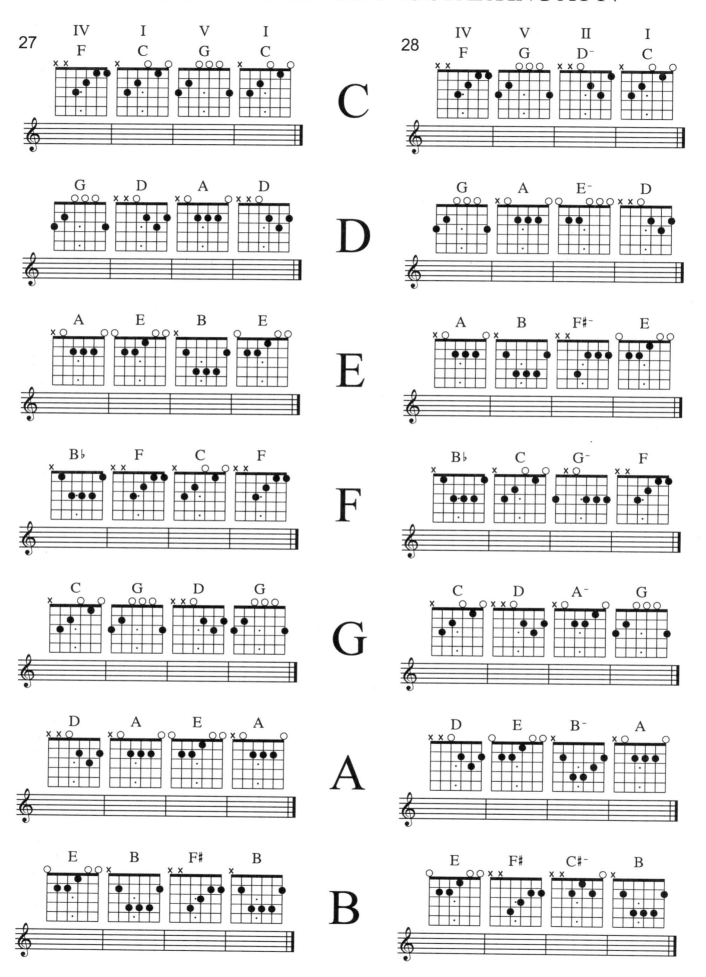

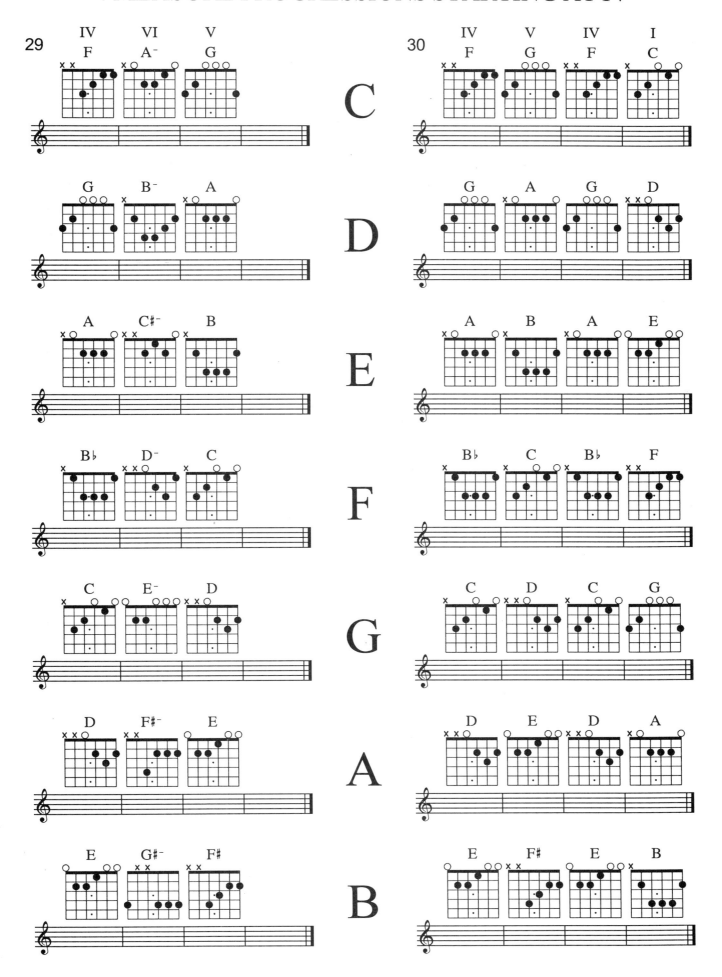

4 MEASURE PROGRESSIONS STARTING AT IV

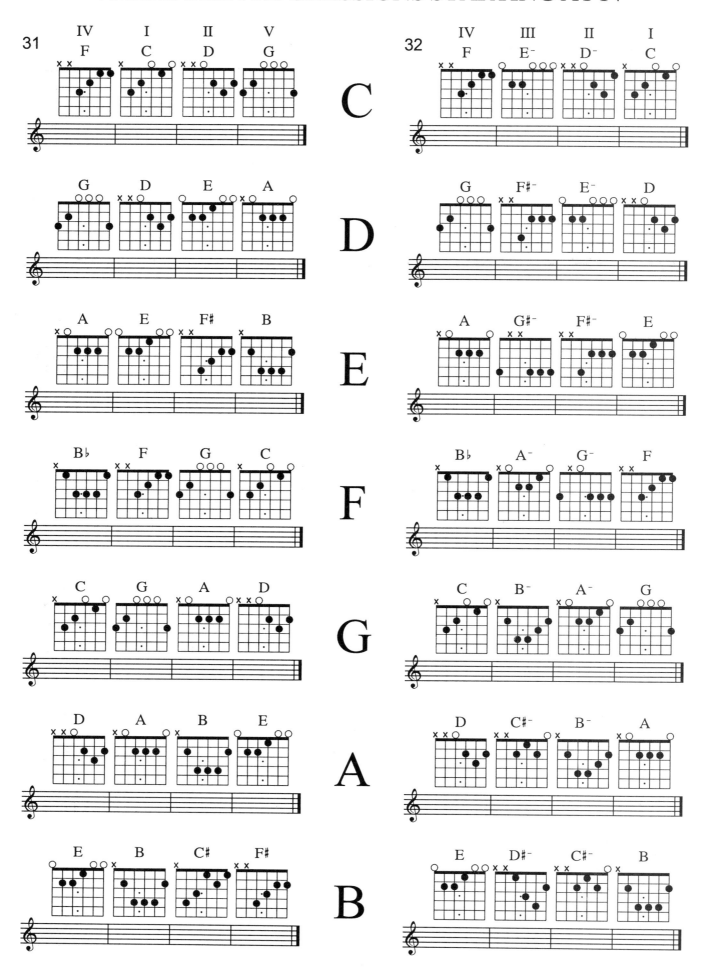

4 MEASURE PROGRESSIONS STARTING AT V

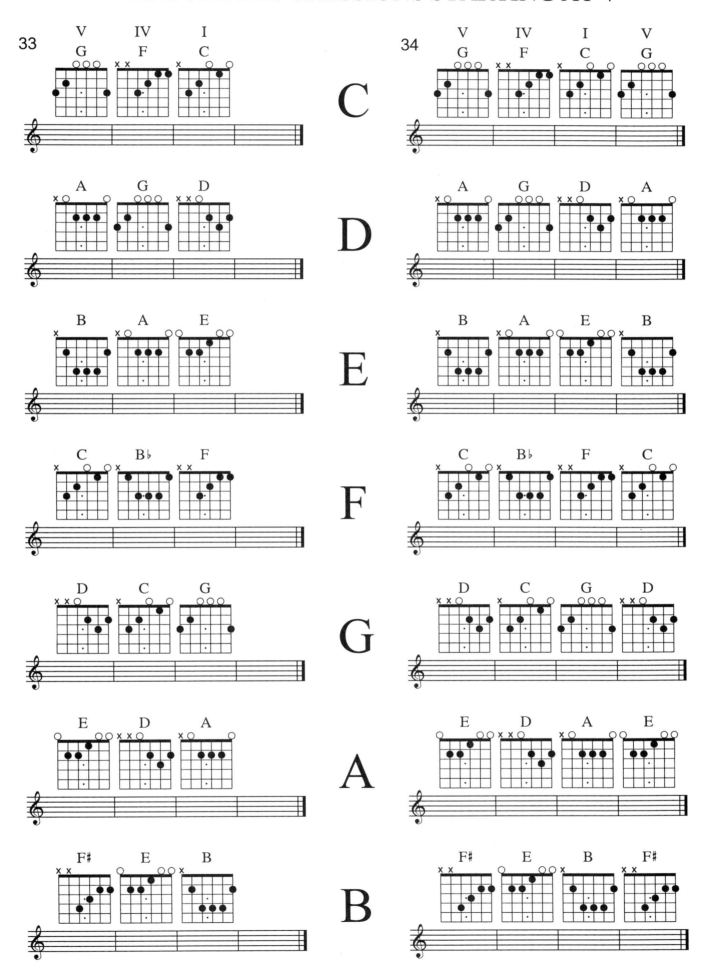

4 MEASURE PROGRESSIONS STARTING AT V

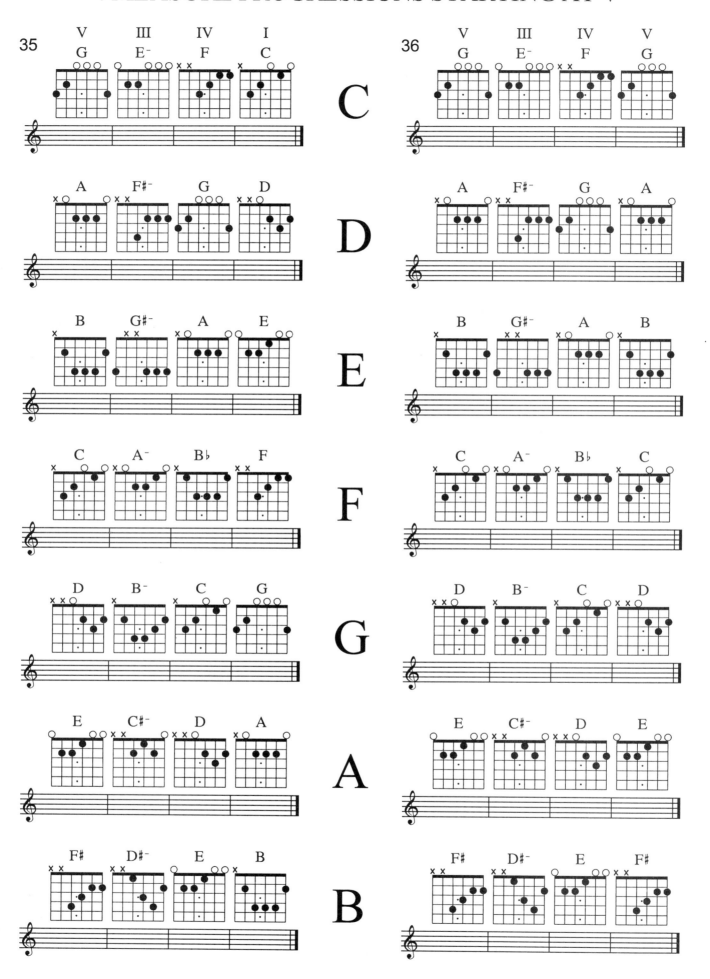

130

4 MEASURE PROGRESSIONS STARTING AT V

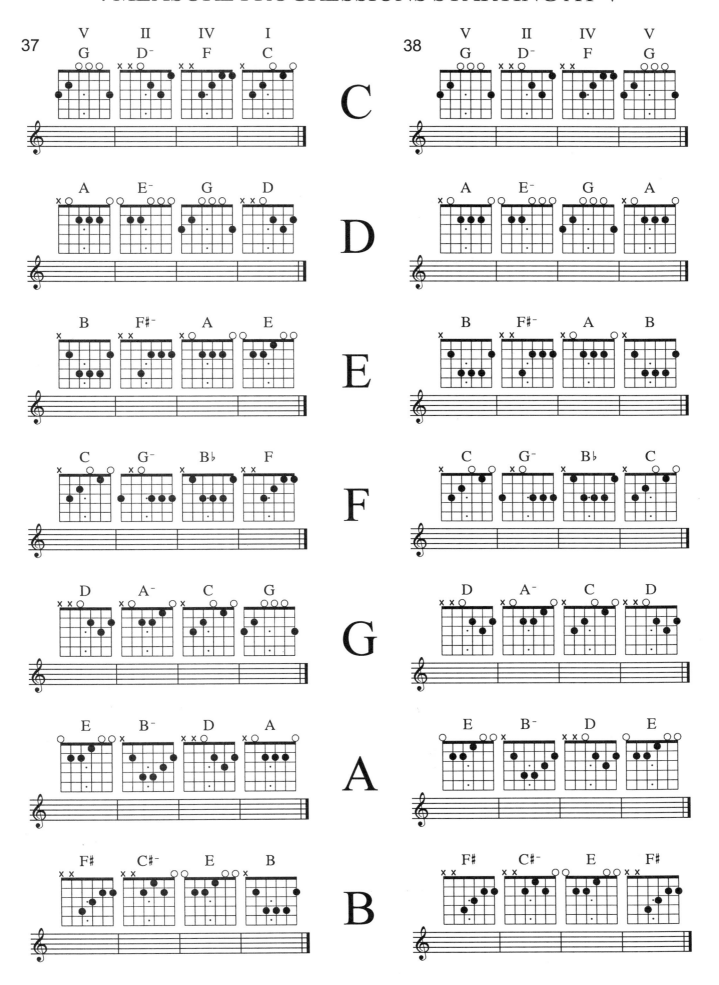

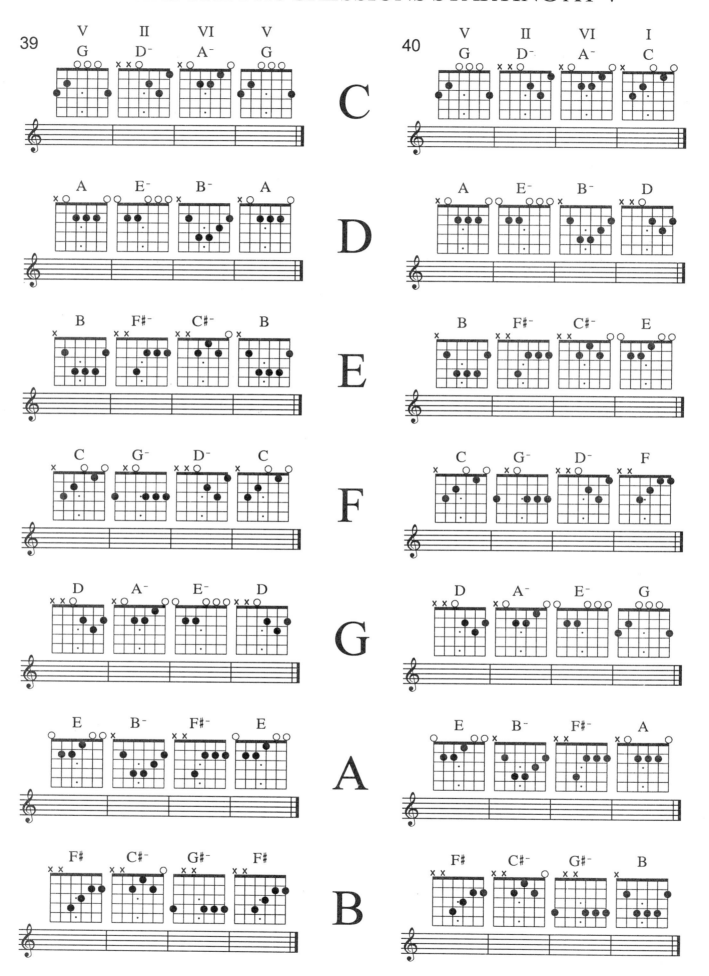

4 MEASURE PROGRESSIONS STARTING AT VI

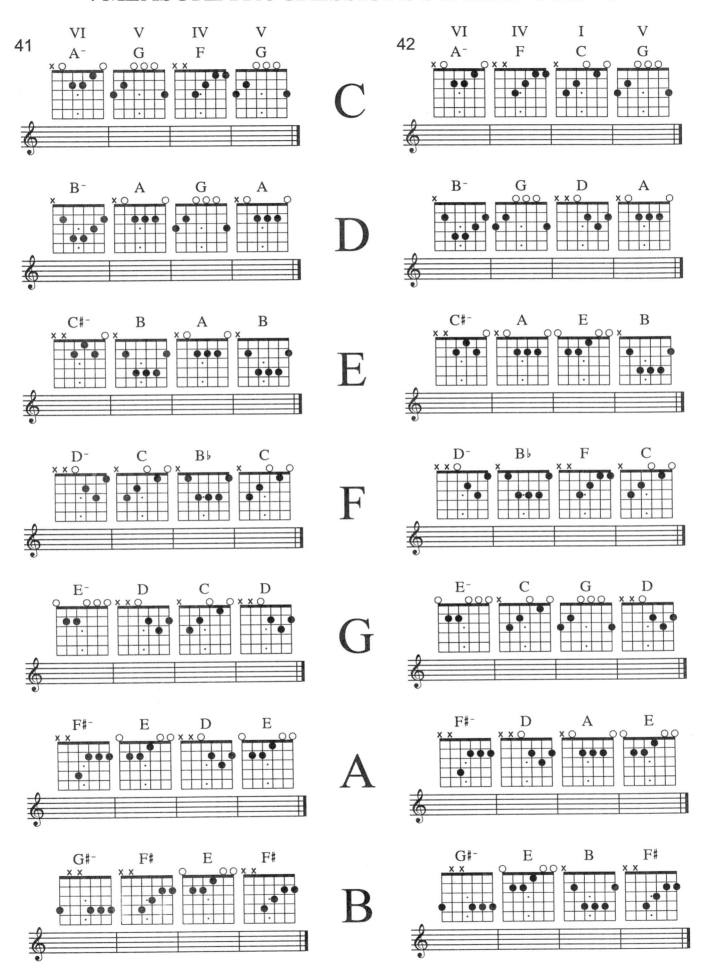

4 MEASURE PROGRESSIONS STARTING AT VI

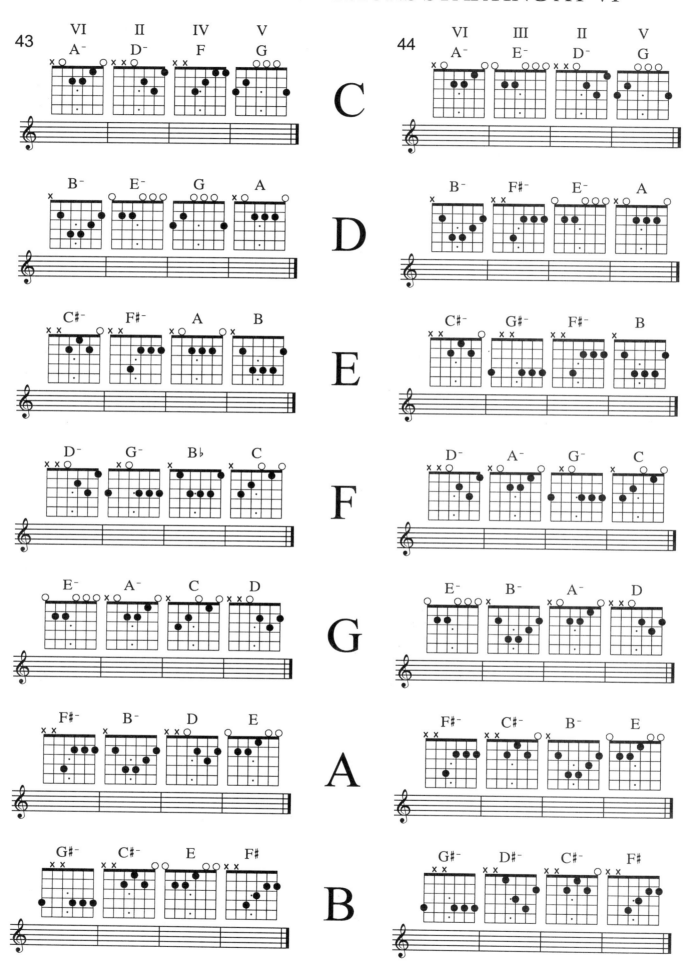

4 MEASURE PROGRESSIONS STARTING AT VI

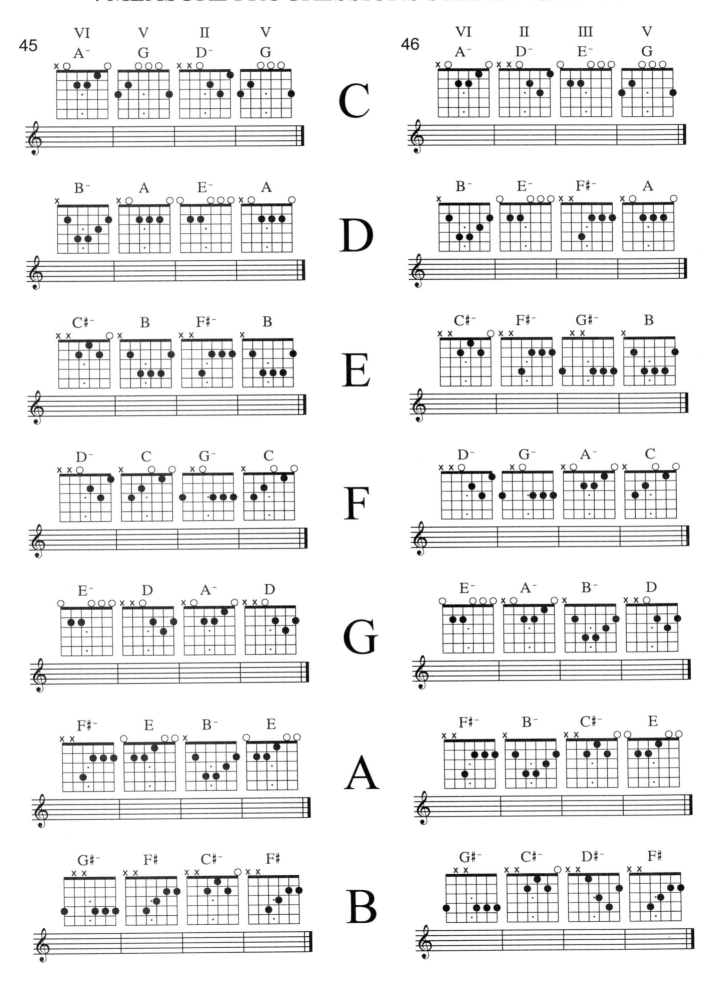

4 MEASURE PROGRESSIONS STARTING AT ♭VII

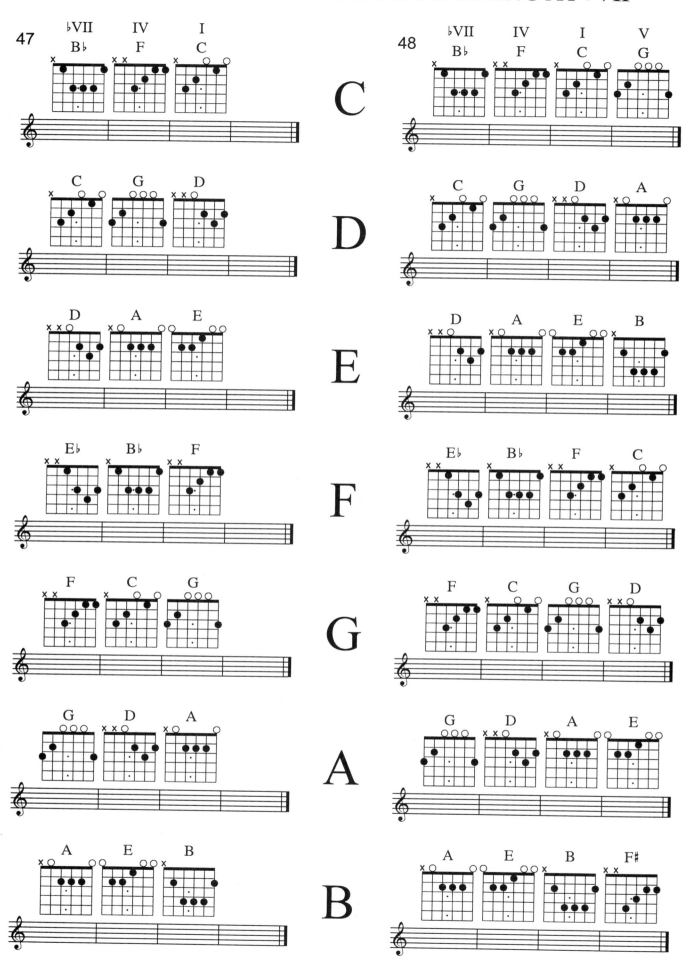

4 MEASURE PROGRESSIONS STARTING AT ♭VII

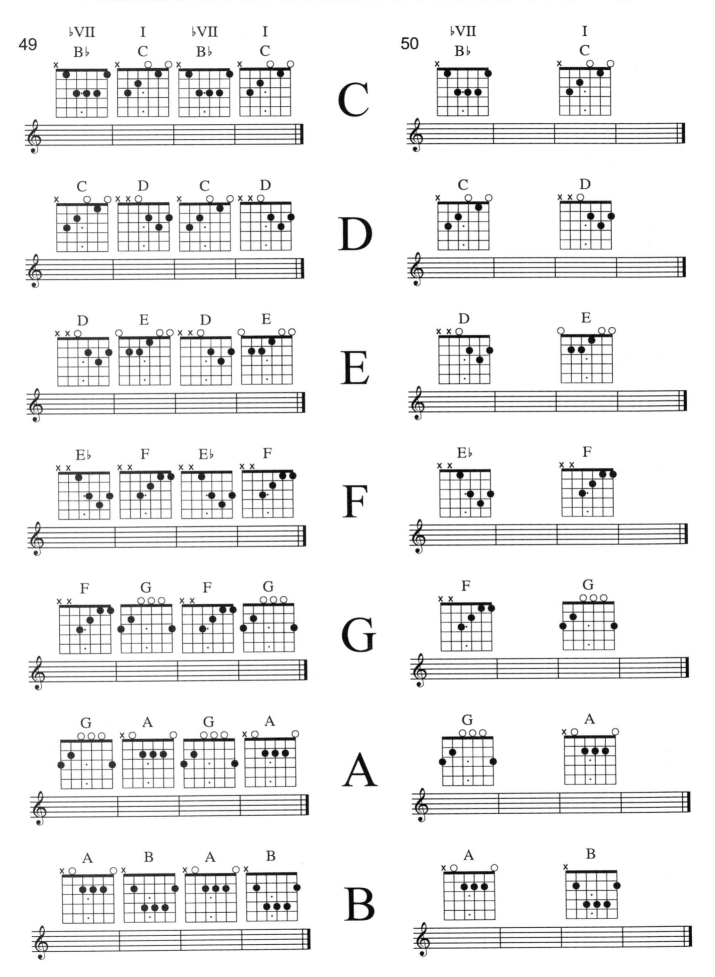

SOLOING AND COMPATIBILITY

In order to solo over progressions we need to understand scales, chords, and scale-chord compatibility. Well we've covered the basics of scales and chords so you're two thirds of the way there. In fact, when we extracted the chords from the modes to learn our first diatonic progression we demonstrated scale-chord compatibility. In essence, the scale we use to solo over the chord must contain the tones of that chord and visa versa. For a more in depth study of compatibility check out **The Guitar Grimoire® - Chords & Voicings.**

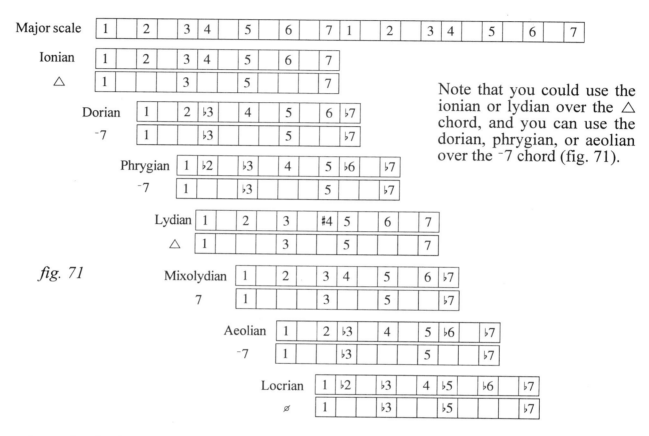

Note that you could use the ionian or lydian over the △ chord, and you can use the dorian, phrygian, or aeolian over the ⁻7 chord (fig. 71).

fig. 71

Our starting point for improvising or soloing over progressions is the one chord jams that were so popular in the late 60's and 70's. In fact they're still used in concert a lot, because they are so much fun and the crowd soaks it up. Anyway if we are doing a jam in A Minor, we use the A minor pentatonic to solo. Or we can use one of the minor modes (dorian or aeolian) (fig. 72).

A MINOR PENTATONIC

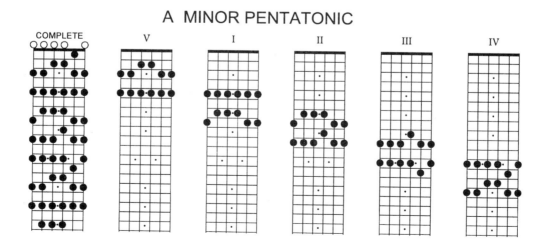

fig. 72

That's fine for one chord jams, but what about when you are changing chords? All right, let's start with a basic 12 bar blues progression. This would be a 12 measure progression with a I, IV, V root motion (fig. 73).

fig. 73

We'll do it in the key of A using basic triad open chord voicings. This means that the chord voicings use open strings (fig. 74).

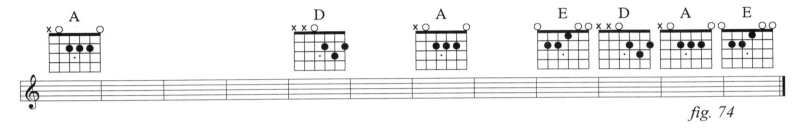

fig. 74

Well, for the "bluesy" sound you can still use the minor pentatonic scale over that progression. The only thing to remember is that when you are playing over the IV chord you will place your emphasis on the 4 tone. When you are playing over the V chord your emphasis will be on the 5 tone. Looking at the interval map for the minor pentatonic in the key of A, you can see it a little better (fig. 75).

For a much better demonstration of this, check out the **Guitar Grimoire - Progressions and Improvisation** video. You can demonstrate things easier on video than in a book.

fig. 75

A Minor Pentatonic

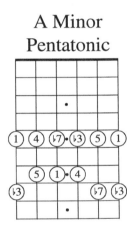

When you are trying to generate a country, or southern rock sound that's a different matter. First of all you will be using major pentatonics. However, you must use the corresponding pentatonic for whatever chord you are playing. In other words, when you are playing an "E", you play a E major pentatonic. And when you are using an "A", you would use an A major pentatonic. And when you are playing a "G" you will use a G Major pentatonic, etc. But if you play a minor chord you will use the corresponding minor pentatonic.

The same holds true when soloing with mixolydians, as in, you play the corresponding scale chord combination, E & E, A & A, etc.

On the following pages are examples of basic 12 bar progressions with open chord voicings in the keys of C, D, E, F, G, A, B. At the top of the page are four variations of the same basic progression. At the bottom of the page are corresponding major pentatonic "windows" for soloing. What I mean is, staying in the same position while changing scales. On the facing page are the mixolydian "windows". Observe that all of the 12 bar progressions, including their variations, are merely combinations of four measure progressions pieced together.

12 BAR PROGRESSIONS: KEY OF C

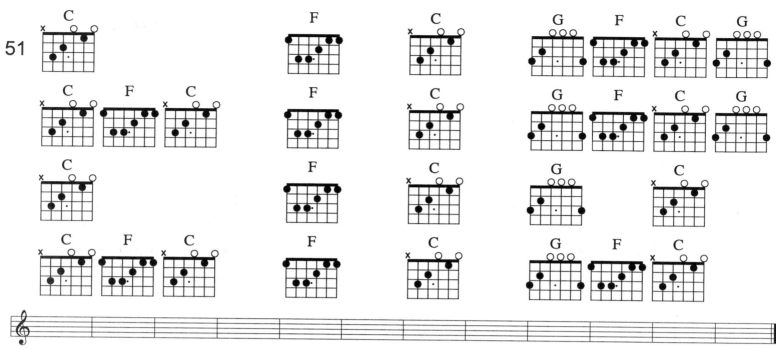

51

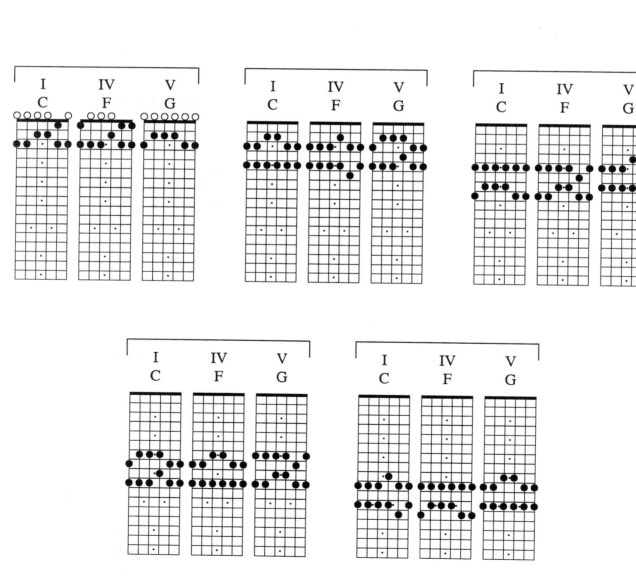

MIXOLYDIAN SOLOING PATTERNS: KEY OF C

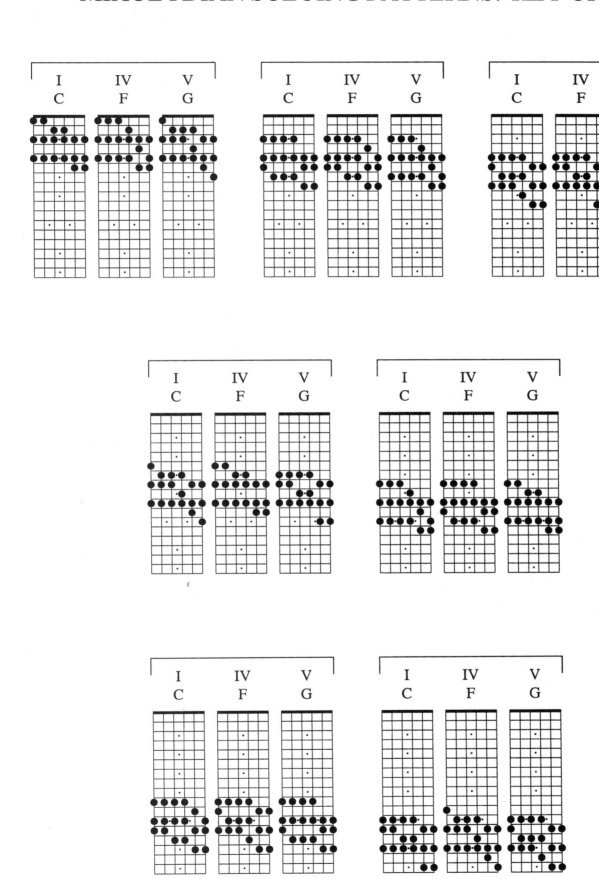

12 BAR PROGRESSIONS: KEY OF D

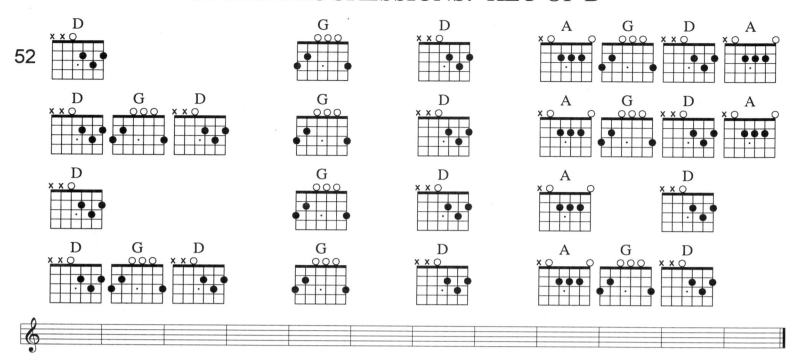

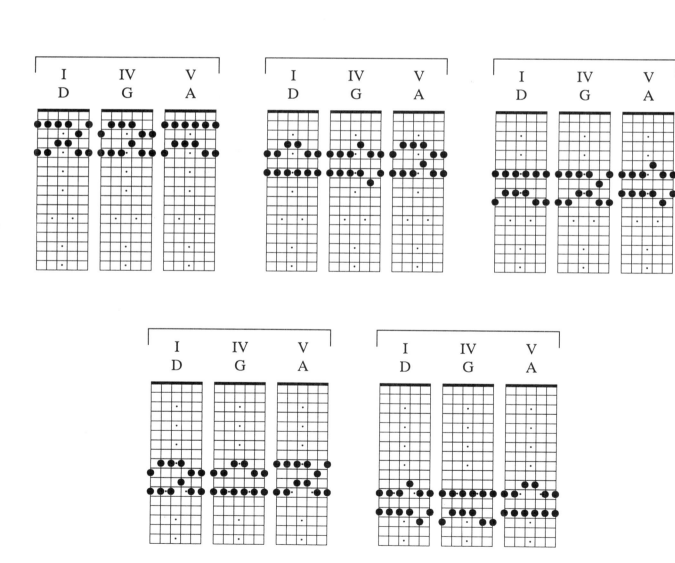

MIXOLYDIAN SOLOING PATTERNS: KEY OF D

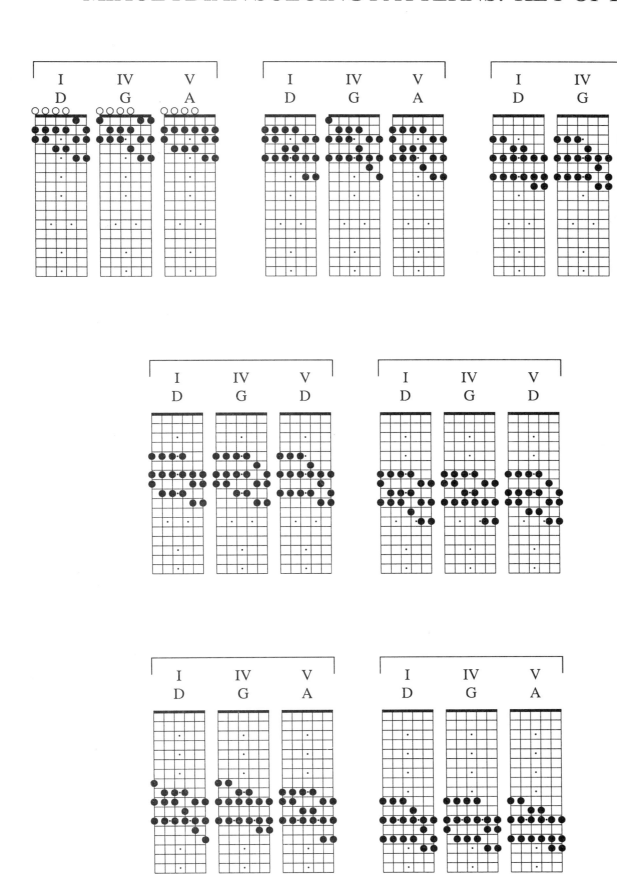

12 BAR PROGRESSIONS: KEY OF E

53

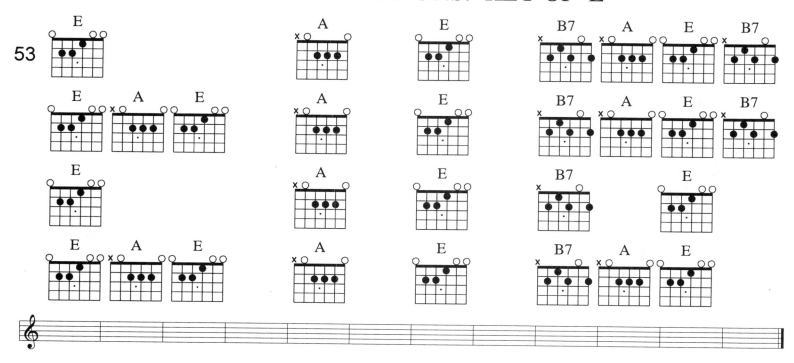

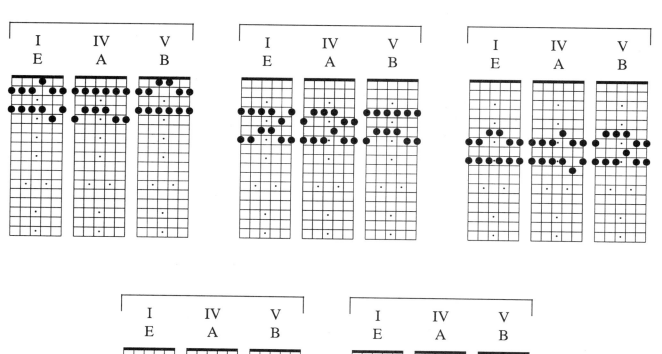

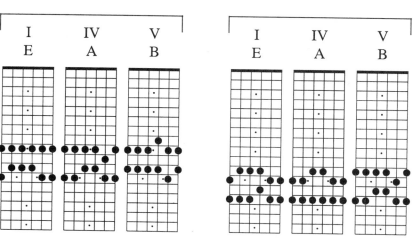

MIXOLYDIAN SOLOING PATTERNS: KEY OF E

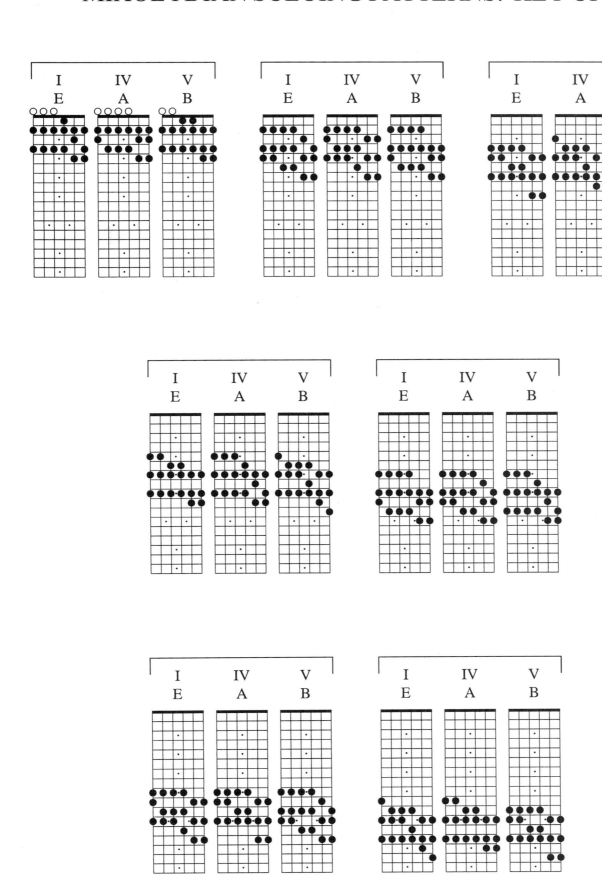

12 BAR PROGRESSIONS: KEY OF F

54

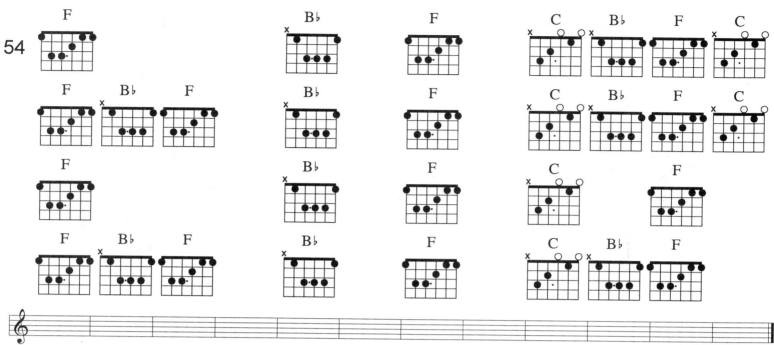

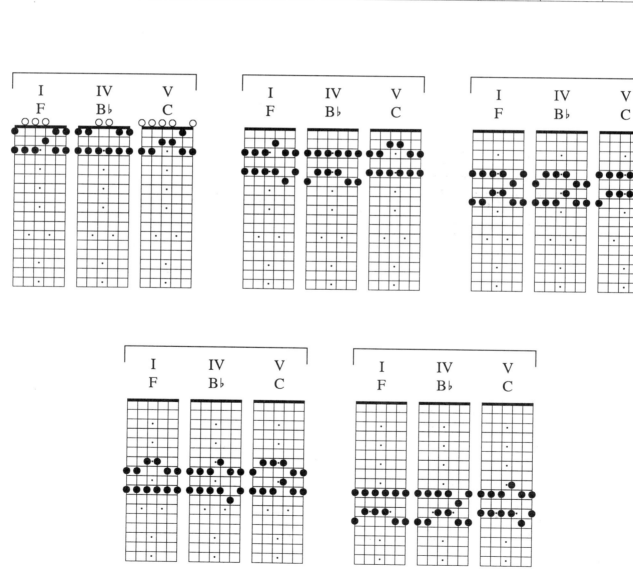

MIXOLYDIAN SOLOING PATTERNS: KEY OF F

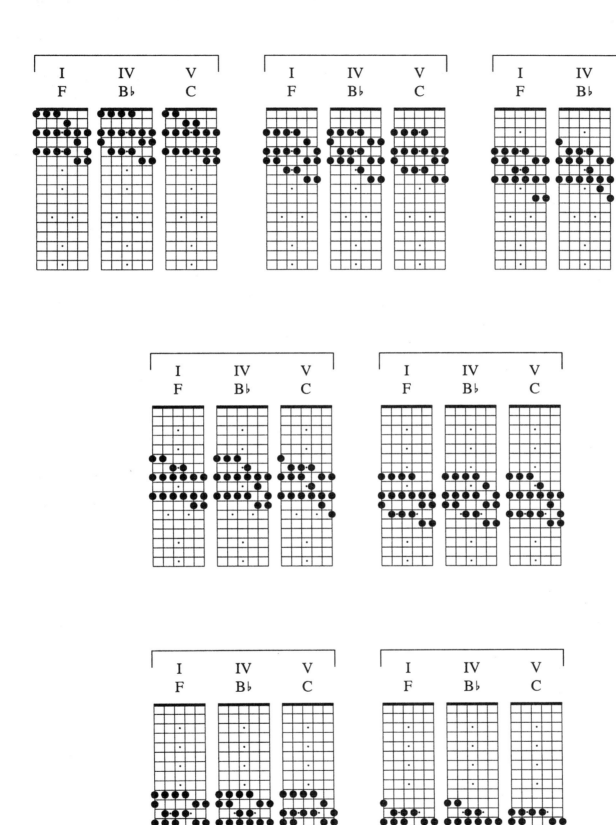

12 BAR PROGRESSIONS: KEY OF G

55

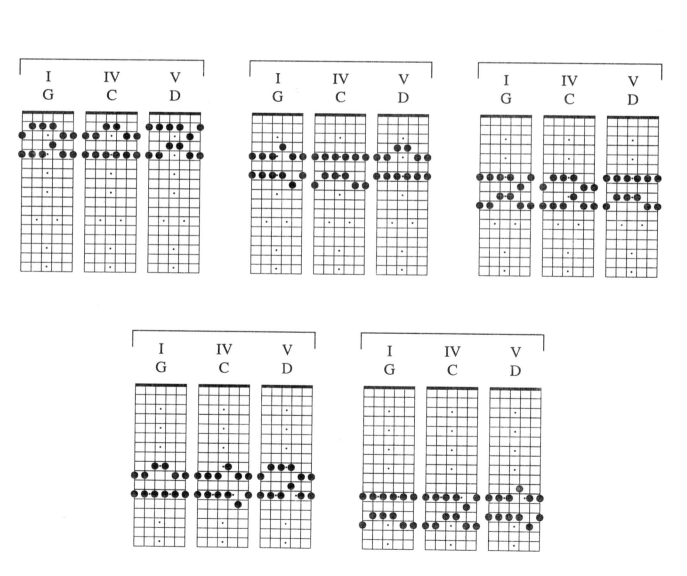

MIXOLYDIAN SOLOING PATTERNS: KEY OF G

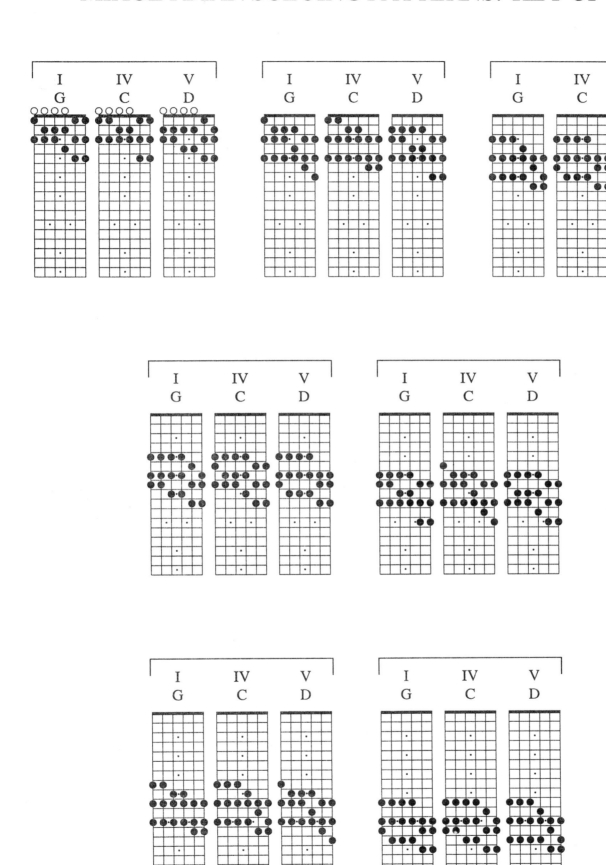

149

12 BAR PROGRESSIONS: KEY OF A

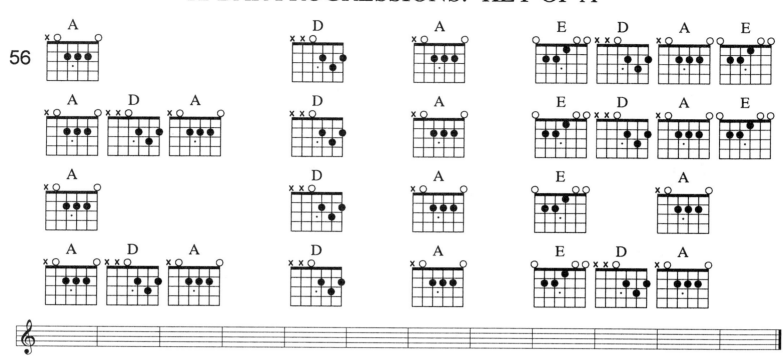

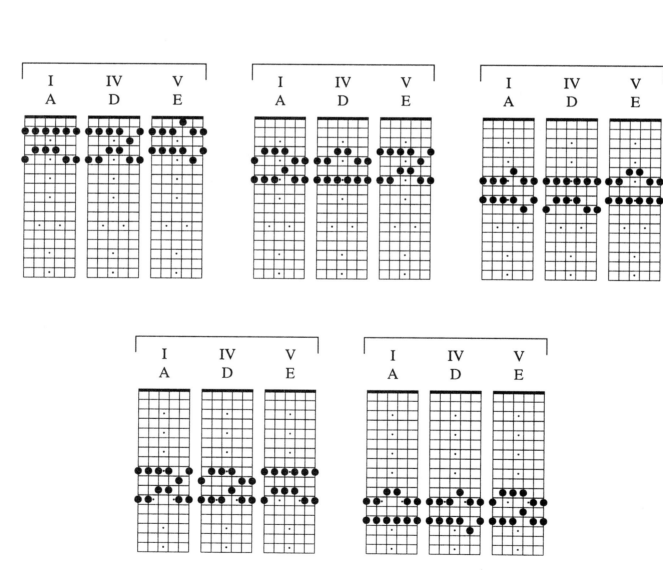

MIXOLYDIAN SOLOING PATTERNS: KEY OF A

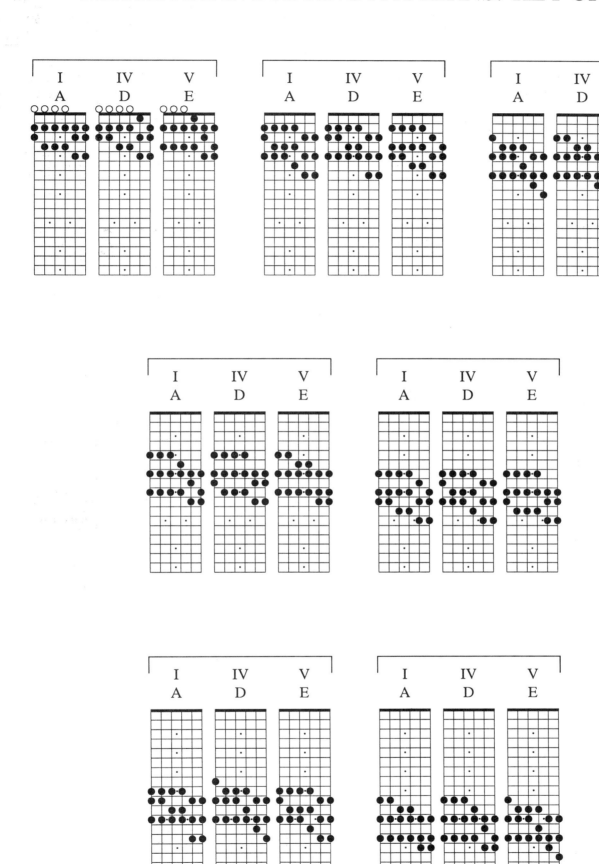

12 BAR PROGRESSIONS: KEY OF B

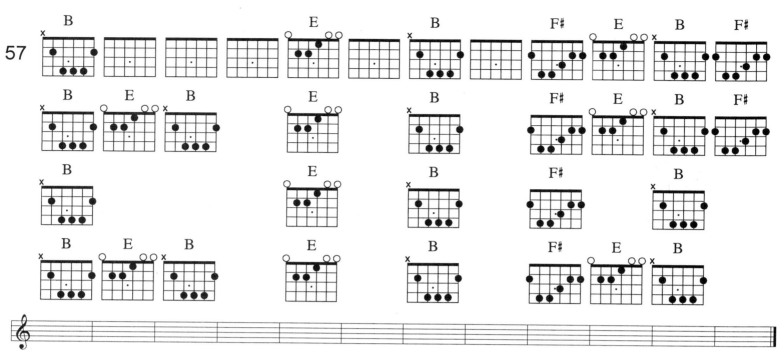

57

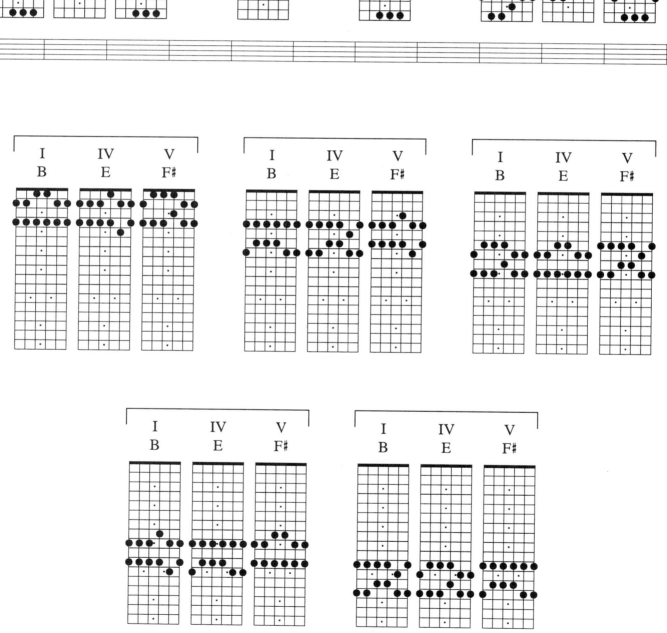

MIXOLYDIAN SOLOING PATTERNS: KEY OF B

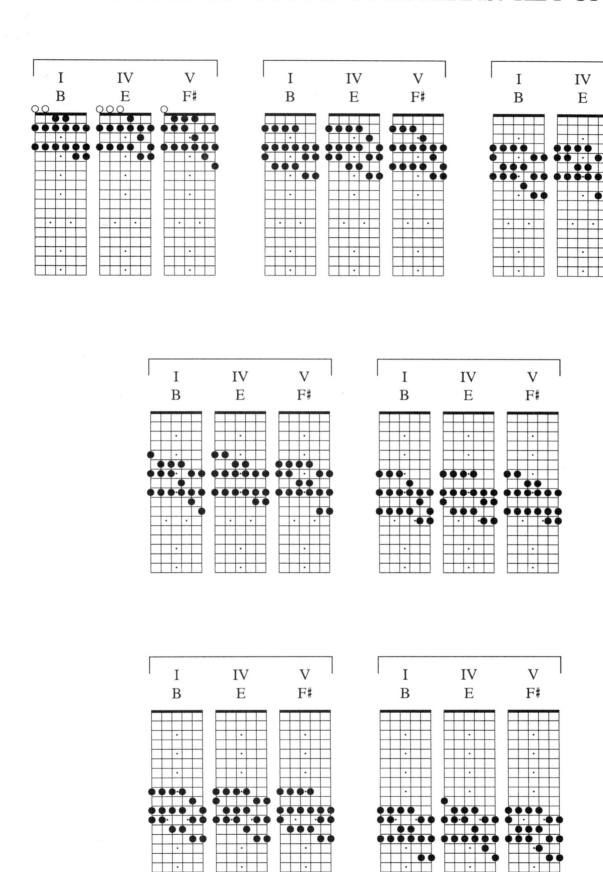

UNDERSTANDING THE NOTES

Before the advent of recording devices, such as tape recorders and now hard disk recorders, the only way to record your composition was to write it down. In order to do this a system of notation had to be created. The present notation system evolved from other systems. After trying to create my own "ultimate" system I then fully realized why the old Masters finally ended up with the notation system that is still in use today. If you want to know more about the history of its evolution, then scope out your school or local library. My goal is to get you to understand the system itself.

Understanding notation, or "reading music", can be quite confusing to the beginner. In fact many a "would be" excellent musician have been discouraged from pursuing music because the study of notation, "reading music", was prematurely dumped on them. That's why I teach my students how to play their instruments first, helping them develop manual dexterity and self esteem before teaching notation.

In order to understand notation you must first understand the mathematics of music. In other words harmony & theory. If you don't understand this all hope is not lost. Go back to the beginning of the book.

What makes notation so confusing to beginners is dealing with the sharps and flats. The main reason it gets so confusing is that you're dealing with the "math formula" as well as the notation. For instance, the formula for the Major scale is 1,2,3,4,5,6,7 which has no sharps or flats and works great in the key of C. But when we shift the formula, which still has no sharps or flats, to the key of C#, we now have seven sharps in notation even though the formula itself has no sharps.

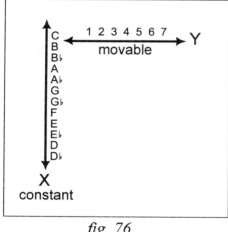

fig. 76

The reason for this is simple, we are dealing with a "X" and "Y" axis, in other words pitch and formula.

The "X" axis, which represent pitch degrees is constant and never moves. The "Y" axis, on the other hand, represents the formula axis and can be moved up and down along the pitch axis. This forms the basis for what we call "modulating" or changing keys (fig. 76). This is also called transposing.

Figure 77 demonstrates how the pitch remains constant, while the formula moves.

You can see how impractical having a separate line for each pitch is. The amount of space wasted is great.

We can save space by using the spaces as well as the lines.

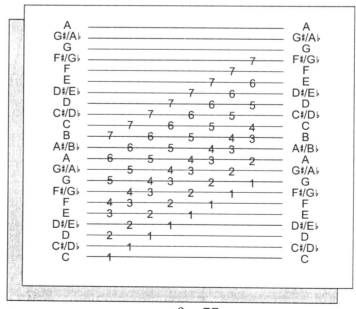

fig. 77

fig. 78

By utilizing spaces as well as lines and eliminating the sharps & flats, we come up with the diagram in figure 78.

Where did the sharps & flats go? Don't worry about that for now, we'll cover that in a moment.

Looking at figure 22, we can see that a bunch of lines & spaces could still get quite confusing. The way we get around that is by zoning or sectioning the lines & spaces. We accomplish this by using symbols known as clefs (fig. 79). This symbol ♭, is the treble clef and this symbol 𝄢, is the bass clef.

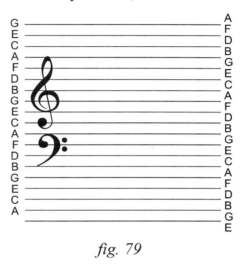

fig. 79

Even still, this could be quite a clutter with all the lines & spaces. So therefore, we have to single out certain lines from the rest. In figure 80, we see that the lines within the area of the clefs become constants, and the other lines are added as needed. The lines that never change are called stave lines, and the add on lines are called ledger lines.

The stave in the treble range is used for the keyboardists right hand and instruments such as guitar while the stave in the bass range is used for the keyboardists left hand and such instruments as the bass guitar.

Even if you just want to play guitar you should learn both clefs and their ledger lines since you need to communicate with other musicians.

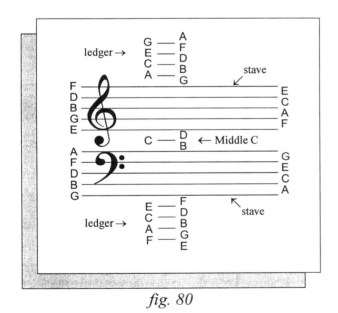

fig. 80

There is an easy way to memorize the lines and spaces. The trick is to make phrases using the pitch letter as the first letter of a word. For instance, the lines of the treble clef can be the phrase, "EVERY GOOD BOY DOES FINE". The lines of the bass clef can be the phrase, "GREAT BIG DOGS FIGHT ANIMALS". The spaces of the treble clef spell the word FACE, while the spaces of the bass clef make up the phrase of "ALL CARS EAT GAS".

Normally, the treble and bass clefs are not so close together. Remember, the first ledger line below the treble clef, and the first ledger line above the bass clef are the same note. This particular note is referred to as "MIDDLE C".

155

STAFF LINES & SPACES

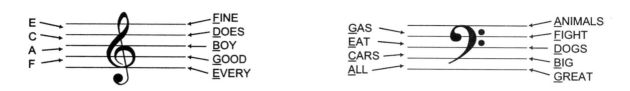

LEDGER LINES & SPACES

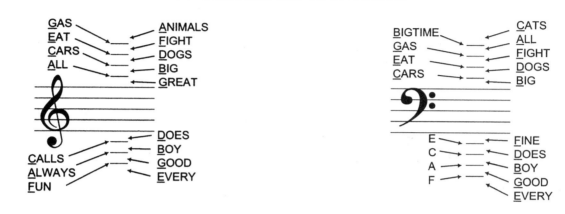

When we want to alter the pitch we use flat & sharp symbols on the line or space in front of the note.

Normally when writing notation, notes that have a double sharp or flat are impractical. In other words, a double flat A would simply be written as a G, and a double sharp G would be written as an A.

The charts that follow show the relationship between the notes, written notes and the fretboard.

PITCH INDICATOR CHART

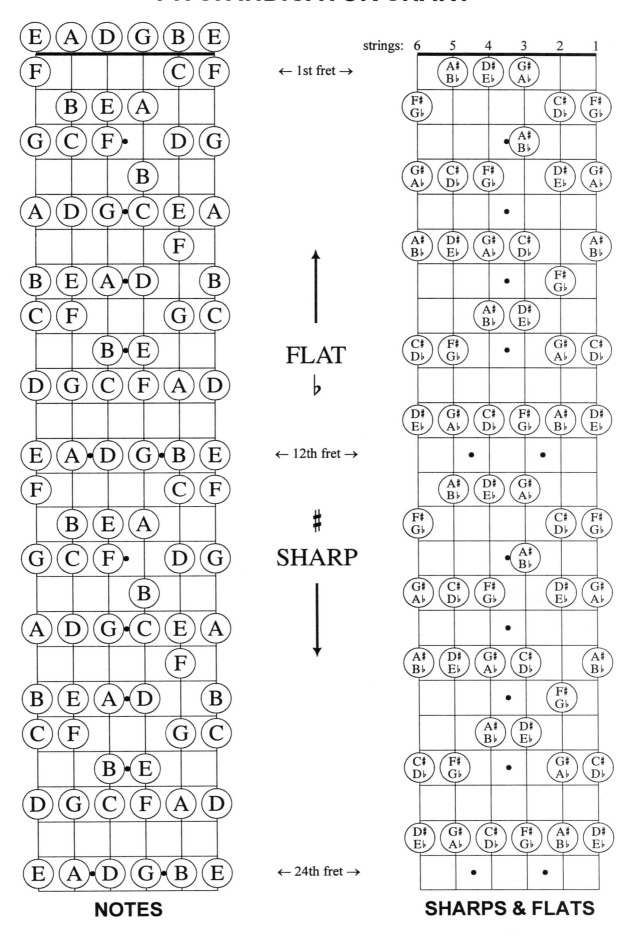

NOTES

SHARPS & FLATS

157

NOTATED FRETBOARD CHART

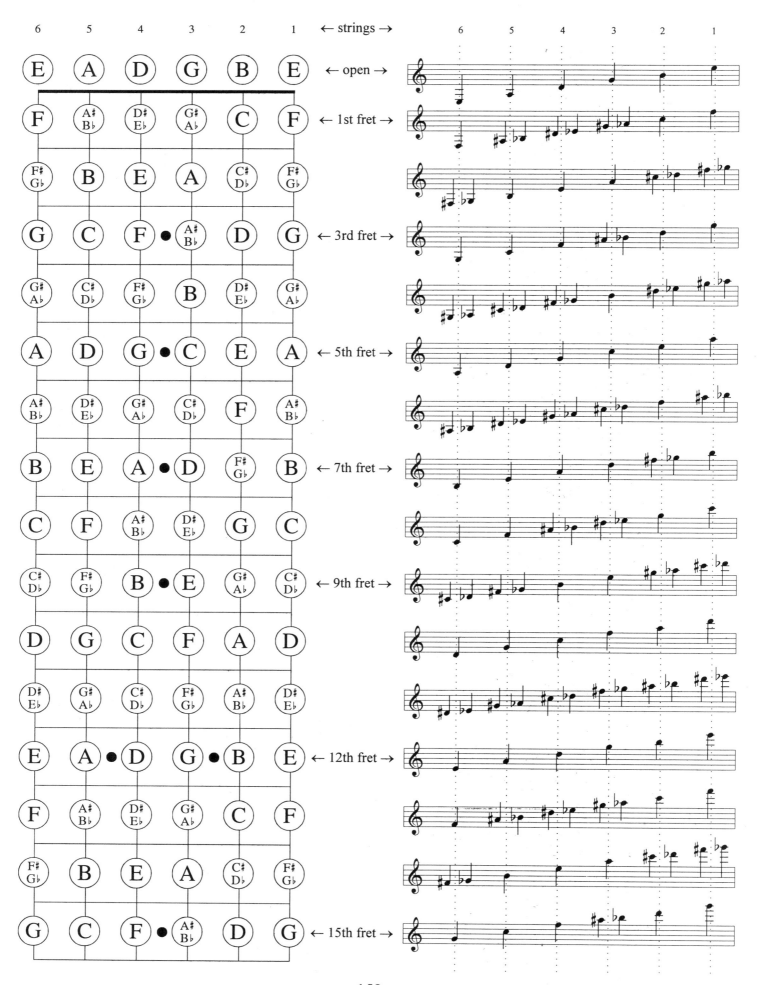

158

KEY SIGNATURES

The circle of fifths is also used for key signatures. Key signatures are located at the beginning of a score or song just after the clefs. Sometimes they are also in the middle of the composition when the song changes keys.

Key signatures tell what key you are in at a glance. This is especially important when using fake books where only the melody is written. Sonically there are only 12 keys; however, in notation there are 15 different key signatures as demonstrated in fig. 81 and fig. 82. This is because of the notes known as "the enharmonics", you know the notes such as C♯ & D♭ which sound the same but are written differently. These are the standard key signatures.

Compare the ♭II , ♭V , and VII positions of fig. 81 and fig. 82. Remember, C♯ & D♭ sound the same, in fact, they are the same. Yet when written they are very different as is the case with F♯ and G♭ and also with B and C♭.

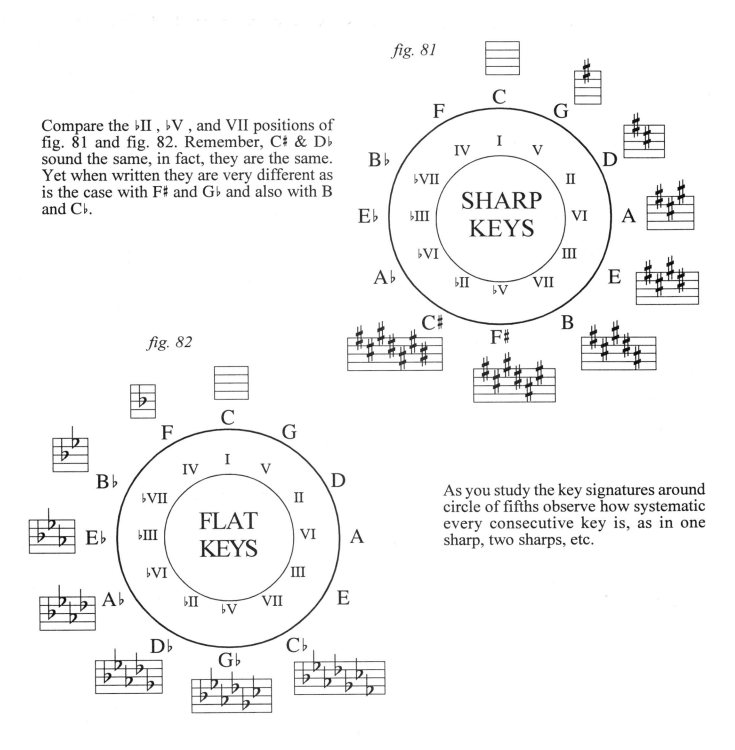

fig. 81

fig. 82

As you study the key signatures around circle of fifths observe how systematic every consecutive key is, as in one sharp, two sharps, etc.

159

What exactly are the key signatures telling us? Let's start with the formula for the Major scale on the "C". At a glance we can see that the notes, (C,D,E,F,G,A,B), are played as is and are unaltered by sharps or flats. Therefore the key of "C" has no sharps or flats. When we take the formula for the Major scale and start it on the "G" pitch, note, or tone, we have to sharp the "F" in order to retain the intervallic spacing of the Major scale (fig.83).

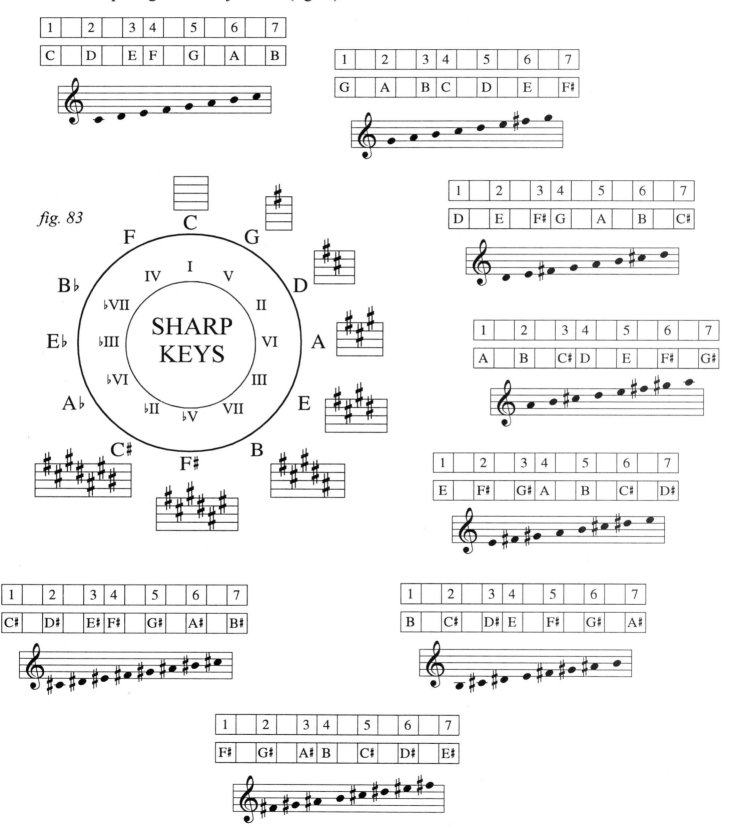

fig. 83

The same holds true for the flat keys as demonstrated below (fig. 84).

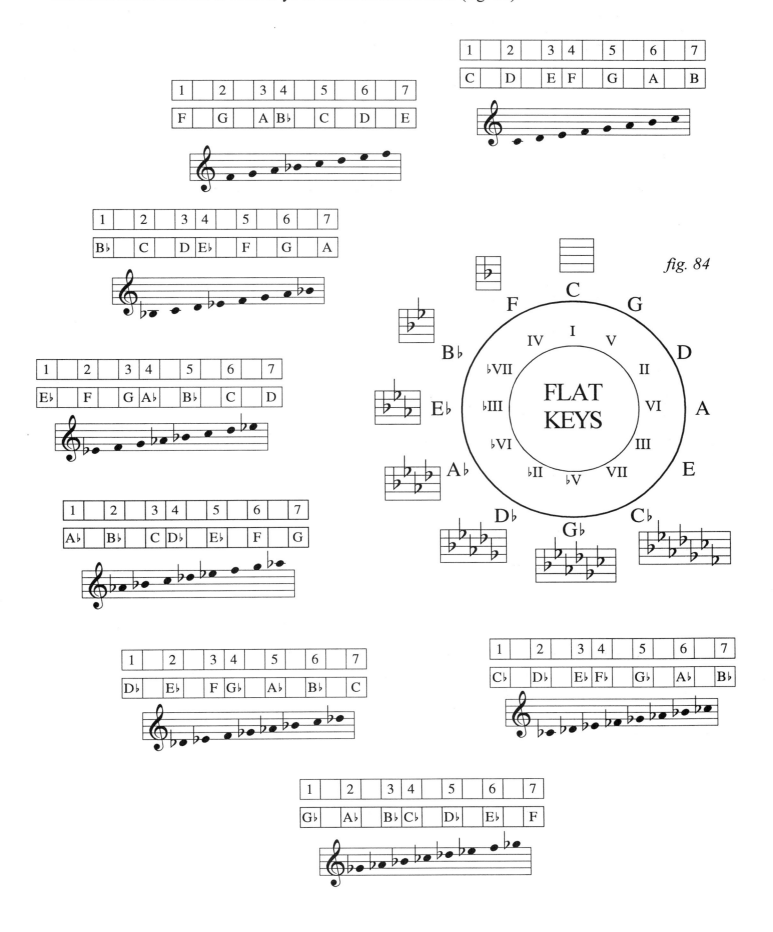

fig. 84

I once asked a guitar teacher if there was a key of G# or D# etc., and was told that there were no such keys. This was not a true statement as the diagram below demonstrates (fig. 85).

A more accurate answer would have been that we don't use or write in these keys because they are impractical and redundant. However, theoretically, these keys do exist. In fact you can get crazy keys such as C×××××× and beyond. Something that's fun to do when you are extremely curious or absolutely bored.

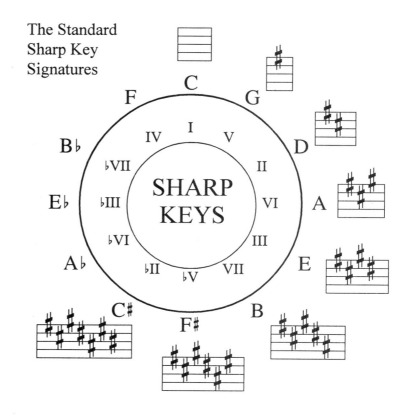

The Standard Sharp Key Signatures

fig. 85

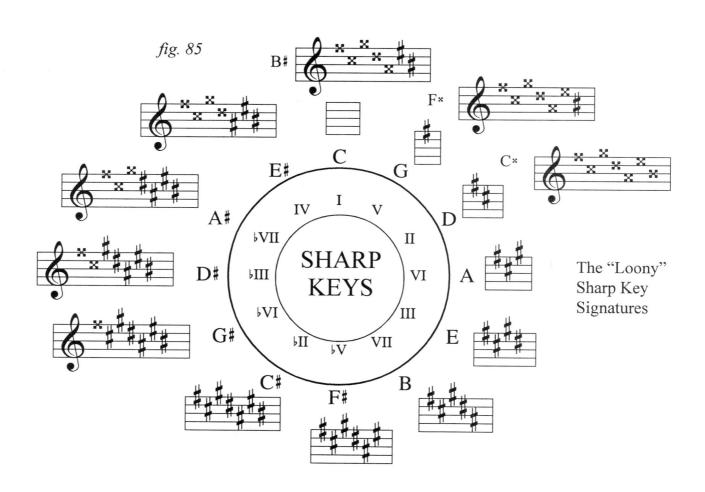

The "Loony" Sharp Key Signatures

The same holds true for the flat keys for those of you who are completeness freaks such as me (fig. 86).

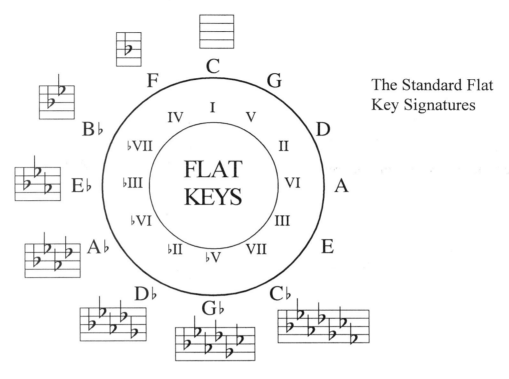

The Standard Flat
Key Signatures

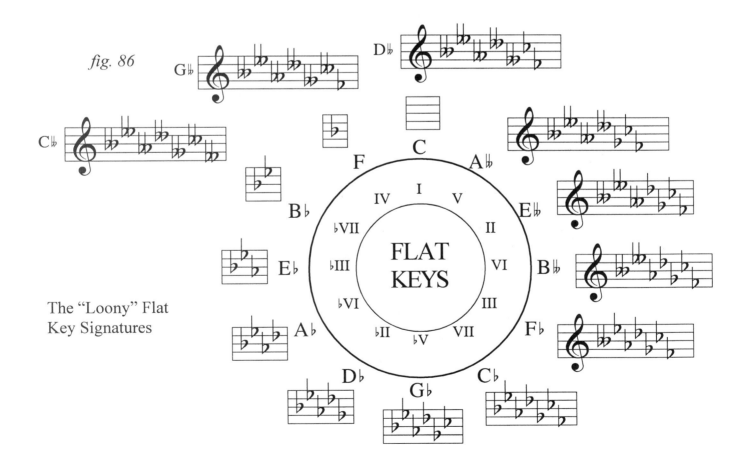

fig. 86

The "Loony" Flat
Key Signatures

CIRCLE OF FIFTHS IN ALL 15 KEYS

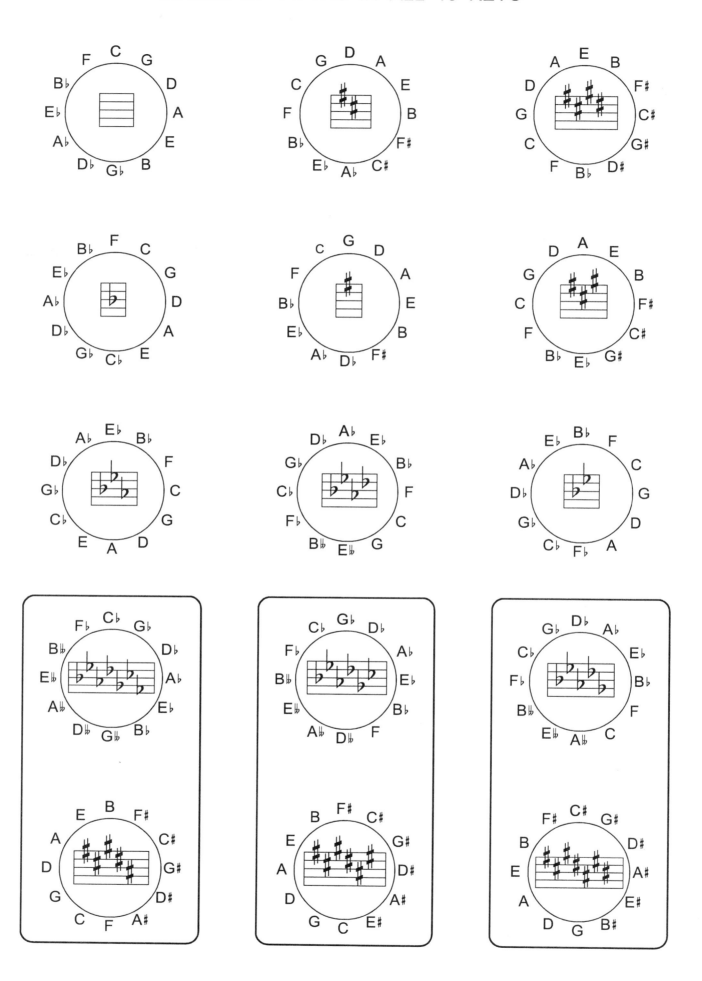

THE PATTERNS OF THE MAJOR SCALE NOTATED IN ALL KEYS

F MAJOR

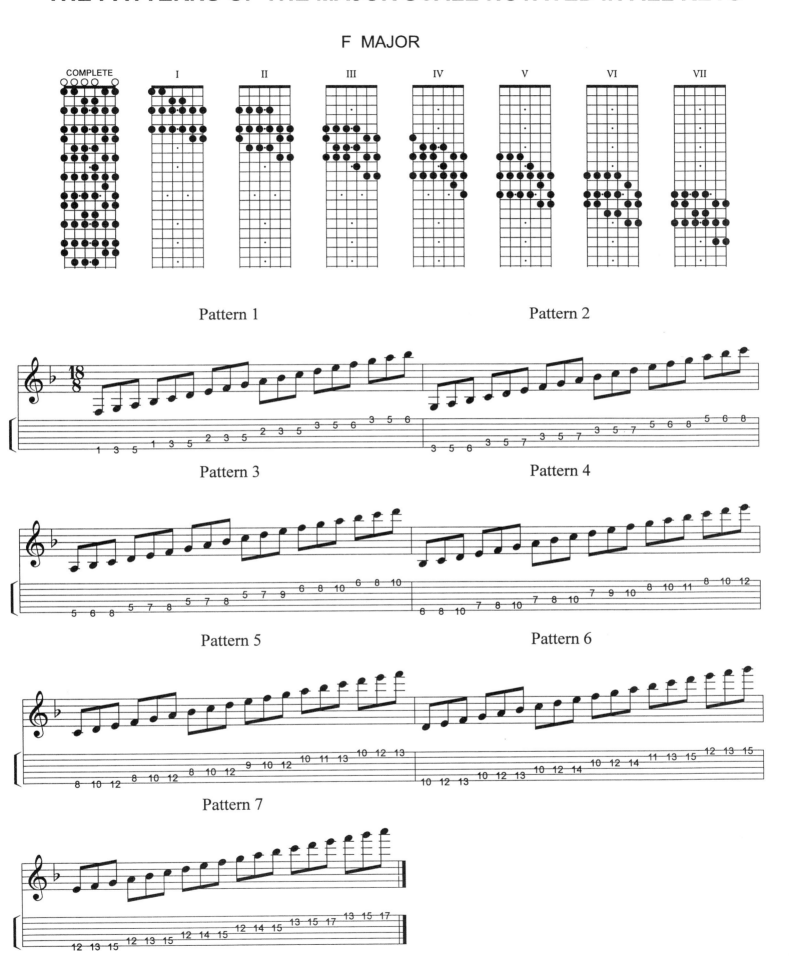

F# MAJOR

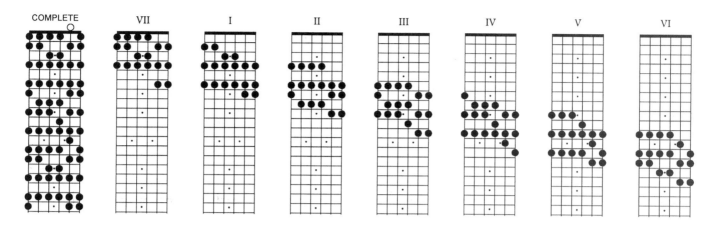

Pattern 7   Pattern 1

Pattern 2   Pattern 3

Pattern 4   Pattern 5

Pattern 6

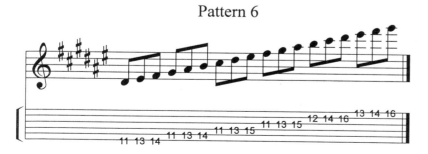

G♭ MAJOR

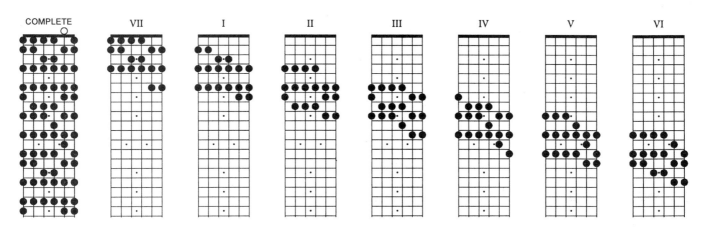

Pattern 7   Pattern 1

Pattern 2   Pattern 3

Pattern 4   Pattern 5

Pattern 6

G♭ Major is the same as F♯ Major. It is included here for the sake of studying the notation.

G MAJOR

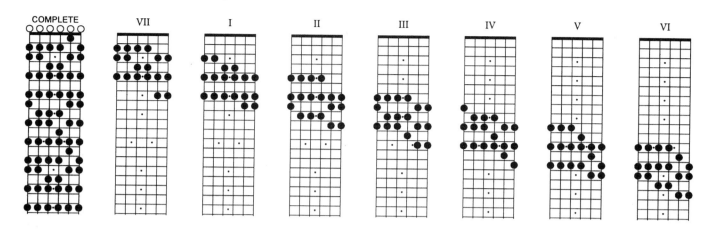

Pattern 7 · Pattern 1

Pattern 2 · Pattern 3

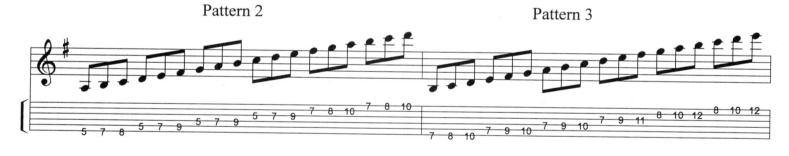

Pattern 4 · Pattern 5

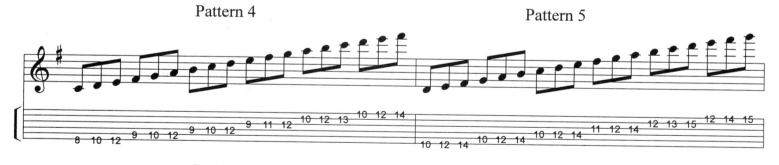

Pattern 6

A♭ MAJOR

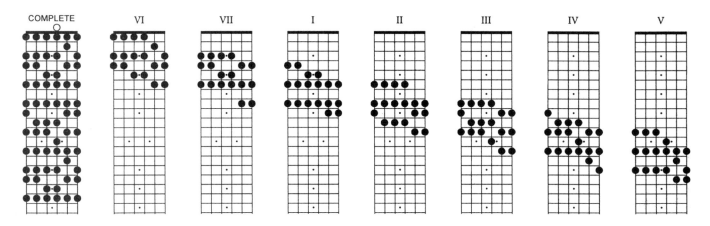

Pattern 6   Pattern 7

Pattern 1   Pattern 2

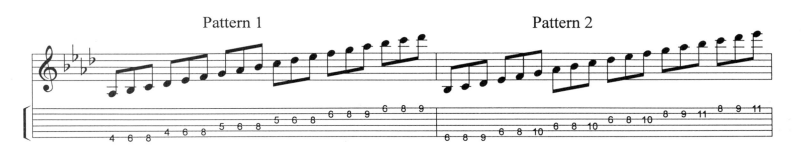

Pattern 3   Pattern 4

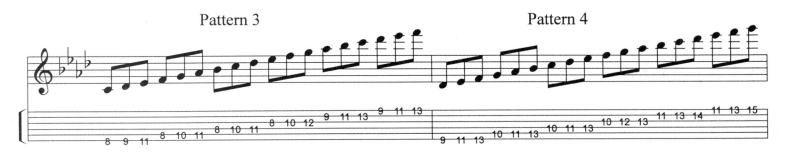

Pattern 5

A MAJOR

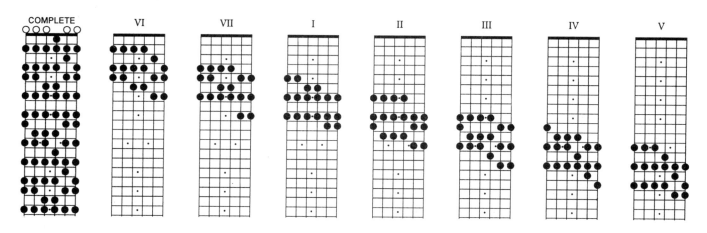

Pattern 6   Pattern 7

Pattern 1   Pattern 2

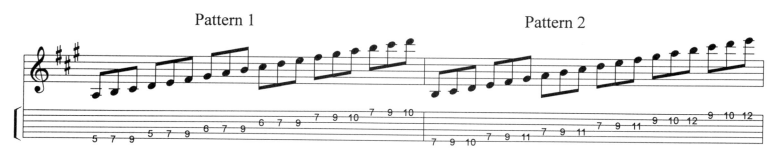

Pattern 3   Pattern 4

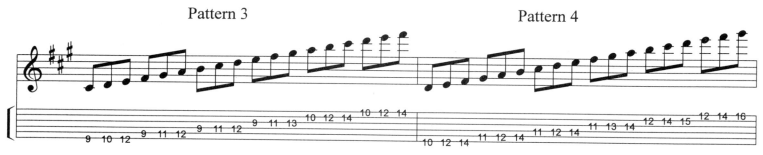

Pattern 5

B♭ MAJOR

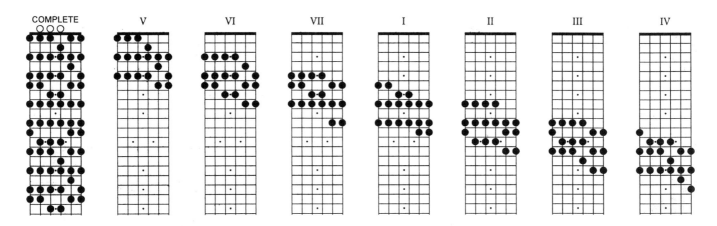

Pattern 5   Pattern 6

Pattern 7   Pattern 1

Pattern 2   Pattern 3

Pattern 4

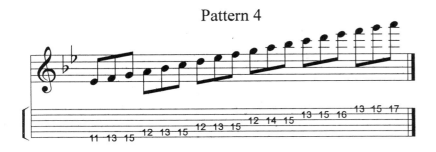

B MAJOR

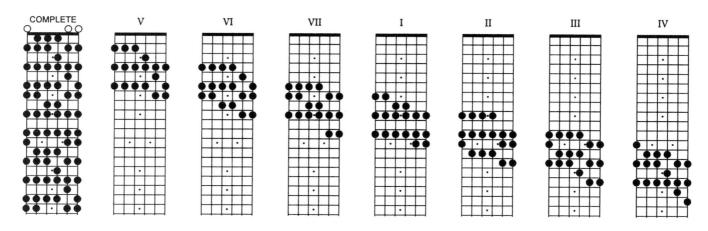

Pattern 5   Pattern 6

Pattern 7   Pattern 1

Pattern 2   Pattern 3

Pattern 4

C♭ MAJOR

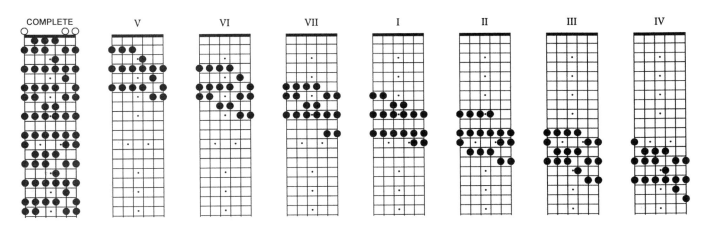

Pattern 5

Pattern 6

Pattern 7

Pattern 1

Pattern 2

Pattern 3

Pattern 4

C♭ Major is the same as B Major. It is included here for the sake of studying the notation.

C MAJOR

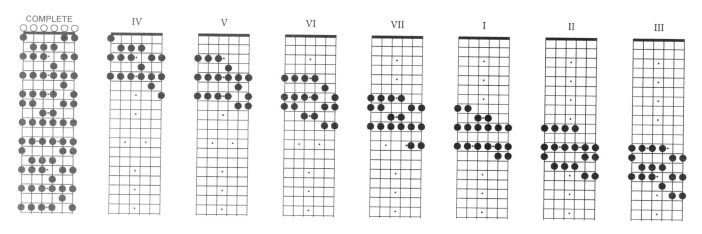

Pattern 4

Pattern 5

Pattern 6

Pattern 7

Pattern 1

Pattern 2

Pattern 3

C# MAJOR

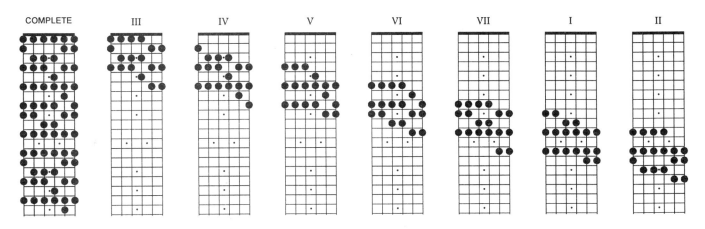

Pattern 3

Pattern 4

Pattern 5

Pattern 6

Pattern 7

Pattern 1

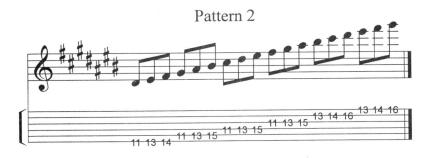

Pattern 2

Db MAJOR

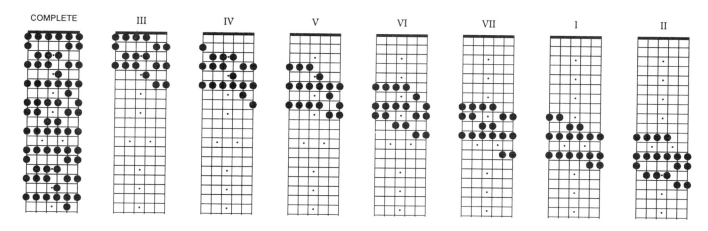

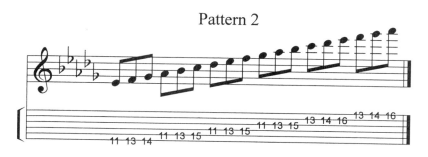

Db Major is the same as C# Major. It is included here for the sake of studying the notation.

D MAJOR

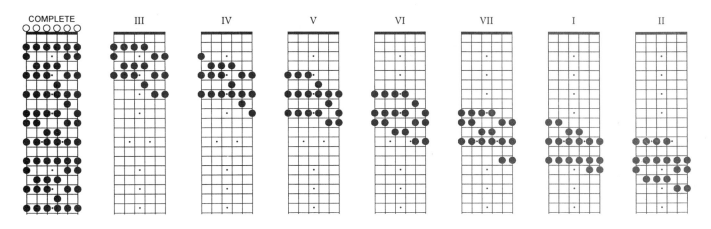

Pattern 3   Pattern 4

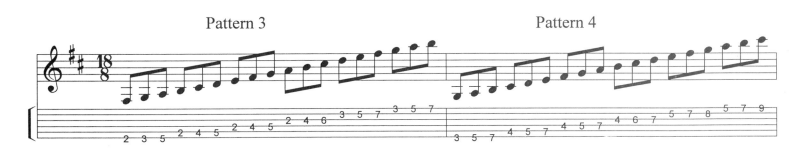

Pattern 5   Pattern 6

Pattern 7   Pattern 1

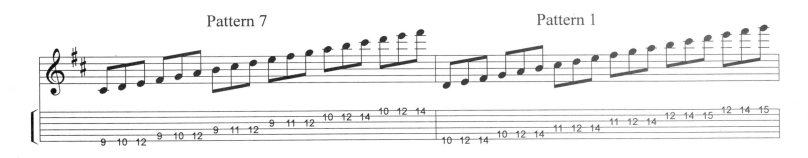

Pattern 2

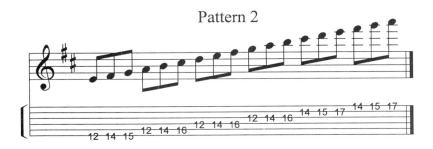

Eb MAJOR

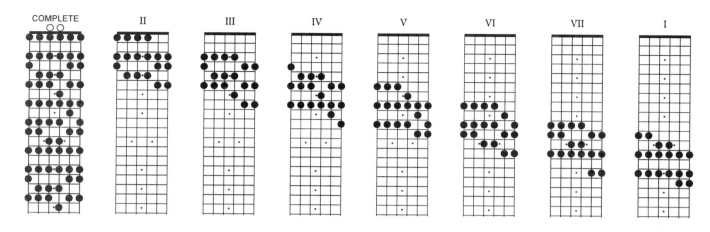

Pattern 2   Pattern 3

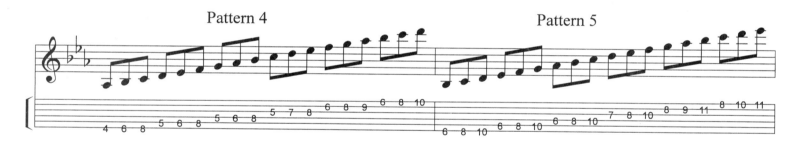

Pattern 4   Pattern 5

Pattern 6   Pattern 7

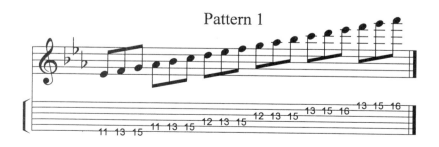

Pattern 1

E MAJOR

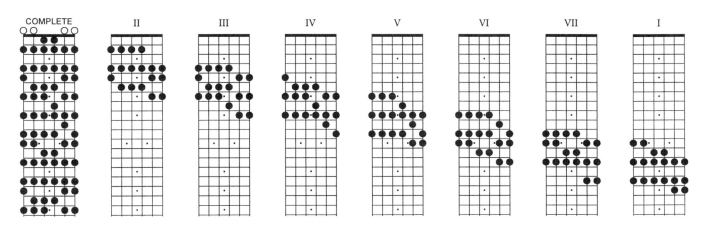

Pattern 2   Pattern 3

Pattern 4   Pattern 5

Pattern 6   Pattern 7

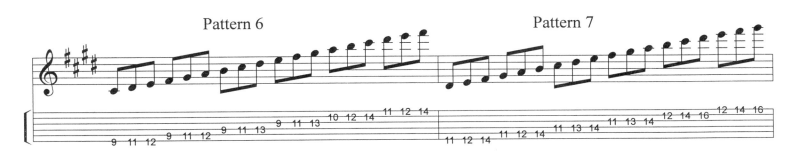

Pattern 1

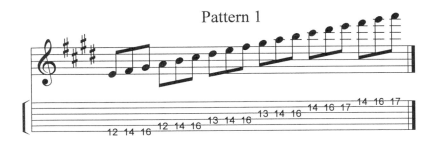

NUMERIC ANALYSIS OF CHORDS

	1	2	♭3	3	4	♭5	5	♯5/♭6	6	♭7	7	8	9
M	1			3			5						
–	1		♭3				5						
sus2	1	2					5						
sus	1				4		5						
♭5	1			3		♭5							
°	1		♭3			♭5							
5⁄8	1						5					8	
+	1			3				♯5					
♭6	1			3			5	♭6					
–♭6	1		♭3				5	♭6					
6	1			3			5		6				
–6	1		♭3				5		6				
°7	1		♭3			♭5			♮7				
Q(3)	1				4					♭7			
7	1			3			5			♭7			
–7	1		♭3				5			♭7			
7sus2	1	2					5			♭7			
7sus	1				4		5			♭7			
7♭5	1			3		♭5				♭7			
ø	1		♭3			♭5				♭7			
7⁺	1			3				♯5		♭7			
△	1			3			5				7		
–△	1		♭3				5				7		
△sus2	1	2					5				7		
△sus	1				4		5				7		
△♭5	1			3		♭5					7		
△°	1		♭3			♭5					7		
△⁺	1			3				♯5			7		
–△⁺	1		♭3					♯5			7		
7⁄6	1			3			5		6	♭7			
9⁄6	1			3			5		6				9
–9⁄6	1		♭3				5		6				9

NUMERIC ANALYSIS OF CHORDS continued

	1	2	3	4	5	6	7	1	2	3	4	5	6	7
9	1		3		5		b7		9					
-9	1		b3		5		b7		9					
b9	1		3		5		b7		b9					
-b9	1		b3		5		b7		b9					
#9	1		3		5		b7		#9					
△9	1		3		5		7		9					
-△9	1		b3		5		7		9					
△b9	1		3		5		7		b9					
-△b9	1		b3		5		7		b9					
△#9	1		3		5		7		#9					
b5 #9	1		3	b5			b7		#9					
b5 b9	1		3	b5			b7		b9					
#5 b9	1		3			#5	b7		b9					
#5 #9	1		3			#5	b7		#9					
11	1		3		5		b7		9		11			
-11	1		b3		5		b7		9		11			
#11	1		3		5		b7		9		#11			
-#11	1		b3		5		b7		9		#11			
△11	1		3		5		7		9		11			
-△11	1		b3		5		7		9		11			
△#11	1		3		5		7		9		#11			
-△#11	1		b3		5		7		9		#11			
13	1		3		5		b7		9		11		13	
-13	1		b3		5		b7		9		11		13	
13#11	1		3		5		b7		9		#11		13	
-13#11	1		b3		5		b7		9		#11		13	
△13	1		3		5		7		9		11		13	
-△13	1		b3		5		7		9		11		13	
△13#11	1		3		5		7		9		#11		13	
-△13#11	1		b3		5		7		9		#11		13	

ALT* { (b5 #9, b5 b9, #5 b9, #5 #9)

* the ALT chords can be used interchangeably

NUMERIC ANALYSIS OF SCALES

Scale	1	♭2	2	♭3	3	4	♭5	5	♭6	6	♭7	7
MAJOR (IONIAN)	1		2		3	4		5		6		7
DORIAN	1		2	♭3		4		5		6	♭7	
PHRYGIAN	1	♭2		♭3		4		5	♭6		♭7	
LYDIAN	1		2		3		♯4	5		6		7
MIXOLYDIAN	1		2		3	4		5		6	♭7	
AEOLIAN	1		2	♭3		4		5	♭6		♭7	
LOCRIAN	1	♭2		♭3		4	♭5		♭6		♭7	
MELODIC	1		2	♭3		4		5		6		7
DORIAN ♭2	1	♭2		♭3		4		5		6	♭7	
LYDIAN AUGMENTED	1		2		3		♯4		♯5	6		7
LYDIAN DOMINANT	1		2		3		♯4	5		6	♭7	
HINDU	1		2		3	4		5	♭6		♭7	
LOCRIAN ♮2	1		2	♭3		4	♭5		♭6		♭7	
SUPER LOCRIAN	1	♭2		♭3	♭4		♭5		♭6		♭7	
HARMONIC MINOR	1		2	♭3		4		5	♭6			7
LOCRIAN ♮6	1	♭2		♭3		4	♭5			6	♭7	
IONIAN ♯5	1		2		3	4			♯5	6		7
DORIAN ♯4	1		2	♭3			♯4	5		6	♭7	
PHRYGIAN ♮3	1	♭2			3	4		5	♭6		♭7	
LYDIAN ♯2	1			♯2	3		♯4	5		6		7
ALT ♮7	1	♭2		♭3	♭4		♭5		♭6	♭♭7		
HARMONIC MAJOR	1		2		3	4		5	♭6			7
DORIAN ♭5	1		2	♭3		4	♭5			6	♭7	
PHRYGIAN ♭4	1	♭2		♭3	♭4			5	♭6		♭7	
LYDIAN ♭3	1		2	♭3			♯4	5		6		7
DOMINANT ♭2	1	♭2			3	4		5		6	♭7	
LYDIAN AUG ♯2	1			♯2	3		♯4		♯5	6		7
LOCRIAN ♮7	1	♭2		♭3		4	♭5		♭6	♭♭7		
HUNGARIAN MINOR	1		2	♭3			♯4	5	♭6			7
ORIENTAL	1	♭2			3	4	♭5			6	♭7	
IONIAN AUG ♯2	1			♯2	3	4			♯5	6		7
LOCRIAN ♮3 ♮7	1	♭2	♭♭3			4	♭5		♭6	♭♭7		
DOUBLE HARMONIC	1	♭2			3	4		5	♭6			7
LYDIAN ♯6 ♯2	1			♯2	3		♯4	5			♯6	7
ALT ♮5 ♮7	1	♭2		♭3	♭4			5	♭6	♭♭7		
HUNGARIAN MAJOR	1			♯2	3		♯4	5		6	♭7	
ALT ♮6 ♮7	1	♭2		♭3	♭4		♭5	♭♭6		♭♭7		
LOCRIAN ♮2 ♮7	1		2	♭3		4	♭5		♭6			7
ALT ♮6	1	♭2		♭3	♭4		♭5			6	♭7	
MELODIC AUG	1		2	♭3		4			♯5	6		7
DORIAN ♭2 ♯4	1	♭2		♭3			♯4	5		6	♭7	
LYDIAN AUG ♯3	1		2			♯3	♯4		♯5	6		7

Scale	1	♭2	2	♭3	3	4	♭5	5	♭6	6	♭7	7
NEAPOLITAN MINOR	1	♭2		♭3		4		5	♭6			7
LYDIAN ♮6	1		2		3		♯4	5			♯6	7
DOMINANT AUG	1		2		3	4			♯5	6	♭7	
HUNGAR GYPSY	1		2	♭3			♯4	5	♭6		♭7	
LOCRIAN ♮3	1	♭2			3	4	♭5		♭6		♭7	
IONIAN ♯2	1			♯2	3	4		5		6		7
ALT ♮3 ♮7	1	♭2	♭♭3		♭4		♭5		♭6	♭♭7		
NEAPOLITAN MAJOR	1	♭2		♭3		4		5		6		7
LYDIAN AUG ♯6	1		2		3		♯4		♯5		♯6	7
LYDIAN DOM AUG	1		2		3		♯4		♯5	6	♭7	
LYDIAN MINOR	1		2		3		♯4	5	♭6		♭7	
MAJOR LOCRIAN	1		2		3	4	♭5		♭6		♭7	
ALT ♮2	1		2	♭3	♭4		♭5		♭6		♭7	
ALT ♮3	1	♭2	♭♭3		♭4		♭5		♭6		♭7	
ENIGMATIC MINOR	1	♭2		♭3			♯4	5			♯6	7
MODE 2	1		2			♯3	♯4			×5	♯6	7
MODE 3	1			♯2	3			×4	♯5	6	♭7	
MODE 4	1	♭2			3	4	♭5	♭♭6		♭♭7		
MODE 5	1			♯2	3	4	♭5		♭6			7
MODE 6	1	♭2	♭♭3	♭3		4			♭6	♭♭7		
MODE 7	1	♭2	♭♭3		♭4			5	♭6			7
ENIGMATIC	1	♭2			3		♯4		♯5		♯6	7
MODE 2	1			♯2		♯3		×4		×5	♯6	7
MODE 3	1		2		3		♯4	5	♭6	♭♭7		
MODE 4	1		2		3	4	♭5	♭♭6			♭7	
MODE 5	1		2	♭3	♭4	4			♭6		♭7	
MODE 6	1	♭2	♭♭3	♭3			♭5		♭6		♭7	
MODE 7	1	♭2	♭♭3			4		5		6		7
COMPOSITE II	1	♭2			3		♯4	5	♭6			7
MODE 2	1			♯2		♯3	♯4	5			♯6	7
MODE 3	1		2	♭3	♭4			5	♭6	♭♭7		
MODE 4	1	♭2	♭♭3			4	♭5	♭♭6			♭7	
MODE 5	1	♭2			3	4	♭5			6		7
MODE 6	1			♯2	3	4			♯5		♯6	7
MODE 7	1	♭2	♭♭3			4		5	♭6	♭♭7		
IONIAN ♭5	1		2		3	4	♭5			6		7
DORIAN ♮4	1		2	♭3	♭4			5		6	♭7	
PHRYGIAN ♮3	1	♭2	♭♭3			4		5	♭6		♭7	
LYDIAN ♭2	1	♭2			3		♯4	5		6		7
SUPER LYDIAN AUG	1			♯2		♯3	♯4		♯5		♯6	7
AEOLIAN ♮7	1		2	♭3		4		5	♭6	♭♭7		
LOCRIAN ♮6	1	♭2		♭3		4	♭5	♭♭6			♭7	

182

Scale	1	2	3	4	5	6	7	8	9	10	11	12
LOCRIAN ♮7	1	b2		b3		4	b5		b6			7
IONIAN #6	1		2		3	4		5			#6	7
DORIAN AUG	1		2	b3		4			#5	6	b7	
PHRYGIAN #4	1	b2		b3			#4	5	b6		b7	
LYDIAN #3	1		2		#3		#4	5		6		7
DOMINANT #2	1			#2	3	4		5		6	b7	
ALT ALT	1	b2		b3	b4		b5		b6		b7	
PERSIAN	1	b2			3	4	b5		b6			7
MODE 2	1			#2	3	4		5			#6	7
MODE 3	1	b2		b3	b4			5	b6		b7	
MODE 4	1	b2		b3			#4	5	b6			7
MODE 5	1		2		#3		#4	5			#6	7
MODE 6	1			#2	3	4			#5	6	b7	
MODE 7	1	b2		b3		4	b5		b6		b7	
MINOR PENT	1			b3		4		5			b7	
MAJOR PENT	1		2		3			5		6		
MODE 3	1		2			4		5			b7	
MODE 4	1			b3		4			#5		b7	
MODE 5	1		2			4		5		6		
KUMOI	1		2	b3				5		6		
MODE 2	1	b2				4		5			b7	
MODE 3	1				3		b5			6		7
MODE 4	1		2			4		5	b6			
MODE 5	1			b3		4	b5				b7	
HIROJOSHI	1		2	b3				5	b6			
MODE 2	1	b2				4	b5				b7	
MODE 3	1				3	4				6		7
MODE 4	1	b2				4		5	b6			
MODE 5	1				3		#4	5				7
WHOLE TONE	1		2		3		#4		#5		#6	
AUGMENTED	1			#2	3			5	b6			7
MODE 2	1	b2			3	4			#5	6		
PELOG	1	b2		b3	b4			5	b6			
MODE 2	1		2	b3			#4	5				7
MODE 3	1	b2			3	4				6	b7	
MODE 4	1			#2	3				#5	6		7
MODE 5	1	b2				4	b5		b6		b7	
MODE 6	1				3	4		5	b6			7
DOMINANT SUS	1		2			4		5		6	b7	
MODE 2	1			b3		4		5	b6		b7	
MODE 3	1		2		3	4		5		6		
MODE 4	1		2	b3		4		5			b7	
MODE 5	1	b2		b3		4			b6		b7	

Scale	1	2	3	4	5	6	7	8	9	10	11	12
MODE 6	1		2		3			5		6		7
DIMIN: WHOLE-HALF	1		2	b3		4	b5		b6	6		7
HALF-WHOLE DIMIN	1	b2		b3	3		#4	5		6	b7	
8-TONE SPANISH	1	b2		b3	3	4	b5		b6		b7	
MODE 2	1		2	b3	3	4		5		6		7
MODE 3	1	b2	2	b3		4		5		6	b7	
MODE 4	1	b2	2		3		#4		#5	6		7
MODE 5	1	b2		b3		4		5	b6		b7	7
MODE 6	1		2		3		#4	5		6	b7	7
MODE 7	1		2		3	4		5	b6	6	b7	
MODE 8	1		2	b3		4	b5	5	b6		b7	
BEBOP LOCRIAN ♮2	1		2	b3		4	b5		b6		b7	7
MODE 2	1	b2		b3	3		#4		#5	6	b7	
MODE 3	1		2	b3		4		5	b6	6		7
MODE 4	1	b2		b3		4	b5	5		6	b7	
MODE 5	1		2		3	4	b5		b6	6		7
MODE 6	1		2	b3	3		#4	5		6	b7	
MODE 7	1	b2	2		3	4		5	b6		b7	
MODE 8	1	b2		b3	3		#4	5		6		7
BEBOP DOMINANT	1		2		3	4		5		6	b7	7
BEBOP MINOR	1		2	b3		4		5	b6	6	b7	
BEBOP LOC add 5	1	b2		b3		4	b5	5	b6		b7	
MODE 4	1		2		3	4	b5	5		6		7
MODE 5	1		2	b3	3	4		5		6	b7	
MODE 6	1	b2	2	b3		4		5	b6		b7	
MODE 7	1	b2	2		3		#4	5		6		7
MODE 8	1	b2		b3		4	b5		b6		b7	7
BEBOP DORIAN	1		2	b3		4		5		6	b7	7
MODE 2	1	b2		b3		4		5	b6	6	b7	
MODE 3	1		2		3		#4	5	b6	6		7
MODE 4	1		2		3	4	b5	5		6	b7	
MODE 5	1		2	b3	3	4		5	b6		b7	
MODE 6	1	b2	2	b3		4	b5		b6		b7	
MODE 7	1	b2	2		3	4		5		6		7
MODE 8	1	b2		b3	3		#4		#5		#6	7
BEBOP MAJOR	1		2		3	4		5	b6	6		7
MODE 2	1		2	b3		4	b5	5		6	b7	
MODE 3	1	b2		b3	3	4		5	b6		b7	
MODE 4	1		2	b3	3		#4	5		6		7
MODE 5	1	b2	2		3	4		5		6	b7	
MODE 6	1	b2		b3	3		#4		#5	6		7
MODE 7	1		2	b3		4		5	b6		b7	7
MODE 8	1	b2		b3		4	b5		b6	6	b7	

M

MAJOR
LYDIAN = MAJOR MODE 4
MIXOLYDIAN = MAJOR MODE 5
LYDIAN DOMINANT = MELODIC MODE 4
HINDU = MELODIC MODE 5
PHRYGIAN ♮3 = HARMONIC MINOR MODE 5
LYDIAN ♯2 = HARMONIC MINOR MODE 6
HARMONIC MAJOR
PHRYGIAN ♮4 = HARMONIC MAJOR MODE 3
DOMINANT ♭2 = HARMONIC MAJOR MODE 5
DOUBLE HARMONIC = HUNGARIAN MINOR MODE 5
LYDIAN ♯6 ♯2 = HUNGARIAN MINOR MODE 6
ALT ♯5 ♮7 = HUNGARIAN MINOR MODE 7
HUNGARIAN MAJOR
ALT ♯6 ♮7 = HUNGARIAN MAJOR MODE 2
LYDIAN ♯6 = NEAPOLITAN MINOR MODE 2
IONIAN ♯2 = NEAPOLITAN MINOR MODE 6
LYDIAN MINOR = NEAPOLITAN MAJOR MODE 4
ENIGMATIC MINOR MODE 3
ENIGMATIC MINOR MODE 4
ENIGMATIC MINOR MODE 7
ENIGMATIC MODE 3
ENIGMATIC MODE 4
COMPOSITE II
COMPOSITE II MODE 3
DORIAN ♮4 = IONIAN ♭5 MODE 2
LYDIAN ♭2 = IONIAN ♭5 MODE 4
IONIAN ♯6 = LOCRIAN ♮7 MODE 2
DOMINANT ♯2 = LOCRIAN ♮7 MODE 6
PERSIAN MODE 2
PERSIAN MODE 3
MAJOR PENTATONIC = MINOR PENTATONIC MODE 2
AUGMENTED
PELOG MODE 6
DOMINANT SUS MODE 3
DOMINANT SUS MODE 6
HALF-WHOLE DIMINISHED = DIMINISHED MODE 2
8 TONE SPANISH MODE 2
8 TONE SPANISH MODE 6
8 TONE SPANISH MODE 7
BEBOP LOCRIAN MODE 6
BEBOP LOCRIAN MODE 7
BEBOP LOCRIAN MODE 8
BEBOP DOMINANT
BEBOP DOMINANT MODE 4
BEBOP DORIAN MODE 3 / MODE 4 / MODE 5
BEBOP DORIAN7
BEBOP MAJOR
BEBOP MAJOR MODE 3 / MODE 4 / MODE 5

- (MINOR)

DORIAN = MAJOR MODE 2
PHRYGIAN = MAJOR MODE 3
AEOLIAN = MAJOR MODE 6
MELODIC
DORIAN ♭2 = MELODIC MODE 2
HARMONIC MINOR
DORIAN ♮4 = HARMONIC MINOR MODE 4
LYDIAN ♯2 = HARMONIC MINOR MODE 6
PHRYGIAN ♮4 = HARMONIC MAJOR MODE 3
LYDIAN ♭3 = HARMONIC MAJOR MODE 4
HUNGARIAN MINOR
LYDIAN ♯6 ♯2 = HUNGARIAN MINOR MODE 6
ALT ♯5 ♮7 = HUNGARIAN MINOR MODE 7
HUNGARIAN MAJOR
ALT ♯6 ♮7 = HUNGARIAN MAJOR MODE 2
DORIAN ♭2 ♮4 = HUNGARIAN MAJOR MODE 6
NEAPOLITAN MINOR
HUNGARIAN GYPSY = NEAPOLITAN MINOR MODE 4
IONIAN ♯2 = NEAPOLITAN MINOR MODE 6
NEAPOLITAN MAJOR
ENIGMATIC MINOR MODE 3
ENIGMATIC MODE 2
COMPOSITE II MODE 2
COMPOSITE II MODE 3
DORIAN ♮4 = IONIAN ♭5 MODE 2
AEOLIAN ♮7 = IONIAN ♭5 MODE 6
LOCRIAN ♮6 = IONIAN ♭5 MODE 7
PHRYGIAN ♮4 = LOCRIAN ♮7 MODE 4
DOMINANT ♯2 = LOCRIAN ♮7 MODE 6
PERSIAN MODE 2
PERSIAN MODE 4
MINOR PENTATONIC
KUMOI
AUGMENTED
HALF-WHOLE DIMINISHED
8 TONE SPANISH MODE 2 / MODE 3 / MODE 5
8 TONE SPANISH MODE 8
BEBOP LOCRIAN ♮2 MODE 3
BEBOP LOCRIAN ♮2 MODE 4 / MODE 6
BEBOP LOCRIAN ♮2 MODE 8
BEBOP MINOR = BEBOP DOMINANT MODE 2
BEBOP LOCRIAN add 5 = BEBOP DOMINANT MODE 3
BEBOP DOMINANT MODE 5 / MODE 6
BEBOP DORIAN
BEBOP DORIAN MODE 2 / MODE 5
BEBOP MAJOR MODE 2
BEBOP MAJOR MODE 3 / MODE 4 / MODE 7

sus2

MAJOR
DORIAN = MAJOR MODE 2
LYDIAN = MAJOR MODE 4
MIXOLYDIAN = MAJOR MODE 5
AEOLIAN = MAJOR MODE 6
MELODIC
LYDIAN DOMINANT = MELODIC MODE 4
HINDU = MELODIC MODE 5
HARMONIC MINOR
DORIAN ♮4 = HARMONIC MINOR MODE 4
HARMONIC MAJOR
LYDIAN ♭3 = HARMONIC MAJOR MODE 4
HUNGARIAN MINOR
LYDIAN ♯6 = NEAPOLITAN MINOR MODE 2
HUNGARIAN GYPSY = NEAPOLITAN MINOR MODE 4
LYDIAN MINOR = NEAPOLITAN MAJOR MODE 4
ENIGMATIC MINOR MODE 7
ENIGMATIC MODE 3
ENIGMATIC MODE 4
ENIGMATIC MODE 7
COMPOSITE II MODE 3
COMPOSITE II MODE 4
COMPOSITE II MODE 7
DORIAN ♮4 = IONIAN ♭5 MODE 2
PHRYGIAN ♮3 = IONIAN ♭5 MODE 3
AEOLIAN ♮7 = IONIAN ♭5 MODE 6
IONIAN ♯6 = LOCRIAN ♮7 MODE 2
LYDIAN ♯3 = LOCRIAN ♮7 MODE 5
ALT ALT = LOCRIAN ♮7 MODE 7
PERSIAN MODE 2
PERSIAN MODE 5
PERSIAN MODE 7
MAJOR PENTATONIC = MINOR PENTATONIC MODE 2
MINOR PENTATONIC MODE 3 / MODE 5
KUMOI
KUMOI MODE 4
HIROJOSHI
PELOG MODE 2
DOMINANT SUS
DOMINANT SUS MODE 3 / MODE 4 / MODE 6
8 TONE SPANISH MODE 2 / MODE 3 / MODE 6 / MODE 7
8 TONE SPANISH MODE 8
BEBOP LOCRIAN ♮2 MODE 3
BEBOP LOCRIAN ♮2 MODE 6 / MODE 7
BEBOP DOMINANT
BEBOP MINOR = BEBOP DOMINANT MODE 2
BEBOP DOMINANT MODE 4 / MODE 5 / MODE 6
BEBOP DOMINANT MODE 7
BEBOP DORIAN
BEBOP DORIAN MODE 3 / MODE 4 / MODE 5 / MODE 7
BEBOP MAJOR
BEBOP MAJOR MODE 2 / MODE 4 / MODE 5 / MODE 7

SUS

MAJOR
DORIAN = MAJOR MODE 2
PHRYGIAN = MAJOR MODE 3
MIXOLYDIAN = MAJOR MODE 5
AEOLIAN = MAJOR MODE 6
MELODIC
DORIAN ♭5 = MELODIC MODE 2
HINDU = MELODIC MODE 5
HARMONIC MINOR
PHRYGIAN ♮3 = HARMONIC MINOR MODE 5
HARMONIC MAJOR
DOMINANT ♭2 = HARMONIC MAJOR MODE 5
DOUBLE HARMONIC = HUNGARIAN MINOR MODE 5
NEAPOLITAN MINOR
IONIAN ♯2 = NEAPOLITAN MINOR MODE 6
NEAPOLITAN MAJOR
ENIGMATIC MINOR MODE 2
ENIGMATIC MODE 4 / MODE 7
COMPOSITE II MODE 2 / MODE 4 / MODE 7
PHRYGIAN ♮3 = IONIAN ♭5 MODE 3
AEOLIAN ♮7 = IONIAN ♭5 MODE 6
LOCRIAN ♮6 = IONIAN ♭5 MODE 7
IONIAN ♯6 = LOCRIAN ♮7 MODE 2
LYDIAN ♯3 = LOCRIAN ♮7 MODE 5
DOMINANT ♯2 = LOCRIAN ♮7 MODE 6
PERSIAN MODE 2 / MODE 5 / MODE 7
MINOR PENTATONIC
MINOR PENTATONIC MINOR MODE 3 / MODE 5
KUMOI MODE 2 / MODE 4
HIROJOSHI MODE 4
PELOG MODE 6
DOMINANT SUS MODE 1 / MODE 2 / MODE 3 / MODE 4
8 TONE SPANISH MODE 2 / MODE 3 / MODE 5
8 TONE SPANISH MODE 7 / MODE 8
BEBOP LOCRIAN ♮2 MODE 3 / MODE 4 / MODE 7
BEBOP DOMINANT
BEBOP MINOR = BEBOP DOMINANT MODE 2
BEBOP LOCRIAN add 5 = BEBOP DOMINANT MODE 3
BEBOP DOMINANT MODE 4 / MODE 5 / MODE 6
BEBOP DORIAN
BEBOP DORIAN MODE 2 / MODE 4 / MODE 5 / MODE 7
BEBOP MAJOR
BEBOP MAJOR MODE 2 / MODE 3 / MODE 5 / MODE 7

♭5

LYDIAN = MAJOR MODE 4
LYDIAN AUGMENTED = MELODIC MODE 3
LYDIAN DOMINANT = MELODIC MODE 4
SUPER LOCRIAN = MELODIC MODE 7
ALT ♮7 = HARMONIC MINOR MODE 7
LYDIAN AUGMENTED ♯2 = HARMONIC MAJOR MODE 6
ORIENTAL = HUNGARIAN MINOR MODE 2
LYDIAN ♯6 ♯2 = HUNGARIAN MINOR MODE 6
HUNGARIAN MAJOR
ALT ♯6 ♮7 = HUNGARIAN MAJOR MODE 2
ALT ♯6 = HUNGARIAN MAJOR MODE 4
LYDIAN ♯6 = NEAPOLITAN MINOR MODE 2
LOCRIAN ♮3 = NEAPOLITAN MINOR MODE 7
ALT ♯3 ♮7 = NEAPOLITAN MINOR MODE 7
LYDIAN AUGMENTED ♯6 = NEAPOLITAN MAJOR MODE 2
LYDIAN DOMINANT AUG = NEAPOLITAN MAJOR MODE 3
LYDIAN MINOR = NEAPOLITAN MAJOR MODE 4
MAJOR LOCRIAN = NEAPOLITAN MAJOR MODE 5
ALT ♮2 = NEAPOLITAN MAJOR MODE 6
ALT ♮3 = NEAPOLITAN MAJOR MODE 7
ENIGMATIC MINOR MODE 4
ENIGMATIC MINOR MODE 5
ENIGMATIC
ENIGMATIC MODE 3 / MODE 4
COMPOSITE II
COMPOSITE II MODE 5
IONIAN ♭5
LYDIAN ♭2 = IONIAN ♭5 MODE 4
ALT ALT = LOCRIAN ♮7 MODE 7
PERSIAN
KUMOI MODE 3
HIROJOSHI MODE 5
WHOLE TONE
HALF-TONE DIMINISHED
8 TONE SPANISH
8 TONE SPANISH MODE 4
8 TONE SPANISH MODE 6
BEBOP LOCRIAN ♮2 MODE 2
BEBOP LOCRIAN ♮2 MODE 5
BEBOP LOCRIAN ♮2 MODE 6
BEBOP LOCRIAN ♮2 MODE 8
BEBOP DOMINANT MODE 4 / MODE 7
BEBOP DORIAN MODE 3 / MODE 4 / MODE 8
BEBOP MAJOR MODE 4 / MODE 6

° (DIMINISHED)

LOCRIAN = MAJOR MODE 7
LOCRIAN ♮2 = MELODIC MODE 6
SUPER LOCRIAN = MELODIC MODE 7
LOCRIAN ♮6 = HARMONIC MINOR MODE 2
DORIAN ♯4 = HARMONIC MINOR MODE 4
LYDIAN ♯2 = HARMONIC MINOR MODE 6
ALT ♮7 = HARMONIC MINOR MODE 7
DORIAN ♭5 = HARMONIC MAJOR MODE 2
LYDIAN ♭3 = HARMONIC MAJOR MODE 4
LYDIAN AUGMENTED ♯2 = HARMONIC MAJOR MODE 6
LOCRIAN ♮7 = HARMONIC MINOR MODE 7
HUNGARIAN MINOR
LYDIAN ♯6 ♯2 = HUNGARIAN MINOR MODE 2
HUNGARIAN MAJOR
ALT ♯6 ♮7 = HUNGARIAN MAJOR MODE 2
LOCRIAN ♮2 ♮7 = HUNGARIAN MAJOR MODE 3
ALT ♮6 = HUNGARIAN MAJOR MODE 4
DORIAN ♭2 ♯4 = HUNGARIAN MAJOR MODE 6
HUNGARIAN GYPSY = NEAPOLITAN MINOR MODE 4
ALT ♮2 = NEAPOLITAN MAJOR MODE 6
ENIGMATIC MINOR
ENIGMATIC MINOR MODE 5
ENIGMATIC MODE 6
COMPOSITE II MODE 2
SUPER LYDIAN AUGMENTED = IONIAN ♭5 MODE 5
LOCRIAN ♮6 = IONIAN ♭5 MODE 7
LOCRIAN ♮7
PHRYGIAN ♮4 = LOCRIAN ♮7 MODE 4
PERSIAN MODE 4
KUMOI MODE 5
WHOLE-HALF DIMINISHED
HALF-WHOLE DIMINISHED
8 TONE SPANISH
8 TONE SPANISH MODE 8
BEBOP LOCRIAN ♮2
BEBOP LOCRIAN ♮2 MODE 2
BEBOP LOCRIAN ♮2 MODE 4
BEBOP LOCRIAN ♮2 MODE 6
BEBOP LOCRIAN ♮2 MODE 8
BEBOP LOCRIAN add 5 = BEBOP DOMINANT MODE 3
BEBOP DOMINANT MODE 8
BEBOP DORIAN MODE 6
BEBOP DORIAN MODE 8
BEBOP MAJOR MODE 2
BEBOP MAJOR MODE 4
BEBOP MAJOR MODE 6
BEBOP MAJOR MODE 8

+ (AUGMENTED)

LYDIAN AUGMENTED = MELODIC MODE 3
HINDU = MELODIC MODE 5
SUPER LOCRIAN = MELODIC MODE 7
IONIAN ♮5 = HARMONIC MINOR MODE 3
PHRYGIAN ♮3 = HARMONIC MINOR MODE 5
ALT ♮7 = HARMONIC MINOR MODE 7
HARMONIC MAJOR
PHRYGIAN ♮4 = HARMONIC MAJOR MODE 3
LYDIAN AUGMENTED ♯2 = HARMONIC MAJOR MODE 6
IONIAN AUGMENTED ♯2 = HUNGARIAN MINOR MODE 3
DOUBLE HARMONIC = HUNGARIAN MINOR MODE 5
ALT ♯5 ♮7 = HUNGARIAN MINOR MODE 7
DOMINANT AUGMENTED = NEAPOLITAN MINOR MODE 3
LOCRIAN ♮3 = NEAPOLITAN MINOR MODE 5
ALT ♯3 ♮7 = NEAPOLITAN MINOR MODE 7
LYDIAN AUGMENTED ♯6 = NEAPOLITAN MAJOR MODE 2
LYDIAN DOMINANT AUG = NEAPOLITAN MAJOR MODE 3
LYDIAN MINOR = NEAPOLITAN MAJOR MODE 4
MAJOR LOCRIAN = NEAPOLITAN MAJOR MODE 5
ALT ♮2 = NEAPOLITAN MAJOR MODE 6
ALT ♮3 = NEAPOLITAN MAJOR MODE 7
ENIGMATIC MINOR MODE 3
ENIGMATIC MINOR MODE 5
ENIGMATIC MINOR MODE 7
ENIGMATIC
ENIGMATIC MODE 3
ENIGMATIC MODE 5
COMPOSITE II
COMPOSITE II MODE 3
COMPOSITE II MODE 6
PERSIAN
PERSIAN MODE 3
PERSIAN MODE 6
WHOLE TONE
AUGMENTED
AUGMENTED MODE 2
PELOG
PELOG MODE 4 / MODE 6
8 TONE SPANISH
8 TONE SPANISH MODE 4
8 TONE SPANISH MODE 7
BEBOP LOCRIAN ♮2 MODE 2 / MODE 5 / MODE 7
BEBOP DORIAN MODE 3 / MODE 5 / MODE 8
BEBOP MAJOR
BEBOP MAJOR MODE 3 / MODE 6

♭6

HINDU = MELODIC MODE 5
PHRYGIAN ♮3 = HARMONIC MINOR MODE 5
HARMONIC MAJOR
PHRYGIAN ♮4 = HARMONIC MAJOR MODE 3
DOUBLE HARMONIC = HUNGARIAN MINOR MODE 5
ALT ♯5 ♮7 = HUNGARIAN MINOR MODE 7
LYDIAN MINOR = NEAPOLITAN MAJOR MODE 4
ENIGMATIC MINOR MODE 3
ENIGMATIC MINOR MODE 7
ENIGMATIC MODE 3
COMPOSITE II
COMPOSITE II MODE 3
PERSIAN MODE 3
AUGMENTED
PELOG MODE 6
8 TONE SPANISH MODE 7
BEBOP LOCRIAN ♮2 MODE 7
BEBOP DORIAN MODE 3
BEBOP DORIAN MODE 5
BEBOP MAJOR
BEBOP MAJOR MODE 3

-♭6

PHRYGIAN = MAJOR MODE 3
AEOLIAN = MAJOR MODE 6
HARMONIC MINOR
PHRYGIAN ♮4 = HARMONIC MAJOR MODE 3
HUNGARIAN MINOR
ALT ♭5 ♮7 = HUNGARIAN MINOR MODE 7
NEAPOLITAN MINOR
HUNGARIAN GYPSY = NEAPOLITAN MINOR MODE 4
ENIGMATIC MINOR MODE 3
COMPOSITE II MODE 3
AEOLIAN ♮7 = IONIAN ♭5 MODE 6
PHRYGIAN ♮4 = LOCRIAN ♮7 MODE 4
PERSIAN MODE 4
HIROJOSHI
AUGMENTED
PELOG
DOMINANT SUS MODE 2
8 TONE SPANISH MODE 5
8 TONE SPANISH MODE 8
BEBOP LOCRIAN ♮2 MODE 3
BEBOP MINOR = BEBOP DOMINANT MODE 2
BEBOP LOCRIAN add 5 = BEBOP DOMINANT MODE 3
BEBOP DOMINANT MODE 6
BEBOP DORIAN MODE 2
BEBOP DORIAN MODE 5
BEBOP MAJOR MODE 3
BEBOP MAJOR MODE 7

6

MAJOR
LYDIAN = MAJOR MODE 4
MIXOLYDIAN = MAJOR MODE 5
LYDIAN DOMINANT = MELODIC MODE 4
LYDIAN ♭2 = HARMONIC MINOR MODE 6
DOMINANT ♭2 = HARMONIC MAJOR MODE 5
HUNGARIAN MAJOR
ALT ♯6 ♮7 = HUNGARIAN MAJOR MODE 2
IONIAN ♯2 = NEAPOLITAN MINOR MODE 6
ENIGMATIC MINOR MODE 3
ENIGMATIC MINOR MODE 4
ENIGMATIC MODE 3
COMPOSITE II MODE 3
DORIAN ♮4 = IONIAN ♭5 MODE 2
LYDIAN ♭2 = IONIAN ♭5 MODE 4
DOMINANT ♮2 = LOCRIAN ♮7 MODE 6
ALT ALT = LOCRIAN ♮7 MODE 7
PERSIAN MODE 3
MAJOR PENTATONIC = MINOR PENTATONIC MODE 2
DOMINANT SUS MODE 3
DOMINATN SUS MODE 6
HALF-WHOLE DIMINISHED
8 TONE SPANISH MODE 2
8 TONE SPANISH MODE 6
8 TONE SPANISH MODE 7
BEBOP LOCRIAN ♮2 MODE 6
BEBOP LOCRIAN ♮2 MODE 8
BEBOP DOMINANT
BEBOP DOMINANT MODE 4
BEBOP DOMINANT MODE 5
BEBOP DOMINANT MODE 7
BEBOP DORIAN MODE 3
BEBOP DORIAN MODE 5
BEBOP DORIAN MODE 7
BEBOP MAJOR
BEBOP MAJOR MODE 4
BEBOP MAJOR MODE 5

-6

DORIAN = MAJOR MODE 2
MELODIC
DORIAN ♭2 = MELODIC MODE 2
DORIAN ♯4 = HARMONIC MINOR MODE 4
LYDIAN ♭2 = HARMONIC MINOR MODE 6
LYDIAN ♭3 = HARMONIC MAJOR MODE 4
ALT ♯5 ♮7 = HUNGARIAN MINOR MODE 7
HUNGARIAN MAJOR
ALT ♯6 ♮7 = HUNGARIAN MAJOR MODE 2
DORIAN ♭2 ♮4 = HUNGARIAN MAJOR MODE 6
IONIAN ♯2 = NEAPOLITAN MINOR MODE 6
NEAPOLITAN MAJOR
ENIGMATIC MINOR MODE 3
ENIGMATIC MODE 2
COMPOSITE II MODE 2
DORIAN ♮4 = IONIAN ♭5 MODE 2
AEOLIAN ♮7 = IONIAN ♭5 MODE 6
DOMIANT ♯2 = LOCRIAN ♮7 MODE 6
KUMOI
HALF-WHOLE DIMINISHED
8 TONE SPANISH MODE 2
8 TONE SPANISH MODE 6
BEBOP LOCRIAN ♮2 MODE 3
BEBOP LOCRIAN ♮2 MODE 4
BEBOP LOCRIAN ♮2 MODE 6
BEBOP LOCRIAN ♮2 MODE 8
BEBOP MINOR = BEBOP DOMINANT MODE 2
BEBOP DOMINANT MODE 5
BEBOP DORIAN
BEBOP DORIAN MODE 2
BEBOP MAJOR MODE 2
BEBOP MAJOR MODE 4

°7

LOCRIAN ♮6 = HARMONIC MINOR MODE 2
DORIAN ♯4 = HARMONIC MINOR MODE 4
LYDIAN ♯2 = HARMONIC MINOR MODE 6
ALT ♮7 = HARMONIC MINOR MODE 7
DORIAN ♭5 = HARMONIC MAJOR MODE 2
LYDIAN ♯3 = HARMONIC MAJOR MODE 4
LYDIAN AUGMENTED ♯2 = HARMONIC MAJOR MODE 6
LOCRIAN ♮7 = HARMONIC MAJOR MODE 7
HUNGARIAN MAJOR
ALT ♯6 ♮7 = HUNGARIAN MAJOR MODE 2
ALT ♮6 = HUNGARIAN MAJOR MODE 4
DORIAN ♭2 ♮4 = HUNGARIAN MAJOR MODE 6
WHOLE-HALF DIMINISHED
HALF-WHOLE DIMINISHED
BEBOP LOCRIAN ♮2 MODE 2
BEBOP LOCRIAN ♮2 MODE 4
BEBOP LOCRIAN ♮2 MODE 6
BEBOP LOCRIAN ♮2 MODE 8
BEBOP MAJOR MODE 2
BEBOP MAJOR MODE 4
BEBOP MAJOR MODE 6
BEBOP MAJOR MODE 8

7 (DOMINANT)

MIXOLYDIAN = MAJOR MODE 5
LYDIAN DOMINANT = MELODIC MODE 4
HINDU = MELODIC MODE 5
PHRYGIAN ♮3 = HARMONIC MINOR MODE 5
PHRYGIAN ♮4 = HARMONIC MAJOR MODE 3
DOMINANT ♭2 = HARMONIC MAJOR MODE 5
LYDIAN ♯6 ♭2 = HUNGARIAN MINOR MODE 6
HUNGARIAN MAJOR
LYDIAN ♮6 = NEAPOLITAN MINOR MODE 2
LYDIAN MINOR = NEAPOLITAN MAJOR MODE 4
ENIGMATIC MINOR MODE 3
ENIGMATIC MODE 4
DORIAN ♮4 = IONIAN ♭5 MODE 2
IONIAN ♮6 = LOCRIAN ♮7 MODE 2
DOMINANT ♮2 = LOCRIAN ♮7 MODE 6
PERSIAN MODE 2
HALF-WHOLE DIMINISHED
8 TONE SPANISH MODE 6
8 TONE SPANISH MODE 7
BEBOP LOCRIAN ♮2 MODE 6
BEBOP LOCRAIN ♮2 MODE 7
BEBOP DOMINANT
BEBOP DOMINANT MODE 5
BEBOP DORIAN MODE 4
BEBOP DORIAN MODE 5
BEBOP MAJOR MODE 3
BEBOP MAJOR MODE 5

-7

DORIAN = MAJOR MODE 2
PHRYGIAN = MAJOR MODE 3
AEOLIAN = MAJOR MODE 6
DORIAN ♭2 = MELODIC MODE 2
DORIAN ♯4 = HARMONIC MINOR MODE 4
PHRYGIAN ♮4 = HARMONIC MAJOR MODE 3
LYDIAN ♯6 ♭2 = HUNGARIAN MINOR MODE 6
HUNGARIAN MAJOR
DORIAN ♭2 ♮4 = HUNGARIAN MAJOR MODE 6
HUNGARIAN GYPSY = NEAPOLITAN MINOR MODE 4
ENIGMATIC MINOR
ENIGMATIC MINOR MODE 3
ENIGMATIC MODE 2
COMPOSITE II MODE 2
DORIAN ♮4 = IONIAN ♭5 MODE 2
LOCRIAN ♮6 = IONIAN ♭5 MODE 7
PHRYGIAN ♮4 = LOCRIAN ♮7 MODE 4
DOMINANT ♯2 = LOCRIAN ♮7 MODE 6
PERSIAN MODE 2
MINOR PENTATONIC
DOMINANT SUS MODE 2
DOMINANT SUS MODE 4
HALF-WHOLE DIMINISHED
8 TONE SPANISH MODE 3
8 TONE SPANISH MODE 5
8 TONE SPANISH MODE 8
BEBOP LOCRIAN ♮2 MODE 2
BEBOP LOCRIAN ♮2 MODE 6
BEBOP MINOR = BEBOP DOMINANT MODE 2
BEBOP LOCRIAN add 5 = BEBOP DOMINANT MODE 3
BEBOP DOMINANT MODE 5
BEBOP DOMINANT MODE 6
BEBOP DORIAN
BEBOP DORIAN MODE 2 / MODE 5
BEBOP MAJOR MODE 2
BEBOP MAJOR MODE 3
BEBOP MAJOR MODE 7

7sus2

DORIAN = MAJOR MODE 2
MIXOLYDIAN = MAJOR MODE 5
AEOLIAN = MAJOR MODE 6
LYDIAN DOMINANT = MELODIC MODE 4
HINDU = MELODIC MODE 5
DORIAN ♯4 = HARMONIC MINOR MODE 4
LYDIAN ♮6 = NEAPOLITAN MINOR MODE 2
HUNGARIAN GYPSY = NEAPOLITAN MINOR MODE 4
LYDIAN MAJOR = NEAPOLITAN MAJOR MODE 4
ENIGMATIC MODE 4
COMPOSITE II MODE 4
DORIAN ♮4 = IONIAN ♭5 MODE 2
PHRYGIAN ♮3 = IONIAN ♭5 MODE 3
IONIAN ♮6 = LOCRIAN ♮7 MODE 2
PERSIAN MODE 5
MINOR PENTATONIC MODE 3
DOMINANT SUS
DOMINANT SUS MODE 4
8 TONE SPANISH MODE 3 / MODE 6 / MODE 7
8 TONE SPANISH MODE 8
BEBOP LOCRIAN ♮2 MODE 6 / MODE 7
BEBOP DOMINANT
BEBOP MINOR = BEBOP DOMINANT MODE 2
BEBOP DOMINANT MODE 5 / MODE 6
BEBOP DORIAN
BEBOP DORIAN MODE 4 / MODE 5
BEBOP MAJOR MODE 2 / MODE 5 / MODE 7

CHORD - SCALE COMPATIBILITY CHART page 3

7sus

DORIAN = MAJOR MODE 2
PHRYGIAN = MAJOR MODE 3
MIXOLYDIAN = MAJOR MODE 5
AEOLIAN = MAJOR MODE 6
DORIAN ♭2 = MELODIC MODE 2
HINDU = MELODIC MODE 5
PHRYGIAN ♮3 = HARMONIC MINOR MODE 5
DOMINANT ♭2 = HARMONIC MAJOR MODE 5
ENIGMATIC MODE 4
COMPOSITE I MODE 2
COMPOSITE II MODE 4
PHRYGIAN ♮3 = IONIAN ♭5 MODE 3
LOCRIAN ♮6 = IONIAN ♭5 MODE 7
IONIAN ♮6 = LOCRIAN ♮7 MODE 2
DOMINANT ♮2 = LOCRIAN ♮7 MODE 6
PERSIAN MODE 2
PERSIAN MODE 5
MINOR PENTATONIC
MINOR PENTATONIC MODE 3
KUMOI MODE 2
DOMINANT SUS
DOMINANT SUS MODE 2
DOMINANT SUS MODE 4
8 TONE SPANISH MODE 3
8 TONE SPANISH MODE 5
8 TONE SPANISH MODE 7
8 TONE SPANISH MODE 8
BEBOP LOCRIAN ♮2 MODE 4
BEBOP LOCRIAN ♮2 MODE 7
BEBOP DOMINANT
BEBOP MINOR = BEBOP DOMINANT MODE 2
BEBOP LOCRIAN add 5 = BEBOP DOMINANT MODE 3
BEBOP DOMINANT MODE 5
BEBOP DOMINANT MODE 6
BEBOP DORIAN
BEBOP DORIAN MODE 2
BEBOP DORIAN MODE 4
BEBOP DORIAN MODE 5
BEBOP MAJOR MODE 2
BEBOP MAJOR MODE 3
BEBOP MAJOR MODE 5 / MODE 7

7♭5

LYDIAN DOMINANT = MELODIC MODE 4
ORIENTAL = HUNGARIAN MINOR MODE 4
LYDIAN ♮6 ♮2 = HUNGARIAN MINOR MODE 6
HUNGARIAN MAJOR
ALT ♮6 = HUNGARIAN MAJOR MODE 4
LYDIAN ♮6 = NEAPOLITAN MINOR MODE 2
LOCRIAN ♮3 = NEAPOLITAN MINOR MODE 5
LYDIAN AUGMENTED ♮6 = NEAPOLITAN MAJOR MODE 2
LYDIAN DOMINANT AUG = NEAPOLITAN MAJOR MODE 3
LYDIAN MINOR = NEAPOLITAN MAJOR MODE 4
MAJOR LOCRIAN = NEAPOLITAN MAJOR MODE 5
ALT ♮2 = NEAPOLITAN MAJOR MODE 6
ALT ♮3 = NEAPOLITAN MAJOR MODE 7
ENIGMATIC / ENIGMATIC MODE 4
WHOLE TONE
HALF-WHOLE DIMINISHED
8 TONE SPANISH
8 TONE SPANISH MODE 6
BEBOP LOCRIAN ♮2 MODE 2
BEBOP LOCRIAN ♮2 MODE 6
BEBOP DORIAN MODE 4
BEBOP DORIAN MODE 8

∅

LOCRIAN = MAJOR MODE 7
LOCRIAN ♮2 = MELODIC MODE 6
SUPER LOCRIAN = MELODIC MODE 7
LOCRIAN ♮6 = HARMONIC MINOR MODE 2
DORIAN ♮4 = HARMONIC MINOR MODE 4
DORIAN ♭5 = HARMONIC MAJOR MODE 2
LYDIAN ♮6 ♮2 = HUNGARIAN MINOR MODE 6
HUNGARIAN MAJOR
ALT ♮6 = HUNGARIAN MAJOR MODE 4
DORIAN ♭2 ♮4 = HUNGARIAN MAJOR MODE 6
HUNGARIAN GYPSY = NEAPOLITAN MINOR MODE 4
ALT ♮2 = NEAPOLITAN MINOR MODE 6
ENIGMATIC MINOR
ENIGMATIC MINOR MODE 6
COMPOSITE II MODE 2
SUPER LYDIAN AUGMENTED = IONIAN ♭5 MODE 5
LOCRIAN ♮6 = IONIAN ♭5 MODE 7
PHRYGIAN ♮4 = LOCRIAN ♮7 MODE 4
KUMOI MODE 5
HALF-WHOLE DIMINISHED
8 TONE SPANISH
8 TONE SPANISH MODE 8
BEBOP LOCRIAN ♮2
BEBOP LOCRIAN ♮2 MODE 2
BEBOP LOCRIAN ♮2 MODE 4
BEBOP LOCRIAN ♮2 MODE 5
BEBOP LOCRIAN add 5 = BEBOP DOMINANT MODE 3
BEBOP DOMINANT MODE 8
BEBOP DORIAN MODE 6 / MODE 8
BEBOP MAJOR MODE 2 / MODE 8

7+

HINDU = MELODIC MODE 5
SUPER LOCRIAN = MELODIC MODE 7
PHRYGIAN ♮3 = HARMONIC MINOR MODE 5
PHRYGIAN ♮4 = HARMONIC MINOR MODE 3
DOMINANT AUGMENTED = NEAPOLITAN MINOR MODE 3
LOCRIAN ♮3 = NEAPOLITAN MINOR MODE 5
LYDIAN AUGMENTED ♮6 = NEAPOLITAN MAJOR MODE 2
LYDIAN DOMINANT AUG = NEAPOLITAN MAJOR MODE 3
LYDIAN MINOR = NEAPOLITAN MAJOR MODE 4
MAJOR LOCRIAN = NEAPOLITAN MAJOR MODE 5
ALT ♮2 = NEAPOLITAN MAJOR MODE 6
ALT ♮3 = NEAPOLITAN MAJOR MODE 7
ENIGMATIC MINOR MODE 3
ENIGMATIC
ENIGMATIC MODE 5
COMPOSITE II MODE 6
PERSIAN MODE 6
WHOLE TONE
8 TONE SPANISH
8 TONE SPANISH MODE 7
BEBOP LOCRIAN ♮2 MODE 2 / MODE 7
BEBOP DORIAN MODE 5 / MODE 8
BEBOP MAJOR MODE 3

△ (DELTA)

MAJOR
LYDIAN = MAJOR MODE 4
LYDIAN ♮2 = HARMONIC MINOR MODE 6
HARMONIC MAJOR
DOUBLE HARMONIC = HUNGARIAN MINOR MODE 5
LYDIAN ♮6 ♮2 = HUNGARIAN MINOR MODE 6
LYDIAN ♮6 = NEAPOLITAN MINOR MODE 2
IONIAN ♮2 = NEAPOLIAN MINOR MODE 6
ENIGMATIC MINOR MODE 7
COMPOSITE II
LYDIAN ♮2 = IONIAN ♭5 MODE 4
IONIAN ♮6 = LOCRIAN ♮7 MODE 2
PERSIAN MODE 2
HIROJOSHI MODE 5
AUGMENTED
PELOG MODE 6
8 TONE SPANISH MODE 2 / MDOE 6
BEBOP LOCRIAN ♮2 MODE 8
BEBOP DOMINANT MODE 4 / MODE 7
BEBOP DORIAN MODE 3 / MODE 7
BEBOP MAJOR
BEBOP MAJOR MODE 4

–△

MELODIC
HARMONIC MINOR
LYDIAN ♮2 = HARMONIC MINOR MODE 6
LYDIAN ♮3 = HARMONIC MAJOR MODE 4
HUNGARIAN MINOR
LYDIAN ♮6 ♮2 = HUNGARIAN MINOR MODE 6
NEAPOLITAN MINOR
IONIAN ♮2 = NEAPOLITAN MINOR MODE 6
NEAPOLITAN MAJOR
ENIGMATIC MINOR
ENIGMATIC MINOR MODE 6
COMPOSITE II MODE 2
PERSIAN MODE 2 / MODE 4
AUGMENTED
PELOG MODE 2
8 TONE SPANISH MODE 2 / MODE 5
BEBOP LOCRIAN ♮2 MODE 3 / MODE 8
BEBOP DORIAN
BEBOP MAJOR MODE 4 / MODE 7

△sus2

MAJOR
LYDIAN = MAJOR MODE 4
MELODIC
HARMONIC MINOR
HARMONIC MAJOR
LYDIAN ♮3 = HARMONIC MAJOR MODE 4
HUNGARIAN MINOR
LYDIAN ♮6 = NEAPOLITAN MINOR MODE 2
ENIGMATIC MINOR MODE 7
ENIGMATIC MODE 7
IONIAN ♮6 = LOCRIAN ♮7 MODE 2
LYDIAN ♮3 = LOCRIAN ♮7 MODE 5
PERSIAN MODE 5
PELOG MODE 2
DOMINANT SUS MODE 6
8 TONE SPANISH MODE 2 / MODE 6
BEBOP LOCRIAN ♮2 MODE 3
BEBOP DOMINANT
BEBOP DOMINANT MODE 4 / MODE 7
BEBOP DORIAN
BEBOP DORIAN MODE 3 / MODE 7
BEBOP MAJOR
BEBOP MAJOR MODE 4 / MODE 7

△sus

MAJOR
MELODIC
HARMONIC MINOR
HARMONIC MAJOR
DOUBLE HARMONIC = HUNGARIAN MINOR MODE 5
NEAPOLITAN MINOR
IONIAN ♮2 = NEAPOLITAN MINOR MODE 6
NEAPOLITAN MAJOR
ENIGMATIC MODE 7
COMPOSITE II MODE 2
IONIAN ♮6 = LOCRIAN ♮7 MODE 2
LYDIAN ♮3 = LOCRIAN ♮7 MODE 5
PERSIAN MODE 2 / MODE 5
PELOG MODE 6
8 TONE SPANISH MODE 2 / MODE 5
BEBOP LOCRIAN ♮2 MODE 7
BEBOP DOMINANT / BEBOP DOMINANT MODE 4
BEBOP DORIAN / BEBOP DORIAN MODE 7
BEBOP MAJOR / BEBOP MAJOR MODE 8

△♭5

LYDIAN = MAJOR MODE 4
LYDIAN AUGMENTED = MELODIC MODE 3
LYDIAN ♮2 = HARMONIC MINOR MODE 6
LYDIAN AUGMENTED ♮2 = HARMONIC MAJOR MODE 6
LYDIAN ♮6 ♮2 = HUNGARIAN MINOR MODE 6
LYDIAN ♮6 = NEAPOLITAN MINOR MODE 2
LYDIAN AUGMENTED ♮6 = NEAPOLITAN MAJOR MODE 2
ENIGMATIC MINOR MODE 5
ENIGMATIC
COMPOSITE II / COMPOSITE II MODE 5
IONIAN ♭5
LYDIAN ♮2 = IONIAN ♭5 MODE 4
PERSIAN
KUMOI MODE 3
HIROJOSHI MODE 5
8 TONE SPANISH MODE 4 / MODE 6
BEBOP LOCRIAN ♮2 MODE 5
BEBOP DOMINANT MODE 4 / MODE 7
BEBOP DORIAN MODE 3 / MODE 8
BEBOP MAJOR MODE 4 / MODE 6

△°

LYDIAN ♮2 = HARMONIC MINOR MODE 6
LYDIAN ♮3 = HARMONIC MAJOR MODE 4
LYDIAN AUGMENTED ♮2 = HARMONIC MAJOR MODE 6
HUNGARIAN MINOR
LYDIAN ♮6 ♮2 = HUNGARIAN MINOR MODE 6
LOCRIAN ♮2 ♮7 = HUNGARIAN MAJOR MODE 3
ENIGMATIC MINOR / ENIGMATIC MINOR MODE 5
COMPOSITE II MODE 2
SUPER LYDIAN AUGMENTED = IONIAN ♭5 MODE 5
LOCRIAN ♮7
PERSIAN MODE 4
PELOG MODE 2
WHOLE-HALF DIMINISHED
BEBOP LOCRIAN ♮2 / BEBOP LOCRIAN ♮2 MODE 8
BEBOP DOMINANT MODE 8
BEBOP DORIAN MODE 8
BEBOP MAJOR MODE 4 / MODE 6

△+

LYDIAN AUGMENTED = MELODIC MODE 3
IONIAN ♮5 = HARMONIC MINOR MODE 3
HARMONIC MAJOR
LYDIAN AUGMENTED ♮2 = HARMONIC MAJOR MODE 6
IONIAN AUGMENTED ♮2 = HUNGARIAN MINOR MODE 3
DOUBLE HARMONIC = HUNGARIAN MINOR MODE 5
LYDIAN AUGMENTED ♮6 = NEAPOLITAN MAJOR MODE 2
ENIGMATIC MINOR MODE 5 / MODE 7
ENIGMATIC
COMPOSITE II / COMPOSITE II MODE 6
PERSIAN
AUGMENTED
PELOG MODE 4 / MODE 6
8 TONE SPANISH MODE 4
BEBOP DORIAN MODE 3 / MODE 8
BEBOP MAJOR / BEBOP MAJOR MODE 6

–△+

HARMONIC MINOR
LYDIAN AUGMENTED ♮2 = HARMONIC MAJOR MODE 6
HUNGARIAN MINOR
IONIAN AUGMENTED ♮2 = HUNGARIAN MINOR MODE 3
LOCRIAN ♮2 ♮7 = HUNGARIAN MAJOR MODE 3
MELODIC AUGMENTED = HUNGARIAN MAJOR MODE 5
NEAPOLITAN MINOR
ENIGMATIC MINOR MODE 5
COMPOSITE II MODE 6
SUPER LYDIAN AUGMENTED = IONIAN ♭5 MODE 5
LOCRIAN ♮7
PERSIAN MODE 4

INTRODUCING THE GRIMOIRE FRETPAD SERIES

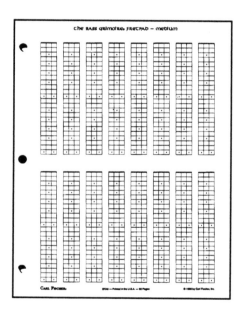

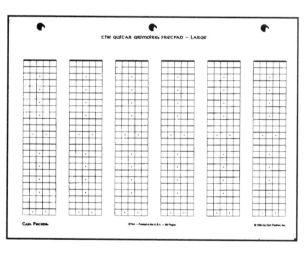

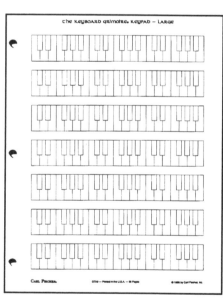

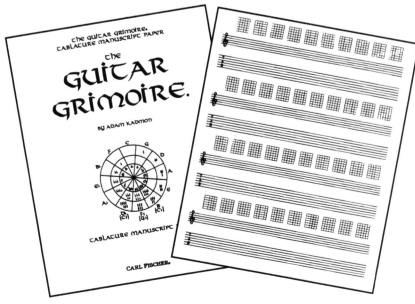

Guitar Grimoire Fretpad — $4.95 each
   GTA2 (small)
   GTA3 (medium)
   GTA4 (large)

Bass Grimoire Fretpad — $4.95 each
   GTA5 (large)
   GTA6 (medium)
   GTA7 (small)

Keyboard Grimoire Fretpad — $4.95 each
   GTA8 (medium)
   GTA9 (large)

The Guitar Grimoire Tablature Manuscript Book
   $4.95